Global Supply Chain Management and International Logistics

The development of international trade is driven by international logistics and management and the provision of the global supply chain. The ultimate objective of global supply chain management is to link the marketplace, distribution network, manufacturing/processing/assembly process and procurement activity in such a way that customers are serviced at a higher level, yet lower cost. Overall, this has introduced a new breed of management in a computer literate environment operating in a global infrastructure.

Addressing this complex topic, Alan Branch's new book fulfills two clear objectives:

- to provide a concise, standard work on the subject, written in lucid language that embraces all the ingredients of a notoriously complex subject with a strategic focus;
- to extol best practices and focus on all areas of the industrial and consumer sectors and their interface with changing international market needs.

Until now, no book dedicated to international logistics and supply chain management was available. Practically oriented, this book features numerous case studies and diagrams from logistic operators. An ideal resource for management students, academics and managers who need a succinct treatment of global operations, Branch's book skillfully illustrates his ideas in practice. It is a book which should be on the shelf of every practitioner and student of the subject.

Alan E. Branch is an international consultant, lecturer and examiner/moderator. He has lectured widely in the UK and overseas, including visiting lectureships at Cardiff University, Reading University, Plymouth University, Leicester University, London City College and Rennes International School of Business in France.

Also available from Routledge:

Elements of Shipping, Eighth Edition, Alan E. Branch. (978–0–415–36286–3)
Maritime Economics: Management and Marketing, Alan E. Branch. (978–0–748–73986–8)

Books by the same author:

Elements of Port Operation and Management
Dictionary of English Arabic Shipping/International Trade/Commercial Terms and Abbreviations
Multilingual Dictionary of Commercial International Trade and Shipping Terms in English, French, German, Spanish
Maritime Economics Management and Marketing
Shipping and Air Freight Documentation for Importers and Exporters, 2nd edn
International Purchasing and Management
Dictionary of Shipping International Business Trade Terms and Abbreviations
Export Practice and Management, 5th revised edn
Dictionary of Commercial Terms and Abbreviations
Elements of Shipping, Eighth Edition

Global Supply Chain Management and International Logistics

Professor Alan E. Branch
FCIT FIEx FILT

International Business/Shipping Consultant

Examiner in International Logistics/Global Supply Chain Management/Shipping/International Marketing/International Purchasing

Visiting Lecturer Cardiff University/Reading University/Plymouth University/Leicester University/Rennes International School of Business, France

Fellow Chartered Institute of Transport and Fellow Institute of Export

Routledge
Taylor & Francis Group

NEW YORK AND LONDON

First published 2009
by Routledge
270 Madison Ave, New York, NY 10016

Simultaneously published in the UK
by Routledge
2 Park Square, Milton Park, Abingdon, Oxon OX14 4RN

Routledge is an imprint of the Taylor & Francis Group, an informa business

Typeset in Times by RefineCatch Limited, Bungay, Suffolk
Printed and bound in the United states of America on acid-free paper by
Edwards Brothers, Inc.

Library of Congress Cataloging in Publication Data
Branch, Alan E.
Global supply chain management and international logistics / Alan E. Branch.
– 1st ed.
    p. cm.
Includes index.
1. Business logistics. 2. International trade. 3. Business logistics–Case
studies. I. Title.
HD38.5.B733 2008
658.7–dc22

2008021843

ISBN10: 0–415–39844–4 (hbk)
ISBN10: 0–415–39845–2 (pbk)
ISBN10: 0–203–88776–X (ebk)

ISBN13: 978–0–415–39844–2 (hbk)
ISBN13: 978–0–415–39845–9 (pbk)
ISBN13: 978–0–203–88776–9 (ebk)

To my grandson Benjamin van Emden

Contents

Preface

During the past 10 years, globalisation of trade has accelerated and in consequence the international environment in which we do business has changed dramatically. It is therefore not surprising that I have received numerous requests from both business executives and academics across the world to write a book on global supply chain management and international logistics and thereby fill a gap in the market. I am most happy to respond to such a request. It is the first title in this field and has been written in the same style as my other 12 titles on international business and shipping, spanning 45 years.

The book, written in a simple language, has a strategic, analytical and pragmatic focus on the best practice code, supplemented by numerous diagrams and case studies of an international nature. It has 12 chapters plus a glossary of terms and abbreviations. Overall, it embraces both industrial and consumer sectors. Moreover, it reflects the growing importance of software-computerised technology in the development of the global supply chain management and international logistics. This embraces the point of origin of the commodity – raw material/componentised products to the manufacturing/ assembly point – in bound logistics, to the ultimate consumer/retailers distribution centre – outbound logistics. The lengthy supply chain, spanning often many international boundaries, embracing numerous regulations and cultures, and several transport modes is a complex operation, embracing third-party (3PL) and fourth-party (4PL) logistic operators. Overall, it embraces managing mobile assets – goods in transit along the entire supply chain. Moreover, it has a strong strategic focus featuring the constant process to deliver measurable results by added value in the logistics network by continuous audit aided by the latest technology such as radio frequency identification (RFID). This embraces the ultimate objective of the global supply chain management, which is to link the marketplace, the distribution network, the manufacturing/processing/assembly process and the procurement activity in such a way that customers are serviced at a higher level and yet lower cost. It demands professionalism, vigilance, creative thinking, pragmatism, efficiency and training at all levels of management. This book seeks to realise this objective. Doing business overseas can only be achieved through complete professionalism.

The 12 chapters include: the global supply chain management and international logistics constituents and environment in the twenty-first century; factors driving logistics and supply chain management; the export sales contract formulation with focus on the global supply chain; advanced communication systems; procurement and competitive product sourcing; selecting the international logistics operator; international transport – trade-offs inherent in international logistics cost – time – speed – inventory information – transport – warehousing; operations management; secure global supply chain; global supply chain software; global trace scene; and developing a strategic focus to reduce cost, improve service and market development.

A fundamental point to bear in mind is the relocation of many industries from North America and Europe to the Far East. They have been developed as the consumer wishes to have a competitively priced product with a wide choice of added value. This has resulted in a massive investment in the logistic infrastructure of high tech to serve these markets and customers. Overall, it must be stressed that logistics is a derived demand as a response to trade and transport in a globalised environment; hence its continuous growth in a expanding global trade environment.

The book is an essential 'aide-memoire' to the discerning international global supply chain executive and international logistics manager operating within the company business plan. It breaks new ground, as it is global and not national, thereby spanning many national boundaries in the logistic and supply chain operation. The emphasis throughout is to develop strategies that focus on efficiency and competitiveness in a global market. It contains useful hints and numerous case studies extolling good practice.

The book is not only ideal for the business community, but also students in college of higher education and universities throughout the world. This includes degree-level undergraduates studying international logistics, international transport, international physical distribution, international marketing and international business. Moreover, it is suitable for students taking professional examinations of the Chartered Institute of Logistics and Transport, the Institute of Export, the Chartered Institute of Purchasing and Supply and the British International Freight Association. It will also prove a popular title for chambers of commerce, trade associations, training agencies and colleges conducting short diploma courses and seminars on global supply chain management and international logistics.

The book focuses strongly on management techniques and strategy, albeit on a pragmatic but thoroughly professional basis. It will prove popular with universities and business schools and continue to expand their international transport/trade/management degree portfolio requiring publications written in a lucid style, which provide a pragmatic yet professional approach to the subject. This includes diploma courses in management studies. In common with my other 12 titles this book is ideal for courses in Malaysia, Hong Kong, Malta, Thailand, Singapore, Turkey, Australia, New Zealand, USA, Pakistan, India, China, Jordan and Saudi Arabia.

Finally, I would like to acknowledge, with grateful thanks, the secretarial help from Mr and Mrs Salter, Mr and Mrs Splarn and, as always, my dear wife Kathleen, in proof reading. This quintet has provided encouragement, forbearance, and above all complete professionalism to produce such a title.

A. E. Branch
Reading
England RG4 8XL   May 2008

Acknowledgements

I am greatly indebted to the various organisations listed below for their enthusiastic assistance, especially:

Containerisation International
Dachser Far East Ltd
Export Master Systems Ltd
International Chamber of Commerce
International Standardization Organization
Red Prairie Corporation
UNCTAD

Chapter 1

Introduction

Introduction and Function of the Book

As we progress through the early part of the twenty-first century the pattern of international trade and services is one of continuous change and challenge. It is becoming more complex and driven by many elements on a global basis. Today, companies and their entrepreneurs engaged on the global business network formulate a strategic approach to conduct their business based on a logistics focus. This embraces supply chain management operations both in material/goods and nonmaterial/service industries. It includes business-to-business (B2B) and business-to-consumer (B2C).

Logistics can be broadly defined as the time-related positioning of resources ensuring that material, people, operational capacity and information are in the right place at the right time in the right quantity and at the right quality and cost. This embraces the ultimate objective of global supply management, which is to link the marketplace, the distribution network, the manufacturing/processing/assembly process and the procurement activity in such a way that customers are serviced at a higher level and yet lower cost. Logistics therefore contribute to a company's relative cost position and create a basis for differentiation providing a 'value-added' activity and competitive advantage. Much of this involves outsourcing products/services in a computer literate environment. Overall, traders/service providers are focusing their attention on developing a global strategy in their search for lower cost and increased profits. This book seeks to realise this objective in a changing global supply chain environment.

An alternative definition by the USA Society of Logistics Engineers is: Logistics is the art and science of management, engineering and technical activities concerned with requirements, design and supplying, maintaining resources to support objectives, plans and operation.

This book, written in a lucid professional style, follows three main aspects: factors driving logistics and supply chain management; the operational aspects and the regulatory network; and finally, the strategic focus. The text contains, throughout, case studies and further recommended reading.

The text draws on the author's experience in the industry spanning 50 years, embracing not only work and consultancy on a worldwide scale in the industry itself, but also as a lecturer/examiner at home and overseas.

Finally, the book is written primarily for the student or businessperson who has limited knowledge of the subject but is keen to develop a viable global/international business, thereby adding value to the company portfolio.

Role of the Supply Chain

The supply chain has been defined as the sequence of events in a goods flow, which adds value to the value of a specific good. These events may include conversion, assembling and/or disassembling and movements and placements. The global supply chain crosses international boundaries. Basically, the supply chain is linking the producer/manufacturer/supplier with the distributor/consumer involving a dedicated service. It is completely transparent with each element of the supply chain throughout the transit. It may be the movement of cars from China to Europe/North America, or the reefer container market embracing food products direct from the supplier to the consumer/supermarket store/distribution centre crossing international boundaries. A global logistics supply pipeline is featured in Figure 3.1 (see page 3), embracing procurement (buying the goods), manufacturing/producing the goods, quality control, handling/loading cargo on container/pallet for shipment by sea/air; delivery to distribution centre; unloading container; delivery to store/warehouse; delivered/bought by consumer. The components of the supply chain are examined in greater depth on page 3. The key to a successful supply chain is customisation, innovation, scalability (integration of unlimited number of clients); multichannel, security and flexibility (see page 3). Other areas, as advanced by Professor Hau Lee, focus on agility, adaptability and alignment (see page 8).

Managing the Supply Pipeline for Global Trade Flows

Managing the flow of goods, information and money across borders is a highly complex, regulated and dynamic process. All companies, large and small, eventually reach a decision point with regard to global trade management. This is the core competency that justifies a continuous investment in people, technology and resources, or it is a process best managed by a partner whose primary focus and business is achieving excellence in global trade management (GTM).

The rationale/benefits of outsourcing all or part of company operations may be summarised as follows. It identifies the driving forces behind a company decision to outsource and the benefits occurring, together with the complexity of global trade flows and challenges.

a   Many companies do not believe that GTM is or should be a core internal competency;

b   The ability to scale GTM resources and capabilities quickly and cost-effectively is a growing challenge;

c   Outsourcing partnerships typically provide companies with better visibility/transparency to their GTM performance than when the processes are managed 'in house';

d   Improves operational performance and process control;

e   Ability to scale global trade activities without adding resources/cost. Examples, including Black & Decker and ITEC, reached a point where they either had to increase the size of their GTM team to keep up with increased trade activities or outsource the function to a third party. A further example arises in an automotive manufacturer, which had been able to increase its global trade activities while reducing its in-house GTM team by 90 per cent;

f   Reduction in customs duties paid (see page 17). This is one area where correct product classifications are essential and involves the International Convention on Harmonized Commodity Description and Coding system administered by the

Table 1.1 Global logistics supply pipeline

The diagram represents the acceptance of an overseas buyer to purchase a quantity of custom built furniture of high value from Europe for a corporate client in the hotel business in India. The goods on arrival have to customise to meet with the corporate client needs. Special packaging and handling arrangements are required. The payment is in USD and under CIF terms. The diagram must not be regarded as an exhaustive global logistics supply pipe line, but merely an insight into one, if rather over simplified. Overall, e-commerce features strongly throughout.

• Export enquiry	• Despatch of quotation	• Procurement acceptance of quotation	• Despatch	• Shipment by air/sea	• Goods arrive	• Despatch to assembly plant	• Goods despatched to customers
• Product specification	• Price	• Logistics input	• Loading on pallet/containers	• Customs clearance	• Delivery to distribution centre	• Goods taken by road/rail to buyer's premises for processing/customisation in destination country	
• Compliance with buyer specification	• Delivery schedule	• Manufacturing/processing goods	• Road/Rail/Canal to seaport/airport	• Buyer makes payment of goods on shipment	• Port charges	• 4PL	
• Credit rating buyer	• Incoterms	• Quality control	• Documentation prepared and despatched electronically to customs etc.	• Title of goods pass to buyer	• Duty paid by buyer		
• Sourcing component parts: cost/delivery	• CIF	• SGS inspection prior to departure	• 3PL	• RFID	• Documentation presented to customs electronically prior to goods arrival		
• Costing/pricing	• UCP 600	• Pre-book ship/flight/container		• 3PL	• Buyer presents import licence to customs		
• Payment terms	• Customs	• 3PL			• 4PL		
• Logistic input	• Routing						
• 3PL engaged	• Packaging						
	• Currency						
	• 3PL						

World Customs Organization. Failure to feature the correct classification results in companies paying too much on duties and taxes, or in some cases underpayment. This is also problematic from a regulatory and corporate responsibility perspective. It embraces customs planning;

g   Better managed broker networks. This yields savings in time and money, and labour can be realised by consolidating import transactions and communications. Better data quality also produces benefits;

h   Faster cycle times. This is a high yield benefit both to the shipper and consumer through quicker transit times. It embraces many elements (see page 78) such as better data quality and customs clearance delays. Moreover, better broker management helps to resolve exceptions quickly;

i   More intelligent business decisions. This focuses on having better visibility of global trade activities, in particular the criteria in regard to sourcing, mergers and acquisitions;

j   Companies that outsource generally do not believe that GTM is or should be a core internal competency;

k   The ability to scale GTM resources and capabilities quickly and cost-effectively is a growing challenge in a global competitive market;

l   Outsourcing partnerships typically provide companies with better visibility to their GTM performance than when the processes are managed 'in-house';

m   As featured in item (f), relative customs compliance across border shipment typically involves accurately completing and filing up to 35 documents interfacing with about 25 parties, including customs agencies, carriers, freight forwarders, brokers, banks and ports, and complying with over 600 laws and 500 trade agreements that are constantly changing (see page 64);

n   Also associated with the customs requirements under item (f) is the classification of products under the Harmonized Tariff Schedule, which poses problems to many companies, particularly those with dynamic product portfolios or products with complex bills of materials. The fact that the product classification varies by country adds yet another layer of complexity;

o   Regional trade agreements and bilateral trade agreements and tariff preferential agreements all add to complexity of customs compliance globally;

p   As supply chains become more fragmented and dispersed, the risk of terrorism, theft, smuggling, counterfeiting and other issues also increases. Today, security-related initiatives exist to counter such situations including (see page 108) Customs–Trade Partnership Against Terrorism (C-TPAT), the Container Security Initiative (CSI) and the Advanced Manifest Rule;

q   Companies that trade globally also face an increased level of financial risk. Duties, taxes, transportation charges and currency exchange rates are contributing factors, but there are other less tangible factors that also influence the bottom line, such as the cost of increased inventory and longer cash to cash cycles due to customs clearance delays;

r   Also achieving compliance with the Sarbanes–Oxley Act of 2002 – a law aimed at improving the accuracy and reliability of corporate financial statements – is depend-ent on having access to timely, accurate and complete information, and establishing process controls – the same success factors required to create more secure and efficient global trade operations;

s   Many companies engage in global trade to reduce costs, particularly to find less expensive sources of raw materials, finished goods, or labour, but viewed from a perspective, total cost may actually increase by going global. There are other factors that companies may fail to consider: staffing a GTM team – trained experienced personnel are difficult to find; investing in GTM technology – companies must invest in GTM software (see page 118) and have a scalable IT infrastructure to automate a variety of trade activities; and missed opportunities for cost avoidance such as failing to take advantage of preferential trade agreements (see page 74) and by misclassifying products and paying too much in duties and taxes;

t   Today, supply chains are becoming more fragmented and dynamic than they were a decade ago. The more countries in the supply chain, the more difficult it becomes to understand and manage the multitude of trade regulations and constraints involved. This is driven by companies in an effort to reduce cost and/or penetrate new markets quickly, and relocate their manufacturing operations and vendor base to low cost countries such as China, India, Brazil and Mexico. Moreover, the manufacturing base exports the product to a third country. This represents a complex operation difficult to manage.

The foregoing must not be regarded as an exhaustive list and will be developed as we progress through the book.

The Global Logistics Operator

The global logistics operator concentrates on six key areas sought by customs.

1   Strategic solutions to the problems of long-distance product sourcing and movement. This is achieved by matching the client's business needs to the latest techniques and expertise to formulate solutions to the problems of long-distance product sourcing and movement. An example is the European-based department stores buying a range of consumer products from the Far East. Key factors are quality control, coping with variations in consumer demand and distributing supplies in a cost-effective manner;

2   Companies that can provide capabilities interfaced across a range of different transport modes including sea, road, rail, canal and air as found in multimodalism;

3   Improvements in quality of service to end customers. This basically centres on customer asset management – ensuring the goods arrive in a quality condition to a prescribed schedule with zero failure rate;

4   Improvements in profits realised through all the marketing and financial benefits to the user inherent in the global logistic system;

5   Management of 'trade-offs' within the supply chain;

6   A fully outsourced logistics management service.

Users of the service include automotive manufacturers, high-street retailers, wines and spirits producers, footwear, fashion garments, sports goods and electronic manufacturers.

   The global logistics operators focus attention on the four key service areas detailed below:

1   *Supply chain management.* This requirement may be illustrated by the leading retail chains sourcing their merchandise from suppliers in Europe, the Far East and the US. The logistics operator's task is to ensure that goods of a saleable quality are

manufactured and transported safely and cost-effectively, and are delivered on time. This key service covers three aspects:

a   vendor management, involving the processing of customers' orders, direct to their supplies and monitoring the production process;
b   information, featuring receipt of customers' orders via EDI/RFID (see page 108) download (this leads to 24-hour monitoring and reporting of status and cost down to item level);
c   communication, permitting customers to receive advance notice of shipments which are off schedule via international email links.

The key benefits are reduced inventory levels, improved visibility of all costs to time level, improved delivery on time and clearer management responsibility. Study the supply pipeline in Figure 1.1.

2   *Delivery and customs clearance.* An example of this requirement is provided by a leading drinks company with over 50 brands worldwide. The objective is to receive and handle stocks and to arrange transport and overseas shipment. The four main features of the service include:

a   inventory management, featuring direct data exchange to provide online reporting;
b   order picking, embracing maximising deliveries of export shipments direct to the end customer;
c   quality control including checking on arrival, arranging, relabelling and repacking as required;
d   security, the adoption of sophisticated arrangements suitable for a high-value commodity.

The key results include delivery only when market demand dictates, secure and cost-effective storage and efficient onward distribution services.

3   *Distribution management.* This is the requirement of a major sportswear company which imports merchandise from suppliers in the Far East. The objective is to improve upstream process controls and maximise direct delivery to high-street stores in Europe. The three main features of the service include:

a   quality control, embracing collecting goods from suppliers and ensuring compliance with specified quality standards;
b   consolidation and delivery, embracing sorting, labelling and packaging goods according to end-customer order requirements and providing delivery direct to the customer;
c   information, embracing full integration via EDI between the customer's purchase order system, their financial and distribution systems and the global supply chain management system.

The ultimate results were improved supplier quality standards, reduced warehousing and handling costs and shortened order cycle times.

4   *Import logistics and outbound distribution.* This is illustrated by a manufacturer of electronic goods, which sources components in the Far East for manufacture in Europe. The objective is to manage the inbound supply of components to exacting production schedules and distribute the finished products across Europe. The three main features of the service include:

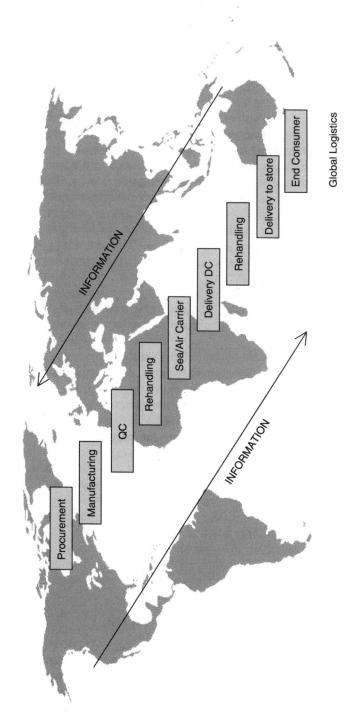

Figure 1.1 Global logistics supply pipeline reproduced courtesy P & O Nedlloyd.

   a   supply chain management, embracing the despatch of orders, the monitoring of production, consolidation and delivery on time to the manufacturing plant;

   b   information, embracing tracking progress in the supply chain so that customers can accommodate changes to the production plan;

   c   consolidation/distribution, featuring maximising container usage to cut costs and distribution 'on time' to retailers.

The key results are proactive control of delivery schedules and reduced shipment costs from the consolidation and integration of inward and outward distribution.

Overall, the global logistics company concentrates on six core products: supply chain management, warehousing, customs clearance, air freight, consolidation and project cargo. It will improve supply chain visibility by developing tailored processes and tracking systems. This will lead to improved buying processes and decision-making, reduced stock levels and improved reaction times in delivering to end users. Overall, it will reduce supply chain costs, thus cutting lead times, creating fast-flow procedures and introducing upstream controls.

To amplify the foregoing, a leading Asian company, Li Et Fung, operating in the Chinese market, engaged in sourcing, borderless trading and virtual manufacturing and supply chain management, identifies seven core principles that underpin the company. These are detailed below:

1   The customer must be at the centre and responsive to market demand;
2   Focus on core competency and outsource new-core activities and develop a position in the supply chain;
3   Develop a low risk and profit-sharing relationship with business partners;
4   Design, implement, evaluate and adjust the work flow, physical goods flow and cash flow in the supply chain;
5   Adopt information technology to optimise the operation of the supply chain;
6   Shorten product lead time and delivery cycles;
7   Lower cost in sourcing, warehousing and transportation.

Underpinning its success is globalisation, which is having the effect of shifting competition between companies away from traditional spheres and more onto the level of efficiency of their supply chains. Moreover, by applying advanced supply chain technologies and global sourcing expertise, it allows clients to focus fully on core competencies, lowers sourcing, warehousing, handling and storage costs, reduces working capital and minimises capital expenditure on distribution assets. The company advocates sourcing from several countries for individual products and in so doing is able to form a dialogue with the management and not the ownership supplying the components.

Comparison between National (Domestic) and International Logistics

As has been alluded to in earlier pages, the business community focuses for growth on a global scale, with many governments facilitating such an objective. Companies realise that trading overseas raises standards at all levels within the company and develops a fast moving management culture change. It encourages adaptability and continuous research to become more competitive in a high-tech fast moving environment.

The national logistics operator serving the local indigenous market usually has the advantage of being aware of the structure of the market, its infrastructure and all its elements, in particular, regulations, all the costing elements from manufacturer/production to the distributor/consumer, the supply chain under the national government, a common language, a range of economic/industrial indices indicating the changing market/trends, taxation levels, employment law, consumer protection and competitive law. Hence the logistics operator/business company remains focused on one country, but must be equally conscious of inwards investment whereby overseas companies penetrate the market with their goods and services.

The international logistics operator in designing the supply chain permeates several countries and may extend to several thousand miles from Australia/China/India/Malaysia to Europe and North America and vice versa. It is a distant market and embraces numerous conventions (see page 145) and complex regulations especially in the area of trade law, international finance, market entry regulations, customs, taxation, language, transport regulations, product specification/regulations, agency law, repatriation of funds, appointment of directors/managers, capital structure of company, unionisation, economic indices/market trends and social structure embracing a developed country, a developing country or less developed country; also, the degree to which the market is high-tech and developed. In consequence it is often the practice to engage the 3PLs and 4PLs.

The international logistics operator must be competent in all areas of the global supply chain. A synergy must be developed between the supplier and distributor together with all elements of the supply chain export/airport, carrier, handling, customs, finance, security warehouse, etc. Transparency is essential throughout the supply chain together with advanced software. Focus must be on inventory management, vendor management, multi-sourcing, outbound logistics, inbound logistics culture and the growing development of RFID (see page 108) to focus on cargo tracking.

As we progress through the book we will identify the skills to develop efficient international logistic design/planning/operation and global supply chain management.

International Transport

International transport comprehension is at the core of developing an efficient global logistics strategy. It is important that the global logistics entrepreneur fully understands the economic characteristics of individual transport modes and the international conventions associated with each. Both will be dealt with fully from a logistics standpoint later in the book (see page 79), but we will now examine succinct key points.

The range of transport modes embrace rail, sea – bulk and containerised cargo – air, inland waterways (usually linked to seaports) and road. Global logistics usually embraces combined transport or multi-modalism such as road/sea/rail, road/air/road, rail/sea/rail, which form the supply chain in transport terms on a door-to-door basis.

International transport law embraces all transport modes. No international uniform regime is in force to regulate liability for loss, damage or delay arising from multi-modal transport. Instead, the present legal framework governing multi-modal transport consists of a complex array of international conventions designed to regulate uni-modal carriage, diverse regional/subregional agreements, national laws and standard term contracts.

A range of legislation now exists and these maybe summarised as follows:

Combined Transport: ICC rules for a combined transport document (see page 83);

UNCTAD MMO convention; UNCTAD/ICC Rules for Multi-modal transport documents; European Union – International Liability; and Convention for Security Containers (see page 107).

International Road Transport: CMR convention governing the international carriage of goods by road signed in Geneva in 1956 and enacted into law in the UK by the Carriage of Goods by Road Act 1965 (see page 83).

International Rail Transport: COTIF Convention Concerning the International Carriage by Rail was signed in Berne in May 1980. It was given legal effect in the UK by the International Transport Conventions Act 1983 (see page 79).

International Air Carriage: is subject to either the Warsaw Convention 1929 or the amended Warsaw Convention 1955. Which of these conventions applies depends on which Convention the countries of departure and arrival have ratified.

Sea Carriage embracing despatch of goods by sea generally involves a Bill of Lading as evidence of the contract and features the various international regulations. Key areas embrace the following (see page 83): the Hague rules (1974), Hague-Visby Rules (1988), Hamburg Rules (1978), and Limitation of Liability for Maritime Claims which is embraced in the Merchant Shipping Act 1995.

International Trade Law

International trade law/regulation is at the core of conducting business overseas and the global logistics entrepreneur must be aware of all its ingredients when formulating a strategic and operational/planning process. Given below is a succinct overview, which will be examined in greater depth later in the book (see page 79).

a   Vienna Convention on Contracts for the International Sale of Goods came into force on 1 January 1988. It was sponsored by UNCITRAL (see page 46).

b   Product liability is the liability of the producer of a product which, owing to a defect, causes injury, damage or loss to the ultimate user. The US and EU have differing directives. Global logistics operators should check out the directives operative in the country of importation (see page 33).

c   Intellectual property rights embrace patents, registered designs and design right, registered trademarks and copyright. These rights make new inventions, designs, brand names and other creations, a form of property. Hence, property owners have the right to decide who can use their property. Overall, they create a system through which innovators can benefit from their work – whether it be an electronic timer, designing a fashion shoe, marketing chocolate bars under a new brand name, creating a new musical or publishing. The World Trade Organization (WTO) are very much in the lead (see page 126). Global logistics operators, when considering overseas markets, should look closely at potential markets in foreign countries.

d   Patents embrace virtually all machine products, and processes – including their individual components/parts – are subject to three conditions: (i) is it new, (ii) is it inventive, (iii) and is it capable of industrial application. Patents are not confined to major technological advances. They embrace agriculture, medicines, paints, electronics and photography. Currently there is no world patent.

e   Designs. These embrace two forms of design protection: (i) a registered design protects the appearance of a product if the product is novel and has its own character. You cannot register a design that is purely functional. (ii) Design right protects the original design of the shape or configuration of items. This includes purely functional items. It does not include two-dimensional designs. Some countries give protection like design right under copyright law

f   Copyright gives rights to the creators or original literary, dramatic, musical and artistic works, published editions of works, sound recordings, films (including videos), broadcasts, cable programmes and computer programmes. They cover copying, adopting, publishing, renting, performing and broadcasting. There is no registration for copyright in the United Kingdom. The protection available in other countries is set out in the national law of that country.

g   Trademarks are signs that distinguish goods and services of one trader from those of others. For example, the contents of a washing powder sold under a particular registered trademark may change many times over the year, but the trademark means that only the company or its licensees can sell a washing powder under that sign. The CE is the symbol all products sold throughout the EU must bear.

The Protocol to the Madrid agreement is a system for the international registration of trademarks. Its pro-centralised register of trademarks is held by the World Intellectual Property Organization in Geneva and allows all trademarks applied for or registered through the National Trademark system to be extended to and protected in the US. The UK is a signatory to the Madrid Protocol and its provisions were implemented by way of the Trademarks (International Registration) (Amendment) Order 2000 (see page 79).

Employment Law

Employment law covers both criminal and civil laws. It embraces a wide area and includes contract of employment, trade unions and their relations with employers and members, work councils, redundancy, health and safety, taxation, and so on. The EU may be regarded as a highly regulated employment market. Internationally, employment law differs widely. Employment law is very relevant to global logistics strategists who are outsourcing their manufacture/assembly/service base on a joint venture, operating alliance, merger and acquisition and setting up a company in another country (see page 79).

Globalisation and International Trade Environment

Logistics and globalisation feed off each other in terms of their development. During the past 25 years, the pattern of international trade has changed dramatically. Hence the need for the logistics operator to comprehend the international trade environment that s/he operates in to devise an efficient supply chain. The area will be dealt with later in the book, but it is desirable that we have an overview at the commencement.

There are various factors that have contributed to the changed international trade environment. This includes e-commerce, open communications systems, politics, technology, economics, cultural and legal and international agencies. This includes the WTO, who have opened up market access, and the ISO, who feature in food chain supply chain management code (see page 74). A further area is the development of economic blocs, such as the North American Free Trade Area (NAFTA), the Association of Southeast Asian Nations (ASEAN) and the Southern Common Market of Latin America (MER-COSUR), and emerging regional trade agreements. The technological area embraces high-tech supply chains.

Globalisation of markets and trade results in the provision of a product or service that can be sold virtually in any market of the world, providing the economic infrastructure and culture can support it. The key to it is the design and specification of the product or service and the added value it provides to the user or consumer (see page 107).

Useful Sources of Information

Chartered Institute of Logistics and Transport <www.ciltuk.org.uk>
Financial Times <news.ft.com/ft-reports>
International Freighting Weekly <www.ifw-net.com>
ISO (International Organization for Standardization) <www.iso.org>
WTO Annual Report Publications <www.wto.int>

Chapter 2

Factors and Challenges Driving Logistics and Supply Chain Management

Factors Driving Global Supply Chain Management

Factors driving logistics in the twenty-first century are focused on companies striving to become more competitive and providing customers with added value in the supply chain. It is more complex and more demanding in a global market environment in comparison with a local domestic market whereby the logistic operator is usually very familiar with the marketplace and its constraints and opportunities.

The key for any global logistics operator is the differential from other players in the marketplace and to have a separate identity. Basically to demonstrate to customers they have a certain added value in the marketplace. This embraces competitiveness and cost featuring efficiency. It may be supply chain cycle time management reduction (see page 24) or lean supply management (see page 27).

An analysis of the competitive advantage identifies three elements, each of which has an interface with the other: customer, company and competitor. The customer requires competitive pricing and the value-added benefit from the purchase, both actual and perceived such as warranty and after sales. S/he may have a wide choice such as from the preferred supplier and the competitor. The differential may be not only cost, but also technology. Hence, the choice differential is how efficient is company A compared with company B.

One particular concept that Michael Porter has brought to a wider audience is the 'value chain':

> Competitive advantage cannot be understood by looking at a firm as a whole. It stems from the many discrete activities a firm performs in designing, producing, marketing, delivering, and supporting its product. Each of these activities can contribute to a firm's relative cost position and create a basis for differentiation . . . The value chain disaggregates a firm into its strategically relevant activities in order to understand the behaviour of costs and the existing and potential sources of differentiation. A firm gains competitive advantage by performing these strategically important activities more cheaply or better than its competitors.

The value chain (Figure 2.1) can be identified into two types – primary activities including inbound logistics, operations; outbound logistics, marketing and sales and service; and support services such as infrastructure, human resource management, technology development and procurement. This is a very complex operation when comparing the domestic supply with the global operator. All the support activities must be logistic literate/focused.

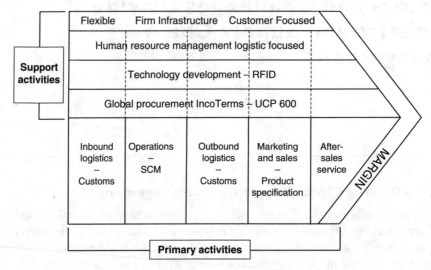

Figure 2.1 The value chain.

As indicated earlier the challenges facing the global supply chain management in the twenty-first century are becoming increasingly complex and very demanding. It all stems [1] from the most senior management in a company to accept and manage change, and to recognise that through the World Trade Organization (WTO) the world has become a global marketplace with trade barriers becoming eliminated, and fewer restrictions on the flow of goods. This also extends to movement of labour, inwards investment, intellectual property, and, moreover, the development of e-commerce – digital trade – and continuous expansion of trade routes such as remodelled container service, development of hub ports, extension of the hub and spoke system, development of new and existing airports, and emerging nations such as Brazil, India, China and Russia and the development of 3PL and 4PL. Trade volume doubles every 12 years and in political terms governments recognise it has political influence globally. A further factor is the growing development of the Free Trade Zone (FTZ), economic zones that favour such countries in the expansion of an export-led economy and industrial expansion/experience. Multinational industries (MNI) have long recognised this situation by reviewing the structure of their production strategy/location/supply chain/market location/productivity, etc. Hence companies today no longer rely on a national production base in a high-cost market, often relying on long supply chain component parts, but relocate closer to their component supply plants and centralise their production. An example arises with Dyson. The final point is business confidence to trade among nations, much of which has emerged through the ICC and the relative political stability, especially in the money markets. It is this background that drives the global supply chain management.

Overall, there are five factors on which to focus, to manage the global network of materials and information flows that transcend many borders and management cultures:

a   The centralisation of a one-production centre – maybe more than one – generates long lead times of supply. The production centre is likely to rely on 'inbound' component sourcing. Ideally, a level of intermediate inventory between the manufacturing and customer/distribution is required to buffer against extended transit times. It needs continuous review. Such multi-country sourcing of inbound complete sourcing needs particular review when the goods cross international borders and attract customs duties and often inherent clearance delays, thereby extending the lead supply time. This customs clearance is eliminated with the FTZ (see page 79) and intra-EU trade operating in a customs-free zone. Hence many companies have set up their production/component assembly/distribution centre in the EU with its 27 countries and population of 520 million, due to its good infrastructure/common product specification CE/custom-free zone/being the wealthiest regional population in the world.

b   Managers are often reluctant to eliminate long-established suppliers, but the strategy of pursuing supplier rationalisation must be pursued with vigour and critical analysis. It will yield administration cost savings and maybe freight/supply chain time benefits. It also poses the question of developing multifunction component units rather than the single function unit as found increasingly in each new generation of technology. It is a route to producing more competitive products and rationalisation of suppliers.

c   A continuous audit review gathering market intelligence must be conducted of both inbound and outbound supply chain embracing all its elements, including the value-added benefit emerging from the 3PL and 4PL. The urgency/importance of such a task manifests itself when comparing national/local suppliers with the global supply chain. The latter embraces the international regulations subject to continuous review/change including customs, the development of infrastructure – trade routes/ new carriers/new transport equipment/handling facilities, new IT providing complete transparency in supply chain and cargo consolidation (see item d).

d   Carriers are driven by the needs of shippers to add value to the service. Three areas present an ongoing challenge: innovation featuring (i) multi-modalism operating alliances, embracing joint services as found in Dubai and Singapore, containerisation – FCL/LCL/road/sea/rail, land bridge – trailer/truck – road/sea/road, land bridge – pallet/IATA container – road/sea/air/road, trailer/truck – road/sea/road, swap body – road/rail/sea/road; (ii) consolidation focusing on small consignments usually through logistics agent; and (iii) hub and spoke system relying on hub airport/seaports being served by feeder services. Overall, the foregoing could reduce freight cost, inventory holding, warehousing, lead time, packaging, insurance, and improve customer service.

e   The procurement officer in product sourcing must have full cognisance to minimise payment exposure to payment of customs duties and taxation. Hence a vigilant customs planning strategy and challenge must be devised to minimise traders' cost of compliance and customs duties, maximise traders' use of facilities and reliefs, avoid risk of seizure and penalties and improve traders' profitability and cash flow.

The key to it is a well trained, organised with a strong interface throughout, dedicated logistic global supply chain team with complete transparency in all the inbound and outbound sectors. This will maximise competitiveness and custom focus.

Customs and Global Supply Chain Management

We have already alluded in this chapter to the significance of customs planning in global supply chain management, but its importance merits a return to subjective deeper analysis, in particular, the need to focus on the need for efficiency and coordinating/

reviewing/auditing the efforts of the procurement manufacture, marketing and distribution aligned to the supply chain management team. Each of these elements may be located in a different country. As materials and goods are moved from one country to another, borders are crossed and any goods or materials shipped/air freighted become subject to customs authorities control.

Political initiatives in liberalising trade and finance, coupled with technological innovations in information, communications and transport technology have stimulated the ongoing process of globalisation and placed more pressure on personnel to add value to the global supply chain.

Customs authorities, by administering and supervising the movement of goods and materials across national frontiers, play a key role. Costs for business can be identified in three areas as follows:

1   Direct cost associated with paying duties embracing: customs duty, excise duty, anti-dumping duty, countervailing duties, CAP levies, import VAT and compensatory interest.
2   Costs for business associated with the compliance of import restrictions and in meeting obligatory customs requirements such as prescribed accounting procedures and information requirements – including statistics – and compulsory document requirements.
3   Costs, which may include opportunity costs, by failing to take advantage of any customs regime or trade concessions. Likewise, the inappropriate use of any customs regime, or procedures, which may give rise to future liabilities.

As goods and materials move across national frontiers managing the customs function is a key factor to success within the efforts of supply chain management. Within each of the supply chain functions, which include procurement, manufacture, marketing and distribution, customs considerations can have a significant impact.

Preferential tariffs for goods and materials may exist in a wide range of countries. For example, the duty rate in the EU on a television tube sourced in Malaysia is 14 per cent, Thailand 9.8 per cent, South Africa 7.3 per cent, and nil in Poland with each country subject to meeting certain conditions. In manufacturing it is prudent to consider any customs regimes that give preferential duty rate advantages. They may suspend, reduce, or defer the duty burden available in the UK and EU, including customs warehousing, inward processing relief, outward processing relief, returned goods relief, standard exchange system and processing under customs control.

When the buyer becomes involved in market sourcing selection, it is important to bear in mind changes in duty rates. Examples include Dubai and China, recent entries to the WTO, which will encourage reduced barriers. Similar opportunities arise for buying sourcing as trade agreements such as MERCOSUR (Southern Common Market – of Latin America), North American Free Trade Area (NAFTA) or ASEAN Free Trade Area (AFTA) further develop, expand and consolidate their customs preferential strategies.

When supply chains take on an international dimension it is essential to take account of customs requirements and procedures, including customs law. Inefficient management of customs control can lead to increased inventory costs, delays at frontiers and loss in supply chain responsiveness. A firm's enhancement in competitiveness arises in cash flow, duty liability and customs clearance time. 'Trade off' considerations that need to be made are the advantages that an available regime may bring, against any compliance, accounting or reporting cost, operating cost and commercial restrictions imposed by the regime. Customs facilities available to the buyer include the following:

a   Import into free circulation (see page 32) – customs duty and import VAT is paid and goods are removed from customs control; some goods may be subject to import licences.
b   Customs warehousing (see page 78) – enables goods to be stored without payment of import duty or VAT until released for free circulation or placed under another customs regime.
c   Free zones (see page 79) – enables goods to be stored and processed without payment of import duty or VAT.
d   Inward processing relief suspension (see page 79) and drawback – allows conditional relief from duty on imported materials and components for use in the manufacture of products for exports; under IPR suspension duty is suspended while under IPR drawback duty is paid and later reclaimed.
e   Processing under customs control – allows specific dutiable components and materials to be imported without payment of duty, processed into finished products and released for free circulation at the duty rate of the finished goods – the rate may be lower than the rate of the components and materials used in the production process.
f   Temporary importation – gives relief from duty for goods imported for a given period of time – maximum 24 hours – and re-exported in the same country.
g   Returned goods relief – allows relief on reimportation of goods previously exported.
h   End use – reduced or zero duty for goods intended for a specified end use.
i   Other – goods are re-exported, destroyed or otherwise disposed of without payment of duty.

Customs facilities available to exporters include the following:

a   Export – goods leaving the EU may be subject to licensing requirements, export duties and commercial policy measures.
b   Outward processing relief – allow relief from duty on EU goods reimported after repair or process abroad.
c   Community Transit – an EC customs procedure, which controls and facilitates the movement of certain goods from one port of the EC to another, delaying duty and VAT payment.
d   ATA carnet – may be used to simplify customs clearance of temporarily exported goods: the carnet replaces normal customs documents both at export and reimport.
e   TIR carnet – subject to certain conditions, this allows goods to travel across national frontiers with the minimum of customs formalities, duty and VAT.

Outside the EU, other customs regimes may exist that could give an international supply chain similar competitive advantages. These embrace free trade zones, distriparks (see page 126), export processing zones, or tariff suspension for industries identified as being essential in developing the governing economy. Any one of these regimes could give the overseas buyer considerable advantage – for example, third country assembly, processing or distribution – in managing cost and duty liabilities and should be considered when planning and managing an international supply chain.

To develop further customs issues, it is essential for the supply chain professional to take into account considerations that go beyond the actual physical handling of goods. There are many customs considerations worthy of attention that could add value to the supply chain. In many instances, customs issues can be deal breakers or makers, depending on trade policies, duty, rates and feasible customs regimes.

Customs law is not static. Rules and regulations are constantly reviewed and businesses need to be aware of developments and changes and their interpretation. Opportunities may exist or evolve that could give a business a competitive advantage and reduce the impact on the supply chain of crossing international borders.

For example, electronic commerce is becoming more widespread globally with traders reporting to customs electronically (see page 114). Usually as a prerequisite, some form of paper trail is required. Electronic reporting and electronic declarations can simplify complying with customs. Electronic reporting is usually subject to customs authorisation.

Another example is customs warehousing (see page 87), which in principle allows the storage of goods free of duty and import VAT. This type of warehouse permits the company's inventory system to be used to track and control inventory for customs warehousing purposes rather than a specific physical location.

Management of the Inventory in the Supply Chain Analysis Including Vendor Management

The management of the inventory in the supply chain is a critical area in the cycle time analysis. This embraces from the time when inventory is needed until it is received, sold and sales payment is received, and is particularly important to company success and longevity. The longer the cycle time the larger the amount of inventory that will be carried to balance against uncertainty.

From an accounting and financial evaluation, inventory is an asset and a positive for businesses. A contract manufacturer turns inventory 3.6 times, a retailer turns inventory 4.1 times, and a wholesaler turns inventory 4.4 times; each have a differing inventory strategy. It embraces raw, work in progress (WIP) or finished product; each have too much money tied up in the inventory.

Development of a strategic focus on inventory is best expressed in companies operating a payment cycle every 90 days resulting in four payments per year. Hence a lot of capital is tied up, which earns nothing while goods remain unsold. Moreover, the working capital to run the company is much increased and thereby is detrimental to the company efficiency and competitive pricing strategy.

Inventory has a limited shelf life. There is a window of opportunity to sell the product. Once that window closes, the sales value falls, and the level of profitability and inventory yield are not maximised. In addition to the capital issue, excess influences service and operations, unnecessary freight costs are incurred to bring the products to the warehouse rather than direct to the buyer/consumer. The inventory works against having a good warehouse layout to reduce order picking. It adds to labour cost. If the company does cycle counting, then such inventory is counted too often and this is wasted time and effort. Too much inventory results in having a distribution centre larger than really necessary to store the extra items. Hence cost and impact are very large. Overall, it restricts agility to respond quickly to changing conditions. Other aspects include insurance cover, risk of obsolescence and discount pricing to dispose of fast-moving goods (FMG) such as the computer, perishable products, etc.

The causes of excess inventory are numerous and diverse. Much depends on the product and level of competition. A key factor is the degree to which the logistic supply chain network has been developed. We will now focus on some of the reasons for excess inventories to be followed by a strategic development:

a   Loss of sales: the new availability of a product to sell encourages the potential buyer to patronise a competitor and the fear of not having an item in stock is stronger than the fear of not being able to sell the item. Moreover, it results in money in the competitor account, thereby improving cash flow. Hence, a hedge factor arises to carry more items and more inventories than is necessary. A further factor is an over-optimistic sales forecast with inadequate market research and intelligence.

b   Price strategy: companies take advantage of lower prices for volumes in excess of what they need or will use in a reasonable time. The strategy is that it is 'too good a deal to pass up', even if it sits forever in inventory. Prima facie economical purchases may actually be uneconomical.

c   Obsolescence is a great risk in overstocking. It results in writing off the inventory, which impacts on profit and loss (P&L) for the year.

d   Absence of a range of effective inventory management measures: this embraces no aggressive measures to measure and manage the inventory, inventory ageing and inventory velocity.

e   Planning: inventory planning is not based on demand management or similar criteria. Basically, it is more of an initiative activity with long lead times for items, especially those imported; this compounds the problem.

f   Supplier performance and analysis is a key area. Suppliers are not managed even when suppliers fail to ship or deliver more than 25 per cent of the procurement on time. Ideally, a zero tolerance or near zero tolerance should be sought, as practised by the Japanese. Firms build in extra time to receive their orders. They carry extra inventory to compensate for the supplier delivery issues. Poor supplier performance generates increased inventories because of its unreliability and extended time to deliver.

g   Absence of any process embracing buying and ordering transactions: it may arise through a perceived or intrinsic need. This embraces companies with no strategic processes for customers, sourcing, or tactical processes for sales and operations planning. Procedures that lack processes, whether for inventory or other purposes, may be used instead. Expediting is another sign of no process. Inventory is used to compensate for the lack of process or for lack of execution.

h   A unified approach embracing one-approach-fits-all: the inventory strategy is not segmented to reflect differences in inventory as to profitability and turn velocity. Consequently, companies end up carrying too much inventory, especially for slower turning items.

Developing a strategic approach is essential with focus on processes at all levels of management throughout the company. A company commitment is required throughout the business, which we will now examine.

i   Inventory analysis. This will identify daily measurement of movement throughout the inventory, especially in terms of velocity, ageing and turns.

j   Developing a lean inventory (see page 27) throughout the business. Excess inventory and additional management time represent waste and add no value to the product.

Many departments can create non-value time and inventory. Lean is very similar to supply chain management (see page 24) with its emphasis on pull (see page 27) for product movement. Lean is a key tool to identifying and reducing unnecessary inventory.

k   An examination of the entire supply chain distinguishes two major elements: the inbound supply chain from the outbound supply chain in designing and implementing the strategy; otherwise the cycle time and resultant inventory become blurred. A further aspect is to develop a multiple transport and stocking programme to reflect the segmentation of the inventory. Companies that have supply chain management as part of the core competency and strategic focus perform better in controlling inventory across the supply chain.

l   Segmenting inventory by velocity and profitability identifies where the inventory exists, why it exists and how it occurs.

m   An important focus of inventory strategy is to make it a key area in the overall company direction with emphasis on customers, sales and profits.

n   To formulate and implement a sales and operations planning programme that embraces both the customer and sourcing strategies.

o   To continuously strive to compress time in the cycle. This embraces focus on uncertainty and inventory buffers that increase the cycle time. Endeavour to reduce the time from the need for inventory until it is sold. This is very important with lead times for critical items especially perishable, fashionable and fast-moving consumer goods (FMCG), and for imports that have long transit times. Compression should occur both internally and externally to the company.

p   To focus on reliability, which contributes to the brand image. Vagaries in the supply chain compound uncertainty and increase inventory.

q   Innovation and creative thinking is often obtained by brainstorming. Do not imitate other companies' practices, and do not be restrained by existing company practices and rules that were developed in a different business environment. Brainstorming must not be confined to middle and senior managers/directors, but throughout the company, especially more recent recruits – fresh from college/university – who have been trained in logistics.

r   Distribution network. The location of the warehouses may have been established years ago under economic conditions that have changed. Their design, layout, often favours a labour-intensive operation and out-of-date transport resource. Many warehouses can increase the total inventory carried because of the extra safety stock. Too few can mean longer transport distances and can have more inventories in transit than on the shelves. Many factors contribute to the location of the warehouse/distribution centre (see page 87). It differs widely in developed countries such as the US and the EU with a good transport infrastructure, as found in France, the Netherlands, Belgium and Germany, and less developed regions as found in many African countries. It also applies in India (see page 137) and Sri Lanka (see page 141). The optimal network for today's business should determine the warehouse location and future needs.

s   Supplier performance is a key part of the inventory management and of the sourcing strategy. Manage purchase orders at all stages of the procurement process, including the supply chain transparency. There is much more to consider than low prices in rent or selection.

t   The effect of global sourcing – long transit times across the Pacific or Atlantic and other trade lands affect the inventories that firms may carry. Analyse the impact of such sourcing and determine how to address the inventory and degree of competitiveness, especially in the area of pricing. Study the Dyson case study (see page 151) relative to the relocation of the production plant of domestic appliances such as washing machines, vacuum cleaners, etc. from England to the Far East – closer to the component sourcing and nearer to the growth markets in the region, including Japan.

u   Outside assistance embracing two options. First, there is the one-time help that can be provided by a supply chain management consulting firm. Secondly, there is the ongoing approach that can be provided by a 4PL or 3PL to manage the inbound or outbound supply chain. The 4PL should be a neutral party whose focus is supply chain management and does not bring a possible 'conflict of interest' by wanting the firm's freight or warehouse activity that some 3PLs do. Third-party logistics and 4PLs that can see the supply chain, not just freight or pallets, can be valuable partners. Increasing inventory turns and velocity is critical to business profitability and survival. Reducing inventory and preventing build-up of unnecessary inventory is not a quick fix.

v   E-commerce. The need to have adequate software in the warehouse is essential, especially bar coding/radio frequency identification (see page 118). It ensures the development of a computer-literate management system and focus. This facilitates planning and especially the interface with the supply chain management.

Management of the inventory should be part of the overall company strategy with focus on customers, sales and profits. It requires commitment and vision. Moreover, it involves all levels of management and constant brainstorming to improve performance.

Factors Contributing to the Development of Logistics

The factors influencing the development of global logistics are numerous. The most salient are detailed below.

1   The development of information technology (IT). RFID has enabled a transformation to take place in communication and data transmission, opening up markets and refocusing strategies in distribution and manufacturing outsourcing and assembly. It has no culture or language barriers, no time zones and is available continuously, bringing together the low- and high-labour cost nations and their skills for the exchange of goods and services.

2   The globalisation of markets with their infrastructure and international trade environment generating business confidence internationally. A major contributor is the WTO (see page 120).

3   The accelerating development of the global container network has offered a new challenge to the global trader. It has placed a fresh focus on global distribution with an emphasis on added value in the distribution chain. The question posed by the international entrepreneur is how can we further improve and extend the conventional multi-modal container service to the benefit of the shipper and in the interest of efficiency. Shippers are already being offered the option of independent software and systems as an alternative to those available from the carrier. This allows suppliers, carriers, manufacturers and retailers to make optimum routing decisions and increases the transparency of goods flows. The financial efficiency of the supply chain network is also being examined. This involves developing a product to

coordinate the flow of funds more efficiently with the movement of goods, thereby allowing the importer and exporter access to cheaper sources of money.

4　The continuous expansion of the integrators TNT and DHL. This has opened up new markets in both the manufacturing and service industries.

5　The decline of the end-to-end/port-to-port liner conference system and the development of the hub and spoke global container network (see page 79), coupled with the expansion of multi-modalism.

6　The emergence of the mega-container operator (see page 156), which exploits the economies of scale and provides the mega-operator the opportunity to provide the 'in-house' global logistics resources such as are found in mega-container operators.

7　The decline of the freight forwarder has emerged as the mega container carriers develop in-house global logistic operations. This has encouraged the trade to entrust the entire distribution arrangement to the shipowner, thereby bypassing the freight forwarder.

8　The development of the free port, free trade zones and distriparks (see page 79) in the port environs has opened up new opportunities of trade distribution for the international entrepreneur. Such designated areas are immune from customs examination and revenue collection until they enter the domestic market in question. They enable the global trader to outsource the product and focus on such areas as the component assembly point, the packaging and distribution point, and the mixing and blending unit for powdered cargoes such as spices.

9　Value is added to the product through the global logistic network. It may be through better packaging arrangements, more outsourcing of componentised products that offer lower costs and better quality, or through the blending and mixing of food products as found in the distriparks in the Port of Rotterdam.

10　Companies, particularly multinationals, are being driven by their logistics departments. Moreover, the multinationals now focus on a simultaneous global product launch across all markets to ensure an early cash return on capital expenditure rather than concentrating on a regional launch over a period of time, for example, phase one Europe, phase two North America and phase three the Far East. This favours the logistic operation.

11　Following on from point 10 is the intense competition emerging in the global product market. Hence, to remain competitive the trader must adopt a global logistic strategy.

12　Satellite production demands a logistic network. It is computer-driven.

13　Shorter product lifecycle, driven by a fashion-conscious international market and continuous technical advancement, favours logistic efficiency.

14　The ongoing technological developments providing a longer shelf life for many consumer products, especially foodstuffs, need a logistically based distribution sourcing mechanism.

15　The global logistic facility offers a one-stop operation and the opportunity to deal with one person – the account executive. Hence, both the importer and exporter develop empathy with the global logistics operator on a tailor-made basis, taking full advantage of their professionalism and experience coupled with a competitively priced operation. Traders can therefore concentrate on their core business of marketing, product development, investment and production.

16　The global logistics operation encourages the rationalisation of distribution networks. This will accelerate as the hub and spoke system develops through the megacarrier operations.

17　Continuing improvements in the global infrastructure, for example port modernisation, the development of inland clearance depots and free trade zones, the provision of new and enlarged airports, the development of road and rail networks, serving the ports and airports, all favour the global logistics operation. The development of multi-modalism involving a stronger interface and integration between transport modes and the emergence of dedicated services also favours global logistics.

18   Undoubtedly, the rapid expansion of IT has been a major driving factor as the global logistic operation is computer-driven.

19   Companies today demand responsiveness from the global operator. The discerning international entrepreneur is demanding the 'total logistics product service' (see item 17). When a trader purchases a service, the trader expects the consignment to be delivered or to be informed of delays or challenges encountered. As trade expands and companies move from a regional to a global market basis to exploit the economies of scale, to remain competitive in price and product specification, and to make further market penetration, the quality of the service becomes paramount. Moreover, the global logistics operator, through experience and professionalism, facilitates the trader's expansion from a regional to a global market base. The global operator will be able to help the trader in planning such market expansion and provide data on the culture, the market environment, import restrictions, customs regulations and the best-practice global logistics operation feasible. Today, traders are logistically literate and demand accreditation to product quality control – which includes distribution through global logistics. Moreover, traders demand a quick response to changing and volatile order levels with cycles of peaks and troughs. Again, the mega-logistic carrier can best respond to such a challenge.

20   Market research confirms that only 30 per cent of changes in suppliers are motivated by a better or cheaper product. Most changes occur due to a poor service quality or inadequate attention to the individual customer. This also favours the mega-logistics global operator.

21   The manufacturer/producer striving to achieve a shorter production cycle realised with the facilitation of many of the ingredients offered by the logistics system.

22   The development of 3PL contractors such as Wincanton Logistics and Exel Logistics.

23   The continuous improvement in supply chain software. The most important concept underlying management of supply is that of integration. This embraces manufacturing resource planning, inventory management and supply chain design. Goods must be able to flow in a highly organised manner between each stage of the supply chain while at the same time achieving the most desirable balance between sales–stocks– production and customer services–cost–working capital. Every supply chain will have a different set of emphases. For example, a manufacturer of high specification value goods may be more interested in speed and security of delivery than achieving the lowest cost. It is essential all parties involved in the supply chain have an agreed set of priorities. Moreover, effective transparent communication and understanding needs to be created of what the supply chain is designed to achieve. Logistic systems are important to be able to send data to where the decisions are taken and to keep all the international business managers and sectors informed about the flow of goods. Figure 2.2 features the supply chain software. Software advances have been accelerated through the rapid globalisation of manufacture and distribution.

24   The development of time-sharing with the logistics contractor. This involves the contractor being linked to the customer's own IT system – receiving order picking and delivery instructions, implementing them and feeding back the results for

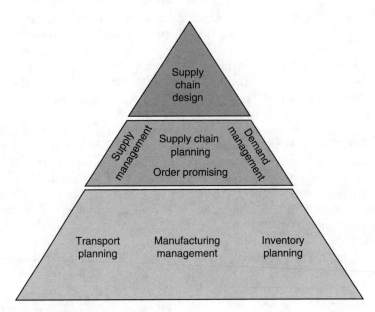

Figure 2.2 A focus of the supply chain software.

Reproduced by courtesy of Synquest.

processing and evaluation. However, this limits their ability to take a proactive approach to their customer's needs.

25   Economic and trading blocs as found in Europe, North America and the Far East are continuing to develop as Member States realise their benefits. Such blocs favour particularly the global logistic trader who can adopt the strategy of selling a single product in a single market, such as the EU, which has no culture or trade barriers and permits the free flow of goods. Supply chain efficiency is here a key factor in sales performance and market penetration.

To conclude our analysis the specific reasons for the increasing interest in supply chain management and global logistics can be summarised as follows:

1   *Concept.* Companies are primarily concerned with reducing delivery times and improving responsiveness to customers, reflecting the shorter product lifecycles they face.
2   *Value.* Equal emphasis is placed upon cost savings (from reduced inventory levels, economies of sale and a reduction in fixed assets) and improved service quality (through reliable delivery, improved stock availability and response times).

To achieve improvements in the management of a supply chain, keeping track of goods at all times is the key. This can be achieved through manual methods or sophisticated electronic data interchange (EDI) tools (see page 114).

Asset Management in the Supply Chain

Asset management is a key area in the global supply chain and warehouse management. It is very much aligned to radio frequency identification (RFID) (see page 108). Overall, it provides a range of benefits in inventory control, asset utilisation, manufacturing work-in-process, loss prevention and security.

The asset management problem – it emerges with many industries conducting and keeping up with existing inventory – has historically been a challenging, resource-intensive process. Many conduct a resource and fiscal decision without having accurate current data available. Many current methods for performing an inventory count or for tracking asset movement do not provide real-time asset visibility. Hence, decisions are based on outdated, inaccurate information. One must acknowledge that in the most advanced supply chain management, warehouse management systems, enterprise resource planning and related software solutions, the accuracy and value of the data from these packages is only as good as the information source input.

Equally challenging is the equipment and asset monitoring to prevent theft or misplacement. Hence the results that the asset is no longer available and the company will incur additional cost to replace it. Endless situations arise of asset loss, such as the hotel that lost hundreds of television sets from their own shipping docks, the manufacturer that was to have much of its electronic equipment stolen via employee exits or shipping docks, or the laboratory unable to locate a piece of test equipment, but later found it locked away in a forgotten storage room. Being able to detect a potential theft before it happens, or locating critical equipment when needed, requires real-time visibility and information relating to the location and status of the item. Additionally, that information must be integrated into the existing host systems so that decisions and actions can be taken in real time.

Security is another area on which to focus attention. Consideration must be given to monitor security personnel; in the event that assistance is needed at a specific location within a facility, the nearest individual can be called upon.

An analysis of the foregoing identifies three key areas: real-time visibility; movement, status or tamper detection; and integration into high-level solutions. This requires a facility to address these areas as found in Red Priarie DL × ® Mobile Resource Management (MRM) software. It is used in conjunction with data capture hardware such as RFID – (active or passive), bar code or global positioning system (GPS); it provides real-time visibility to assets at the site or enterprise level.

The system operates on the basis of the foundation for a data capture ecosystem. It allows users to integrate a variety of data collection mechanisms, embracing the best technology for a given class of assets while maintaining a single, comprehensive data collection exchange and reporting structure.

The managing mobile resource solution is capable of providing a complete solution for the improved management of mobile resources and assets inherent in the supply chain such as pallets, containers, totes, equipment and vehicles. Running as a thin client application (most of software resides on network as opposed to PC, that is, web-deployed applications), the solution has the ability to provide the following: (a) real-time location of any mobile resources; (b) current status and life history of assets; (c) automatic user-definable warnings and alerts; (d) monitoring and enforcement of service schedules; (e) tracking of assets through manufacturing or repair cycles; (f) simple and effective exporting to Excel and Word; (g) performance monitoring; and (h) comprehensive management information and dashboard.

The mechanism procedure of RFID embraces tags placed on assets to be monitored. Depending on the asset type and application requirements, the tags may be active or passive RFID. Active tags have a battery, beacon, on a periodic basis, and can be read from distances of several hundred feet depending on the antenna type and surrounding environment. Passive tags derive their power when they are within the field of the reader. While they are considerably less expensive than active RFID tags, they have considerably less read range capability, with most having maximum read ranges of 10 feet or less. This limitation may require maximising the tags' readability by placing it on the asset where it is more susceptible to damage from moving equipment. Because of the differences in cost and read ranges, care must be taken and time invested to choose the proper tag for the application.

The area to be monitored is divided into zones with a reader placed in each zone such that when a tag is seen by a reader, its location is known, based on the zone definition. Resolution for the zones can vary based on the asset being tagged, antenna type and composition of the surrounding environment.

In a passive RFID application, portals would be set up at the entrances and exits to a given area, such that the tagged asset can only enter or leave the area by passing within the field of the reader. Additionally, bar-code readers could be used to capture asset information and provide this to the system via the MRM software. This assumes that a bar code is placed on each asset and the operation or process provides means for manual scanning of the bar code.

An example of asset management arises in the manufacturing sector in North America, embracing seven locations. The manufacturing process is highly automated and high-tech. Hitherto, it was reliant on manual bar-code scans or manual entries into logs. At certain steps in the process, assembly workers and/or automation tools need to know which unit is being worked on, so the correct function or process step is performed.

To resolve the problem, tags were placed on units being assembled and readers placed at key work cells along the assembly line; when a tag is read, the MRM software interprets which unit is identified at that work cell. It then interacts with the customer's host system, updating the location of other tagged units in the flow using sequencing logic. This information is subsequently shared with other systems in the operation and made available and transmittable via web browser, report or alert. Subsequently, the RFID was used to track totes used to transport parts and tools, and monitor and locate vehicles moving within the facility.

A further example arises with reusable container tracking. A leading manufacturer of residential glass uses metal racks to transport sheets of glass within the facility and for shipping to window manufacturers. The racks are often moved between the manufacturer's various facilities as they are returned from the window manufacturers.

The glass manufacturer has a problem maintaining visibility to the racks inasmuch as they can only account for a percentage of the racks and do not know how many reside at their manufacturing or customer locations. This generates a problem, as individual sites may not have enough racks on hand to support customer orders, impacting the sales cycle and ultimately revenue. Moreover, it contributes to excess inventory as more are purchased to meet demand because of misplaced racks.

To resolve the problem, RFID tags are placed on each rack and readers placed at each dock door. The MRM software is used to provide visibility to the tagged racks as they move into and out of the manufacturer's facilities. The MRM software is integrated into the manufacturer's host systems so that this information can be shared across the enterprise, allowing total visibility to all racks and providing a means for them to make better decisions as they manage incoming orders.

To conclude, active RFID (see page 108) is not a panacea for all asset types or applications. Alternatively, the passive RFID bar code or global positioning systems (GPS) may be needed. The ideal asset management system must make use of multiple technologies, choosing the best data capture solution for each type of asset. This could result in using a combination of bar-code labels, passive RFID, active RFID and GPS, thereby taking advantage of the strengths of each for certain asset types.

Lean Supply Chain Management

Lean supply chain management is the strategic process of developing and managing a cost-effective and efficient supply chain that is competitive in the global marketplace and has a strong empathy with the end user. It involves the ability to identify waste in the supply chain. Overall it focuses on three key areas.

Basically, it extends beyond the supply chain and manufacturing programme, but includes a change throughout the organisation to be logistically focused and literate. Secondly, it embraces the suppliers and customers. Thirdly, the lean principles that must be the basis of the lean supply chain: determine value from the view of the customer, not the view of the company, make the product and information flow, a pull product (see page 14) strategy, do not push it, and manage towards perfection with continuous improvement.

Lean supply chain management is a challenge that must be acknowledged. This is in addition to the usual company issues, such as lack of implementation know-how, resistance to change, lack of a crisis to create urgency, gaining resources and commitment and backsliding.

Areas that need to be addressed include the following:

a   International sourcing – procuring finished goods or raw materials in China, India, Germany, Brazil and elsewhere creates a significant obstacle to lean, especially outside North America. The order to delivery time is long. Time is a waste/ uneconomic resource, and it compounds the inventory waste issue by making firms buffer (carry additional stocks), and carry more inventory than is needed to compensate for the time being lean, with a 20–40-day transit time bringing a unique test to develop lean SCM. It is compounded when experiencing port delays and shortage of specialised containers.

b   Accounting – does not recognise waste as lean does. The need to have continuous financial evaluation and added value identity/opportunities is essential. Inventory represents capital tied up. Accounting systems do not recognise time, particularly in the balance sheet. Rework is not treated the same by accounting.

c   Organisation – supply chain management and lean are processes that cross organisation boundaries. Implementing a process that goes horizontally in a vertically and functionally defined organisation creates gaps in both processes. These gaps create areas where waste can develop and where removing it can be difficult, especially with MNIs who follow a corporate strategy.

d   Number of firms. There are many suppliers and many logistic service providers in a supply chain. Some are visible and some are less visible. Many suppliers or logistics services do not practice a lean strategy. Adopting a lean strategy outside the company into other firms adds to the time and complexity of implementing and becoming lean.

Adopting a lean strategy requires a plan with an objective/strategic focus and that is pragmatic/professional/flexible. This involves evaluating all the ingredients of the supply chain and measuring each element against a benchmark. A key to the plan is the starting point. Overall, a useful tool is the value stream mapping (VSM), which defines the current state of a company's support chain, to identify waste and to lay the foundation in determining its future state flow.

Initial VSM efforts include defining the present value stream for product families, those that share common operations or have large volume impact, either in units or currency value. Formulating the supply chain embraces featuring the various lean tools in the future supply chain flow. This features the infrastructure to support it, training, culture, quality methods, accounting systems and investment policies. Lean tools have differences as to ease of use, time to implement, benefits and risk. It embraces six stages.

a   5 Ss – sort, straighten, sweep/shine, standardise, sustain/self-discipline. This is a visual way to organise waste removal with extra time for travel or employees. It can be used in distribution centres and in offices.
b   Rapid set-up – or changeover – has application in the warehouse to adjust layout for seasonal products, new products and changes in which products are fast-moving and often picked, and the complementary items that go with these fast-overs. Reducing the time can involve housekeeping and maintenance (including 5 Ss), setting up smaller areas for stock-keeping units (SKUs), technology (such as warehouse management systems) and RFID (see page 108)).
c   Standardise – involves efficient work processes that are repeatedly followed to define who, what, how, where and when. This helps firms synchronise the time required to pull and ship all the orders and actual time to do this (cycle time). It can be the basis for employee training.
d   Kanban – present a new, unique way to view 'warehousing' and inventory positioning. A way to coordinate multi-step processes for multiple products. With Kanban, small stocks of inventory are placed in dedicated locations for supply chain control. This approach runs counter to the traditional way of large distribution centres delivering truckloads of products to stores or customers. Instead, mini 'warehouses' are used to position inventory closer to the customer and increase the speed of delivery and inventory turns. Point of sale and other technologies can be the withdrawal signal to trigger both drawing from and replenishing Kanbans. Items placed in supply chain Kanbans could be limited to high inventory such as 'A' items and then using regular warehouses for 'B' and 'C' items. A variation to Kanban is with the import supply chains and differentiating 'A' versus 'B' versus 'C' items, and using faster mode and faster carrier transit methods for select items. This reduces time and inventory with small batch sizes for select items. All inventories are not treated the same way from suppliers nor with regard to warehousing.
e   Workcell – can be defined as a unit larger than an individual operation, but smaller than a department. It is self-contained as to equipment and resources. The potential application, combining multi-operations into a central area, exist where warehouses carry out additional activities such as kitting or assembly.
f   Sigma – an advanced tool that ties to quality. The focus is variation and controlling and preventing errors. Statistical measurement is fundamental. It is used throughout the supply chain, not just in select activities or locations. Sigma takes lean supply chain management to its ultimate level.

Usually, there are complementary or supporting processes with lean supply chain management. The additional processes may include 'strategic sourcing' to manage supplier performance for critical and important items; 'strategic customer' to gain the needed viewpoint of key customers; and 'sales and operations planning' to blend the strategic sourcing and customer with the tactical day-to-day supply chain management.

Overall, lean supply chain management involves continuous focus and flexibility in all areas of the business. It requires a dedicated team to achieve the objective and critical analysis of all areas of the supply chain to improve efficiency and add value to the supply chain. Multi-sourcing yields improvement, but adds to the complexity of the supply chain operation/management. Essentially, the operation must remain seamless throughout. A strategic focus is required.

Getting started with lean and sustaining it with continuous improvement is not easy. Lean takes time and years to accomplish. Often the waste has become incorporated into the daily operation company-wide and is accepted as part of doing business. In some situations there may be too much instability in a supply chain to become lean. The first step is to increase stability before beginning lean. Overall, the benefits are intrinsic, embracing gaining market share, reducing capital tied up in inventory, increasing profitability, improving customer service, increasing capacity and taking time out of the entire company's way of doing things – a management culture change. Planning is an essential ingredient.

Lean Supply Workforce

We have examined lean supply chain management (see page 27) and will examine the demand-driven workforce (see page 101), embracing the demand-driven supply network, incorporating the pull model as distinct from the push model. We will now examine the concept of lean supply workforce. These are all interrelated.

Lean supply workforce traces its history/conception to the Japanese car producer Toyota, which extolled a highly efficient manufacturing workflow process. Its objective is to remove waste from the workflow processes. Today it has become translated into the logistic framework and is found in the global supply chain. It adds value to the supply chain and eliminates waste from the time the order is placed, to the delivery process/end user. Areas on which to focus include unproductive work methods, non-productive or indirect time, and a range of other work habits and conditions – many of which are historical – that don't add value.

Taiichi Ohno – the Toyota production engineer – who developed the idea, identified seven areas on which to focus, which we will now examine briefly:

a   The first objective is to adopt the 'best practice' approach and eliminate historical methods, which many labour forces are keen to preserve or even modify.

b   The next stage is to set goals, standards and adaptable precision. This embraces using the most efficient methods as defined by the best practice. A useful technique is engineered labour standards developed using time studies, an established database of granular movements called master standards data, or a combination of both. These examine individual jobs based on the work content to define an appropriate length of time for each task that reflects weight, cube and dimensions of the product, the equipment used and the distance travelled. Overall, the operations must reflect current and future trends, gain labour force acceptance, and strive towards accuracy, fairness and productivity. It should be noted that historical averages should not be used as they do not reflect best practices and above all do not account for variances in job content.

c   The third element is planning, scheduling and simulation. This embraces the prerequisite to have in place the best practice and creation of accurate standards, which facilitate how long a given job should take or the required number of workforce to undertake a particular job. Technology is available to translate order demand data, seasonal trends, special promotions, and other demand signals into workforce plans that indicate how many people, with what skills, are required to complete the prescribed work within a given time frame such as a shift, day, week or longer period. This planning data can be combined with human resource data on skills, severity, preferred shift or workdays, hours worked in the pay periods, employment regulation (see page 63) and other pertinent information to develop proper staffing schedules. This strategy will eliminate the waste associated with overstaffing or unnecessary overtime or temporary help. A further benefit of understanding work content and time frames is the ability to evaluate the impact of changes on work methods, equipment or layout, and calculate the return on investment (ROI) for these changes.

d   An area where waste can be identified is unproductive time embracing time spent between jobs or indirect time.

e   Quality and safety are key factors to establish best practices. This is realised through employed best-practice methodologies, training workers and supervisors how to properly use the best practices, and by removing barriers to productivity. Workers will try to cut corners to improve their productivity performance, but the cost of mistakes and accidents that ensue, including damaged inventory and equipment, injuries, penalties, returns and other customer service issues, can far outweigh the savings from productivity gains.

f   Educating the workforce in the logistic skills to develop best practice is a key area. This includes not only the initial course programme, but also refresher courses. Continuous training must be given by supervisors to ensure the goals are realised. Overall, the training must be professional and pragmatic and with a view to performance monitoring and coaching.

g   The management must have regular meaningful data to measure the workforce productivity and reliability. This involves a range of analytical tools that will identify problem areas and groups that are high or low performers. For example, it may identify areas of investment, training and changes in the workforce.

Companies focusing on the lean supply workforce strategy frequently devise incentive schemes. This requires accurate performance data.

Finally, in our lean supply workforce analysis, companies frequently experience a reluctance to change, but in most situations the option does not exist if the company and its products are to remain competitive. The driving force is often technology. The following points can be deployed to persuade the workforce/management of the benefits emerging.

i   Modelling and simulation tools enable management to evaluate the true cost of changes to methodologies, equipment, or layout in order to calculate ROI.

ii Proper workforce planning and scheduling reduces overstaffing, overtime and temporary staff.

iii It develops a logistic culture focused on efficiency – particularly cost-consciousness.

iv Transformation to a self-accountability culture eliminates cherry-picking and other work avoidance activities. This improves productivity and morale, since all workers are evaluated fairly and equitably.

   v Elimination of wasted time and effort improves productivity and throughput, thus reducing costs and improving service.

  vi Employment of best practices not only ensures that the most efficient, safe and error-free methodologies are used, it makes operations more consistent. This reduces training cost, improves quality, and enhances customer service.

 vii Self-motivated and accountable workers with higher morale will provide better, more friendly and responsive customer service. This improves customer satisfaction and loyalty.

viii The collaborative partnership established in a performance-focused culture improves the morale and retention of the labour force. Overall, the benefits can significantly impact bottom-line results.

  ix The use of granular standards and discrete measurement software enables activity-based costing. This helps management to better understand the cost to serve each customer by product or service provided. This data can be very helpful in bidding and price negotiations, as well as in determining true margin contributions by product, customer service, location or business unit.

To conclude, our lean workforce analysis is the result of the twenty-first century strive (see page 29) for improved and continuous productivity in all sectors of the business community. It generates a situation where workers are self-motivated and self-accountable, supervisors become coaches, and the management has a more productive workforce with higher esteem and retention qualities. It requires the skill of managing change encapsulated through training, involvement and financial incentive.

Useful Sources of Information

Chartered Institute of Logistics and Transport <www.ciltuk.org.uk>
GAC Logistics <www.gacworld.com>

Chapter 3

Export Sales Contract

Introduction

The formulation of the export sales contract represents the conclusion of some possibly difficult negotiations and accordingly particular care should be taken regarding the preparation of its terms. It must be borne in mind that an exporter's primary task is to sell his or her products at a profit and therefore the contract should fulfil this objective insofar as his or her obligations are concerned. Above all, it should be capable of being executed under reasonable circumstances and ultimately produce a modest profit. Full cognisance must be taken of logistics and the supply chain.

Market Environment

Today, conducting business overseas is logistically driven. Hence, the need to conduct adequate research to ensure the logistic entrepreneur company is compatible with the buyer organization and thereby ensure there is an efficient supply chain on which both parties can build on to conduct business.

The following points are relevant:

a   Who are the main players in the market and what is their profile?

b   Market access and legal/political constraints.

c   Market stability and its infrastructure.

d   Product availability and its stage of development. It may be the first or second stage of development – low- or high-tech. It is also added value in terms of its development. Countries like India (see page 33), Pakistan, China and Sri Lanka (see page 141) are moving from a low-tech to a high-tech environment in many industrial and sociably developed regions with a logistics focus and continuous investment in the logistic infrastructure.

e   Is the market computer and logistically literate, and are importers/buyers flexible and adaptable?

f   Exchange rate stability and importation cost such as import duty (see page 117), sea/airport charges, and sales tax.

g   Membership of economic or trading bloc. Excellent example found in EU – 27 Member States – good infrastructure – single market permitting distribution of goods without border controls embracing customs duty and above all, high-tech and logistically focused (see page 133). North America is likewise logistically focused (see page 136).

h   Whether market is fully developed, underdeveloped, or developing. Fully developed are high-tech, capital-intensive with fully trained workforce. Conversely the less developed countries (LDCs) are agriculturally driven and often a commodity focused economy with low labour costs and low levels of technology. Moreover, they rely on non-convertible currencies.

i   Opportunity for inwards investment embracing joint venture, licensing, franchise, mergers and acquisition or industrial transplant.
j   Perceived benefits of the market such as indigenous resources, strategic geographical location etc.

Market Entry Strategy

Companies must have a logistic strategic focus in their decision-making process of selecting and entering a market, a series of markets, or cluster markets. The following logistic strategic considerations are relevant:

a   To have a customer portfolio with an international base.
b   To increase production thereby lowering unit cost and permitting more competitive pricing.
c   To raise the company profile to attract more capital into the company and provide more funds for new technology.
d   To realise a more volume-based and productive utilisation of the company infrastructure and its logistics/supply chain.
e   To increase market share and dominance.
f   To increase general competitiveness of the company.
g   To ensure the long-term future of the company.
h   To develop a proactive, rather than a reactive, company, which is globally logistically focused and market research-driven, with a continuous focus on client base and marketplace environment.
i   To develop an international brand image.

Many companies tend to develop/target a cluster market concept, each of which is logistically focused and thereby reliant on a distribution centre in one country served by reliable supply chains in neighbouring countries. It also favours a volume market with the opportunity for more productivity and logistic development.

Basically, the role of logistics is the development of systems and supporting coordination processes to ensure the customers' aspirations are met. Planning is an essential factor with well-thought-out and designed logistic systems. Overall, it embraces three basic areas.

The first is to identify customer service needs. The key components and the preferences must be identified. Reliability, cost of service, value added, and performance are key areas. Cluster customer markets of similar service preferences are ideal.

The second is to define customer service objectives. It is a market-driven logistics strategy. This embraces a zero failure rate. This is more difficult to realise with a global supply chain involving the complexity of international regulations compared with a national supply chain operating exclusively in one country such as the USA, Germany, or China. The global supply chain is likely to involve 3PLs and 4PLs, customs duty, differing transport modes, a variety of international trade regulations crossing international boundaries, Incoterms 2000 (see page 46), UCP 600 (see page 52) packaging regulations, products specification, various cultures, differing currencies, etc. It is a challenging operation that the global logistics entrepreneur must overcome. A development in the twenty-first century is tracking, whereby mega-container operators are able, through satellite communications INMARSAT (see page 145), to locate for the customer the whereabouts of the consignment in its international transit and anticipated arrival time at the destination. Software is a key factor in the design of the global logistic system and enables, through e-commerce, continuous communication such as RFID (see page 108).

The cost benefit of the customer service will be explored in greater depth in chapter 3, but a number of salient points are very significant, which we will briefly examine. The first stage is to identify the profitability emerging from individual customers. High-volume customers generate substantial profits, but lower unit cost. The second aspect is to continuously examine ways of reducing cost in the supply chain compatible with providing an acceptable service to the client. This is an important area in global logistics as international transport operators are continuously remodelling their services to become more competitive in transit time. The 'hub and spoke' system in a container operation is an example. Finally, the credit rating of the customer must be sought, engaging Standard & Poors of Stockhom (see page 126), and the country risk as available from Dun & Bradstreet, which monitors country risk (see page 56).

Constituents of the Export Sales Contract

The formulation and execution of the export sales contract involves four elements – insurance of the goods, payment of the goods, the contract of carriage and the export sales contract. All are interrelated and are primarily based on the global logistic operation and the related documentation. This embraces the cargo insurance certificate, the contract of carriage found in a bill of lading, air waybill or consignment, the payment arrangements involving presentation of the bill of lading to the bank to confirm shipment of the goods, and the export sales contract identifying the foregoing arrangements on a timescale basis. There are numerous variations to the foregoing arrangements (see page 79), which provide the logistics operator the ability to reduce cost, improve productivity and above all improve service and competiveness to the customer. The key to it is to fully understand the international trade environment embraced in the supply chain and have complete transparency with all the contributors/participants in the supply chain. This embraces credit rating, risk area, customs, routing, payment arrangements, packaging, transport cost, Incoterms, warehouse management, distribution centres, currency, 3PLs, 4PLs, software, insurance and product specification. A system of checkpoints to develop a cost benefit strategy to the supplier/consumer is an effective way of developing an efficient supply chain.

Details of an export contract are given below:

a   Exporter's (seller's) registered name and address.
b   Importer's (buyer's) registered name and address.
c   Short title of each party quoted in a and b.
d   Purpose of contract – the specified merchandise sold by person in item a to addressee quoted in item b.
e   Number and quantity of goods, precisely and fully described. In particular the contract must mention details of any batches and reconcile goods descriptions with custom tariff description (see page 74).
f   The price. The currency selected must be stable and convertible (see page 52). It may be in the seller's or buyer's currency or third currency acceptable to both parties. The

seller's currency transfers the risk of variation to the buyer; conversely the buyer's currency risk rests with the seller, while the third currency shares the currency risk variation between seller and buyer.

g   Terms of delivery. It is important that the correct Incoterm 2000 (see page 50) is used and the supply chain management keeps it under continuous review.

h   Terms of payment, for example open account, cash with order, letter of credit, open account or documents, against payment or acceptance. Again, salient factor in the design of the supply chain.

i   Delivery date and shipment date or period. This is a critical area with item j and has a strong interface with international transport operation (see page 79).

j   Methods of shipment – container, Ro/Ro, air freight or multi-modal road/container/rail/air.

k   Method of packing. Both parties must be fully aware and agree on packing specification. Skilful packing can improve the load-ability of the cargo unit/container/handling. Stringent regulations apply to dangerous classified cargo shipments (see page 86).

l   Cargo insurance policy/terms. The option exists for the seller/buyer to undertake the insurance and depends on the Incoterm 2000 (see page 50).

m   Import or export licence details or other instructions. The period of their validity must be reconciled with the terms of payment and delivery date or shipment date or period. There is a zero tolerance with the import/export licence extension, which the logistic operator must acknowledge.

n   Shipping, freight and documentary requirements and/or instructions. This includes marking of cargo. A complex area that the logistic operator must be familiar with. This includes pre-shipment documentation (see page 83).

o   Contract conditions, for example sale, delivery, performance (quality) of goods, arbitration, security, etc. This embraces local conditions that will vary with overseas destinations, especially customs clearance (see page 78).

p   Signature. Both parties must ensure that a responsible person at director or managerial level signs the contract and the data should be recorded.

Obviously the terms of the export sales contract will vary by circumstance and must be driven by logistics strategy. It may feature agency involvement, after-sales activities such as the availability and supply of spares, product servicing, training, advertising and promotion cost, and so on. It may embrace outsourcing of components and third-country assembly, embracing inbound and outbound movement. The logistics operator must minimise any risk areas such as political situation, currency fluctuations, unreliable transit schedules, protracted customs clearance, excessive documentation to effect customs clearance, liquidation of the buyer, and absence of adequate software in the supply chain management. Usually, the documents (item h) will be electronically transmitted, feature a performance bond, and the contract is subject to English law, or the national sovereignty of the buyer's/seller's country and an arbitration clause. Each party of the contract must retain a copy.

A sound logistic management strategy is required and full use must be made of computerisation. The tactics adopted include the strategy required for continuous review in the light of changing marketing conditions. Five areas need special attention: cash flow, administration, insurance, risk areas and total cost.

The foregoing embraces: (a) cash flow and the payment cycle and the options available to speed up payment through factoring (see page 51); (b) administration/supply chain management to be professional/focused and strive to improve efficiency; (c) credit insurance can be arranged to lessen payment risk; (d) risk areas such as credit rating evaluation/product liability/currency/political situation; and (e) total cost. The logistics operator designing the supply chain must fully understand the role of the Incoterms and the financial payment and the interface with the international transport operation.

Business-to-Business (B2B) and Business-to-Consumer (B2C)

The process of conducting business globally is electronically driven and there is no doubt it is a main driver in the globalisation of logistics. The web/Internet not only provides a good promotional tool available to procurement companies looking for suppliers, but also for conducting digital trading. Digital trading extends to the digital trade transport network embracing the logistics chain. This includes importers, exporters, freight forwarders and 3PL providers, terminals, carriers, government departments, banks and financial institutions, insurance companies and inspection agencies – online and paperless trading in as short a time as possible. Hence, from the procurement standpoint it ranges from the issue of purchase orders, insurance and letters of credit to inspections, the insurance of government certificates, trade declarations and payment functions.

Scanning the web to obtain potential overseas buyers and analysing potential companies and markets is a key area in the exporter's strategy today. It enables both the MNIs and the small and medium enterprises (SMEs) to operate in the same environment with similar market penetration strategies crossing international barriers and developing the B2B or B2C contact.

Hence, the exporter with a logistic focus in developing market entry strategies must have a high-tech computer resource and software to develop a viable overseas market. Procurement companies are unlikely to do business with suppliers that are not computer logistic-focused/oriented. A market research strategy must be adopted.

During the past decade and much facilitated by e-commerce internationally, we have seen an enormous increase in the B2B and B2C sectors. It is, to the exporter, a very efficient way to develop the international portfolio and in particular eliminates the intermediary with significant cost savings, and accelerates the decision-making process. Moreover, it develops empathy between the two parties and favours strongly a logistic and computer-focused approach. It favours both the MNIs and SMEs.

The B2B e-commerce market is well established and favoured strongly by personnel designing the logistic supply chain as it eliminates the intermediary and encourages transparency. Moreover, it enables the international sales logistics team to concentrate on selling and efficient supply chains development. It is low cost and emerges when the exporter/importer have a good relationship and complete synergy.

The B2C is distinguished from the B2B by the nature of the customer and how the customer uses the product. In business marketing international customers are organisations such as businesses, government bodies and institutions such as hospitals. The B2C market is often through e-commerce such as cars and accessories, home appliances and accessories, books, financial services, tourism, transport and food products. It is very popular in the EU market.

An area of significance with B2B and B2C is to maintain and develop a good website, which is completely logistically focused and have well-trained and professional personnel handling enquiries with a good logistic knowledge. It should be manned 24 hours per day to handle global enquiries in various time windows. The website must be targeted to focus on individual logistic markets and ideally in the language of the buyer. It is often prudent to feature in distant markets a local contact such as an agent/distributor/franchisee who can demonstrate the product to the importer.

It is important to bear in mind that consumer and business markets differ in the nature of the markets, market demand, importer behaviour, exporter/importer relationships, buying power, and market environmental influences such as legal, cultural, political, logistic, exchange control and economic. Also check the country/company credit rating.

Evolution and Revolution of Logistics and Supply Chain Management

As indicated in the earlier chapter it is appropriate briefly to record the growth of logistics and supply chain management. In the 1960s and 1970s the freight forwarding industry witnessed/contributed a rapid growth in door-to-door services. This was driven very much by containerisation, which has changed considerably during this 40-year period. However, logistics has changed at a faster rate as the customer demands more efficiency and value-added benefit in the marketplace. The biggest changes in the logistics industry have occurred in the last 10 years. This is largely due to increased globalisation making the supply chain longer and more complex, rapid developments in IT – particularly the Internet – and the industry consolidation (mergers and acquisitions (M&A)).

Figure 3.1 shows that in the 1960s there was little or no integration between the various function areas within exporting companies with respect to the movement of goods. Integration between departments increased steadily in the following years, until in the 1970s the two distinct functions of materials management and physical distribution became prominent. These gradually merged into a more integrated logistics function by the early to mid-1980s. The high level of fragmentation in the 1960s produced operational inefficiencies and high cost. In the early 1970s logistics costs accounted for 15 per cent of gross domestic product (GDP) in the US, 14 per cent in Australia and 25 per cent in Japan.

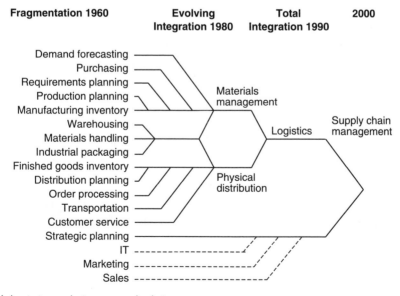

Figure 3.1 Logistics evolution to supply chain management.

Source: Alfred J. Battaglia, Reckitt & Colman.

In the 1960s and 1970s shippers examined distribution cost holistically under the 'total cost concept'. This led to increased integration between different functional areas, which today fall under the single logistics umbrella. Undoubtedly, containerisation was the driving force that simplified inland moves to groupage services and depots, reduced inventories for shippers and eliminated intermediate warehouses. Moreover, the rapid and regulated flow of traffic in the container network, both inland and overseas, permitted a reduced safety stock level. This arose also because more regulated delivery, more rapid response of the system, and total stock, in the pipeline capital assets in transit (see page 18), is reduced by a quicker transit time.

Today, several of the top 10 3PLs are Swiss companies founded in the nineteenth century. Examples include Hausmann – a subsidiary of Panalpina – and CSCL. Air freight was a fast-growing industry in the 1970s. Emery was a leading player, but today focuses attention onto other transport modes. In the container business various subsidiaries and acquisitions over the years were consolidated at Maersk Logistics and APL Logistics in 2000 and 2001, respectively. In 2005, Maersk Logistics merged with the P&O Ned Lloyd Logistics when the two liner companies merged. Today, Maersk Line is a leading player in global logistics.

In the 1990s, just in time (JIT) became known and at the same time distribution services began to include the management of customer inventories and management of cargo flows from suppliers and sub-suppliers. Moreover, globalisation and the use of Internet technology paved the way for global sourcing, which triggered global supply chain management solutions.

Johan Wanninga – Managing Director of Maersk Logistics for the UK and Ireland – has indicated that the evolution of logistics and supply chain management in the last seven years has been faster than at any time in the industry history. Basically, because of labour costs, European and North American retailers had increasingly replaced suppliers in Southern China with those in Northern China and Vietnam (the latter facilitated by WTO access). The 3PL has expanded the number of consolidation centres across China. Supply chain integration has increased significantly. IT developments have facilitated the merging of domestic and international supply chains, particularly where many companies treated them separately in the past. Moreover, retailers have increased control of their supply chains, partly through opening their own sourcing offices in China and South East Asia, with the result that more sales are focused in Asia. With longer supply chains and an expansion of the 'JIT' concept, requiring shorter door-to-door transit times, particularly in the consumer electronics industry, the demand for sea air transport has increased, resulting in transportation times that are 50 per cent faster than by sea, but costing up to seven times higher.

Increased supply chain integration has been aided by the development of the 4PL. Conceived in 1996, outside the progressive automotive industry, there were few examples of working 4PLs in the container industry. Chris Thorby, Managing Director of *Container International*, indicated 'like the traditional 3PL, the 4PL is by definition a service provider, but the 4PLs sphere of activity is substantially more extensive, as it encompasses the design management and in many cases re-engineering of the supply chain on behalf of its shipper customers. However, a much larger change has been the merger and acquisition strategy to produce substantial consolidation among some of the largest global logistics providers. This will continue as the global logistic industry becomes more competitive.'

Currently, according to Professor R. H. Ballou at Weatherhead School of Management, Ohio, 'the SCM promotes co-ordination throughout the entire supply channel. However, SCM currently takes place to a very limited degree. The most likely place for

SCM to occur is between the firm and its first tier suppliers. Currently SCM is practised as logistics and not the broad, theoretical scope envisioned for it. Maybe managers will begin to practice SCM when its benefits are better documented and measured, and the techniques and tools needed to achieve the benefits are refined'. The RFID may prove a vehicle for accelerating change plus rapid expansion of containerisation.

Currently as demonstrated in Figure 3.2, 34 per cent of exporting/importing companies accommodate SCM within the purchasing/procurement department and focus on integration with first-tier suppliers, but only 9 per cent of companies integrate their logistics operation comprehensively up and downstream, that is, from key suppliers to key customers.

Figure 3.3 identifies that the supply chain management function is expected to have a much more prominent position that at the moment. Over the years the supply chain is expected to become a distinct department with responsibility for purchasing, production and logistics. This would benefit companies considerably as the forecast increase on globalisation, outsourcing and free trade between countries will encourage higher shipment volume growth and of course more logistics activity. By 2020, 80 per cent of the goods in the world – according to consultant McKinsey and Company, will be manufactured in a country from where they are consumed, compared with 20 per cent now. Efficiencies will be realised by exporting companies in the future by a shift in management strategy with respect to the supply chain. The current objective of minimising supply chain cost will increasingly be replaced by one in which revenues are enhanced to

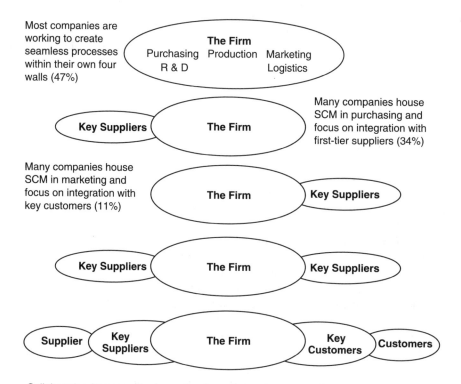

Figure 3.2 Scope of supply chain management as currently practised.

Source: Stanley E. Fawcett and Gregory M. Magnan. The Rhetoric and Reality of Supply Chain Integration (2002).

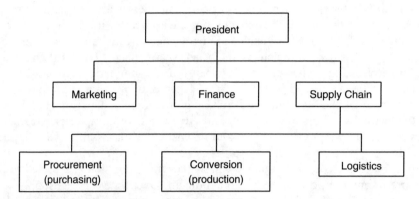

Figure 3.3 A future organisation for supply chain management.

Source: Ronald H. Ballou.

maximise supply chain operations and contributions to profits. This is embraced in the financial formula return on supply chain assets (ROSCA) (see page 13): revenue minus cost divided by assets. Overall, revenue refers to the expenses incurred in the supply chain processes and assets to the investment made in facilities and equipment to support the supply chain process.

With the foregoing change, the freight forwarding industry and 3PLs will be under pressure to maximise efficiencies across the supply chain and add further value to shipper operations. Likewise, increased opportunities will exist for logistic service providers, 3PLs and 4PLs, as the rapid evaluation continues, aided substantially by global container logistic growth and associated infrastructure.

Modern Logistics Concepts

Global logistics is a fast-moving market and it is very much consumer-driven. Areas on which to focus are given below:

a   Optimising resources from store shelf to manufacturing – end to end. Perfecting the consumer experience through innovation.
b   In the retail management to have an adaptive inventory and workforce management that automatically responds to consumer demand in real time. This embraces optimised scheduling and budget management, facilitates learning, synchronises merchandising, controls assets and adjusts promotion forecasts.
c   Distribution management ideology requires a system that will react quickly and seamlessly to changing markets. This features maintaining service level commitments, making efficient use of resources and having adaptive IT systems.

To summarise the foregoing, one must focus on defining balance between enterprise resource planning (ERP) ecosystems and innovative vendor solutions, empowering operational workflow while maintaining services, providing technology solutions that add value to customer base and penetrating the market, providing end-to-end visibility, consistency and striving for improved performance.

There is no doubt that electronic commerce consumer-driven supply chains are changing business practice as found in 'B2B' and 'B2C' (see page 36). The starting point is the consumer. Hitherto, the producers could drive the supply chain. The chain featured producer projection, raw materials/producer, producer warehouse, retail warehouse and retail store. Today it features raw materials, company producer, producer warehouse, retail warehouse and retail outlet. Additionally, the retail store produces the forecast, which is passed down the supply chain from retail distribution centre to manufacturer distribution centre, to manufacturer plant and to raw material supplier.

An analysis of customer-driven supply chain changes in the next five years focused on eight key areas in order of priority:

a Significantly lower cost overall – this embraces a wide range of areas on the global environment – freight charges, customer duty, insurance, payment cycle, packaging and handling/port charges;

b Reduction in lead times. This embraces quicker response rate at the manufacturing/ supply base. It may need a multi-sourcing concept from various suppliers in different countries;

c Higher quality service. The development of B2B, B2C, RFID and better quality control;

d More value-added service. This embraces wider product range choice such as colour, multi-uses producer/products, after sales – customer service, and better user-friendly product/service. An example is global sourcing whereby food products were despatched only in season when they were harvested. Today, they are processed/quality controlled and placed in a controlled temperature warehouse and despatched throughout the 12 months, usually in containers and not as hitherto in bulk shipments at harvest time;

e Smaller orders but higher delivery frequency. This favours cash flow, inventory controls, warehouse management and general competitiveness;

f More flexibility and better response times. This enhances market penetration and general competitiveness;

g More cross-docking. This embraces the movement of the goods from one transport unit to another, obviating any warehouse storage cost, thereby accelerating transit time. This embraces combined transport from ship to rail distribution centre/ICD/ FTZ or hub and spoke system (see page 83). Overall, it reduces downtime in the warehouse/distribution centre. A key factor is forwarding planning and transparency in the supply chain. Usually a good infrastructure presents continuous scope for cross-docking, whereby customs clearance can be undertaken at consumer premises, whereas with an LDC, it tends to be centred at the port and not inland at the buyer premises (see page 79).

h A daily delivery service. This is more practicable in developed countries with a developed logistic culture and more intense competition.

In analysing the foregoing a number of areas arise.

i Development of the pull methodology as distinct from the push technique (see page 101). This eliminates/reduces intermediaries, which tend to be too numerous in the global supply chain. This features, especially, agents in customs procedures, transport operators, transhipment, quality control and government intervention. A growth area is security (see page 107). Additionally, it yields shorter cycles embracing quicker response rate and less risk of asset obsolescence. Finally, it adopts greater synchronisation throughout the chain.

ii Consumer-driven optimisation. This entails the interface of the workforce, inventory and transportation with the business process integration and retail supply chain manufacturing.

The global logistic supply chain is very much engaged in customs. Customs planning is a key area (see page 74). It includes the customs duty, handled warehousing, tax-free supply chain, excise management, customs product specification code and cross-border taxation. It also features synchronisation with trading partner, and as a mobile resource enterprise, asset tracking.

The *Financial Times* produced a five-point checklist to realise a tax efficient supply chain:

i transferring significant cost to the end of the supply chain;
ii use experience available from proven exports, identifying all available customs procedures that will benefit the business;
iii paying all applicable duties and VAT at the latest possible point or removing payment of duty completely;
iv provide software solutions which ensure compliance; and
v the proven logistic leaders pay up to 40 per cent less tax than their competitors.

The latter can embrace sourcing a third country favourable tax regime – a situation whereby the logistic operator must consult a proven tax expert. Taxation is an area the supply chain manager must keep under continuous review in a global changing market, much of which is initiated by national government to raise more revenue and protect home industries and trade balances.

To import completely knocked down (CKD) products for assembly – often on a cluster market basis – can prove cost-effective in customs planning. This can embrace FTZ, ICD, distriparks and economic zones/economic blocs – ASEAN, EU, NAFTA, etc.

Transport management systems are a key area in the development of supply chain evolution. They embrace enterprise transportation planning, routing and scheduling, enterprise transportation management, supply chain analysis and design, carrier bid optimisation, track and trace shipment (RFID) and international trade and logistics featuring customs/duty, denied party, EU/NAFTA/ASEAN preferential trade, export compliance, global multi-mode optimisation, scheduling and tracking visibility and full landed cost (Incoterms – see page 46).

Logistics Department

The overseas buyer must be very conscious of the benefits of operating in a logistics environment and it is appropriate to evaluate the logistics department structure. The role of the basic logistic team includes:

a   assessing the supply chain competitiveness of the organisation;
b   creating a vision of the required supply chain;
c   closing the gaps between vision and the present supply chain reality;
d   prioritising items and appropriate measures;
e   reflecting current and future technology;
f   featuring at directorate level in the organisation structure;
g   a global logistic and multilingual culture at all levels;

h   professionally qualified personnel in all aspects of the global supply chain.

The primary function performed by the global logistics department within the firm includes: (a) traffic management, (b) warehousing, (c) facilities location, (d) global logistics, (e) inventory control, (f) order processing, (g) packaging, (h) purchasing, (i) order entry, (j) product planning, (k) sales forecasting, (l) general management, (m) transparency, and (n) information technology.

The logistics department tends to exhibit both on integrated and process orientation. An integrated orientation seeks to simultaneously manage logistic flows, coordination and complexity within the organisation and with external parties. A process orientation seeks efficiency control and cost reduction. A cost analysis resource is also important for implementing a cost minimisation strategy. This embraces a strategic focus to determine what is driving logistics costs, material costs, production costs, staffing patterns and inventory costs. The structure and focus of the department need to be under continuous review to reflect future trends and add value to the supply chain (see page 13).

An important area is the development of strategic partnerships with external transportation providers (3PL – see page 40), focused on long-term commitments, open (transport) communications and information sharing, and the sharing of risks and rewards. Study Figure 3.1 (see page 37).

Logistics Providers Are Taking on More Responsibilities as the Industry Goes Global

As emphasised on page 37 and Figure 3.2 (see page 39), the logistic industry is fast changing as exporting/importing companies accommodate their purchasing/procurement department and integrate with first suppliers. This is moving towards, as in Figure 3.3 (see page 40), the supply chain management function having a more distinct department in the organisation with responsibility for purchasing, production and logistics with a director on the board. This will drive globalisation and increase the role of 3PLs and particularly 4PLs.

The automotive industry is very much in the 'van of change', driven by relocation of plants. Today the shift is towards production in Eastern Europe – Poland now has six major assembly plants – and the emergence of large-scale assembly in China are two examples of this charge. This has presented a challenge, especially to the 4PLs. The key area is to keep cost under control and ensure flows criss-crossing Europe dovetail to minimise wasted capacity. Planning and system integration are key factors, not only with the parent company PSA Peugeot Citroen, but also with Gefco's many other automotive customers. These include other big name car manufacturers and tier-one supplier Delphi in Turkey. It also operates dedicated two-way shuttles between Toyota plants in France and the UK. Additionally, it manages some major international flows of tier-one supplier Ogihara from Telford to Brazil, while Gefco France has an overseas consolidation centre in Le Havre.

NYK is one of the biggest single industry sectors in the UK. It provides external logistics for several UK-based manufacturers including Aston Martin, Land Rover, Toyota and Jaguar, as well as international plant logistics. NYK also runs cross-dock operations in Germany, France and the Czech Republic, and also picks up from car plants in the latter two countries. The 4PLs have a challenging task and it is paramount they understand their role in the supply chain. It embraces the need to understand detail such as their bills of material and the overall way of working to be able to collaborate not only with the manufacturer, but also their suppliers and other third-party operators.

Car manufacturers impose many constraints, one of which is to place limits on the number of vehicles on site. Hence the paramount need for operators to work together and attend customers' planning and shift meetings. Control of the inventory is the key factor. With carmakers always keeping cost under tight control, planning logistics networks so that cross-dock or stockholding points are in exactly the right place can be critical. Logistics firms need to know far more about the minutiae of their auto-industry customers' operations than they used to.

NYK have engaged packing engineers to look at the design of trays and boxes as to whether to go for collapsible units or cheap-type solutions. Hence the 3PLs employ not only logistic specialists, but also with car manufacturing experience. Agility and precision are also vital with the mega-multinational automotive industry, which commands not only large transport networks, but skilled personnel – often multilingual ones.

IT input is essential, embracing customer IT networks. For example, the bill of materials for a single day's shift can run into half a million line items. Thus, logistics operators' IT systems need to be able to produce data that is not only comprehensive to its own staff, but also produced in the customer's own format.

Automotive is the fastest growing industry and logistics is a major part of the operation. Menlo is best known for its involvement in the Vector joint venture 4PL operation with General Motors, and sits above their supply chain with a view to identifying areas where it can be improved.

A feature of the long-established car manufacturing industry in North America and Europe is the sprawling empire spread over several continents, often with IT systems that do not always connect properly to each other, or with third-party suppliers. The major reason why Japanese manufacturers have been so successful is that they were able to start with a clean sheet in the 1960s and adopt lean manufacturing and logistics principles from the start.

There are some 50 vector logistics engineers in Detroit and the 4PLs' reward structure is based solely on 'gain share'. So far, GM has been the only major motor manufacturer to outsource its strategic supply chain management in this manner. Vector strategy in supply chain management does focus on resource planning systems. In so doing it examines each element of the supply chain – one piece at a time – and endeavours to improve it, rather than trying to tackle the enterprise IT problems in 'a single bang'.

Kuehne and Nagel gets involved in many auto manufacturers' supply chains, not only on long-distance legs, but also in plant logistics themselves. There is now a vogue for sequencing centres, usually located close to the point of manufacture, where materials can be called up in a sequenced manner, which may involve sequencing deliveries right to the line-side. Most motor manufacturers will generally go to more than one logistic company. Overall, it is a very big industry and currently it accounts for 6 per cent of total cost and a large assignment for one logistic operator. However, 3PLs and 4PLs are becoming larger as they undergo merger and acquisition or form operating alliances to widen their global base and become more competitive through economies of scale. A recent 3PL example of how the car industry is responding to the global environment arose with BMW, which has now contracted DHL for the entire part load volume to all its production sites in Europe. In the past, different operators got certain parts of the supply chain – different lanes, different parts or regions. This is the first time a complete supply chain has been handed over to a single operator. Previously, BMW used around

200 different logistics suppliers to handle the business. The difference between a 3PL and 4PL is that the latter don't really control their network.

Finally, as the globalisation of the automotive industry intensifies, it is important to highlight the development of the new generation of pure car and truck carriers. PCTC and NYK have a fleet of 93 car carriers. Modern car carriers have a capacity of up to 7,000 car equivalent units (CEUs), embracing 13 decks. Undoubtedly the new generation of PCTC is contributing to the cost-effective global supply chain. In 2005, 10 million cars were distributed by sea and by 2009 Chinese car production will reach 9 million.

Useful Sources of Information

Alan E. Branch (1998) *Shipping and Air Freight Documentation for Importers and Exporters*, 2nd edn, Witherby & Co Ltd: Livingstone

Alan E. Branch (2005) *Export Practice and Management*, 5th revised edn, Thomson Learning: London

Dachser Far East Ltd <www.dachser.hk>

Financial Times <news.ft.com/ft-reports>

Integrated Distribution Services <www.idslogistics.com>

Lloyds Freight Transport Buyer Asia, from Amazon <amagarea.com>

Chapter 4

Constituents of the Export Sales Contract Continued

Introduction

An important activity of global logistic practice in the design of the global supply chain is the processing of the export consignment through all its numerous procedures. It is an area that must be fully understood by the logistics operator engaged in the international supply chain.

Contract of Affreightment: Terms of Delivery – Incoterms 2000

The basis of a price quotation depends on the correct interpretation of the delivery trade terms. The export marketing manager will, through experience, accumulate information that will enable him or her to quote accurately. It is important to bear in mind each delivery trade term quoted embraces three basic elements: the stage at which title to the merchandise passes from the exporter (seller) to the importer (buyer), a clear definition of the charges and expenses to be borne by the exporter and importer, and finally, the stage and location where the goods are to be passed over to the importer.

The international consignment delivery terms embrace many factors including, in particular, insurance, air or sea freight plus surface transport costs, customs duty, port of disbursements, product cost, packing costs, etc. Moreover, the importance of executing the cargo delivery in accordance with the prescribed terms cannot be overstressed and this involves a disciplined process of progressing the export sales contract order dealt with in Chapter 10. In the ideal situation, the sales export contract order, also embracing the delivery terms, should be undertaken on a critical path analysis (CPA) programme devised by the export marketing manager in consultation with department colleagues within the company, and relevant outside bodies, that is, booking shipping space, processing financial aspects, obtaining export licences, etc.

There must be no ambiguity in the interpretation by either party of the delivery terms quoted, particularly in the area of cost and liabilities. If such problems arise, much goodwill is lost and the exporter could lose the prospect of a repeat order in a competitive market. Moreover, costly litigation could arise. It is essential, therefore, that the exporter (seller) and the importer (buyer) agree to the terms of delivery and their interpretation. Such a situation could be overcome by quoting the provisions of Incoterms 2000, dealt with in the latter part of this section. It must be borne in mind that special provisions in individual export sales contracts will override anything provided in Incoterms 2000. In addition, it should be remembered that breaches of contract, and their consequences, together with the ownership of the goods, are outside the influence of Incoterms 2000.

The need for every global logistics operator to have a thorough knowledge of Incoterms 2000 cannot be overstressed, and likewise the sales and marketing personnel who negotiate the export sales contract terms on behalf of the seller. The booklet Incoterms 2000, No. 560 is available from local chambers of commerce.

An international trade deal can involve up to four contracts and the exporter (seller) must have a broad understanding of each of them. The four contracts are: the contract of carriage, the export sales contract usually involving Incoterms 2000, the insurance contract and the contract of finance. (See ICC booklet No. 600 on Uniform Customs and Practice for Documentary Credits 2007.) There are three main areas of uncertainty in international trade contracts and their interpretation: the uncertainty as to which country's law will be applicable to their contracts, the difficulty emerging from inadequate and unreliable information, and the serious problem of the diversity of interpretation of the various trade terms. The latter point can involve costly litigation and loss of much goodwill when a dispute over the interpretation of such terms arises. Hence study ICC booklet No. 600.

The role of Incoterms 2000, adopted in 96 countries, is to give the business person a set of international rules for the interpretation of the more commonly used terms such as FOB (free on board), CIF (cost insurance freight) and EXW (Ex-works) in foreign trade contracts. Such a range of terms enables the business person to decide which is the most suitable for their needs, knowing that the interpretation of such terms will not vary by individual country. It must be recognised, however, that it is not always possible to give a precise interpretation. In such situations, one must rely on the custom of the trade or port. Business persons are advised to use terms that are subject to varying interpretation as little as possible and to rely on the well-established internationally accepted terms. To avoid any misunderstandings or disputes the parties to the contract are well advised to keep trading customs of individual countries in mind when negotiating their export sales contract. However, parties to the contract may use Incoterms as the general basis of their contract, but may specify variations of them or additions to them relevant to the particular trade or circumstances. An example is the CIF plus war risk insurance. The seller would base his or her quotation accordingly. Special provisions in the individual contract between the parties will override anything in the Incoterms provisions.

An important point to bear in mind is the need for caution in the variation, for example, of CFR (cost and freight), CIF (cost insurance freight) or DDP (delivered duty paid): the addition of a word or letter could change the contract and its interpretation. It is essential that any such variation be explicitly stated in the contract to ensure each party to the contract is aware of its obligations and acts accordingly.

The seller (exporter) and buyer (importer) parties to the contract must remember that Incoterms only define their relationship in contract terms, and have no bearing directly or indirectly on carriers' obligations to them as found in the contract of carriage. However, the law of carriage will determine how the seller should fulfil his or her obligation to deliver the goods to the carrier on board the vessels as found in FOB, CFR and CIF. A further point to be borne in mind by both seller and buyer is that there is no obligation for the seller to procure an insurance policy for the buyer's benefit. However, in practice many contracts request the buyer or seller to arrange insurance from the point of departure in the country of despatch to the point of final destination chosen by the buyer. A summary of the 13 terms are given below (see, also, Figure 4.1; see page 48 Incoterms 2000 group analysis):

Incoterm 2000
Group E
EXW   Ex Works (named place)
Departure from factory – all carriage paid by buyer

Group F
FCA   Free Carrier (named place)
Main carriage unpaid
FAS   Free Alongside Ship (named port of shipment) by seller
FOB   Free On Board (named port of shipment)

Group C
CPT   Carriage Paid to (named place of destination)
Main carriage paid by Seller
CIP   Carriage and Insurance Paid to (named place of destination)
CFR   Cost and Freight (named port of destination)
CIF   Cost, Insurance and Freight (named port of destination)

Group D
DAF   Delivered at Frontier (named place)
Arrival – carriage to
DES   Delivered Ex Ship (named port of destination) delivered paid by
DEQ   Delivered Ex Quay (named port of destination) the seller
DDU   Delivered Duty Unpaid (named place of destination)
DDP   Delivered Duty Paid (named place of destination)

Group E
EXW – Ex Works (. . . named place) – suitable for all modes of transport – buyer collects and responsible for all carriage, the seller to load the goods onto the buyer's collection vehicle.

Group F
FCA Free Carrier (. . . named place) – suitable for all modes of transport – main carriage unpaid.

FAS Free Alongside Ship (. . . named port of shipment) – suitable for maritime and inland waterway transport only – main carriage unpaid.

FOB Free On Board (. . . named port of shipment) – suitable for maritime and inland waterway transport only – main carriage unpaid.

Group C
CPT Carriage Paid to (. . . named place of destination) – suitable for all modes of transport – main carriage paid, the seller to provide the buyer, upon request, with the necessary information for procuring additional insurance.

CIP Carriage and Insurance Paid to (. . . named place of destination) – suitable for all modes of transport – main carriage paid.

CFR Cost and Freight (. . . named port of destination) – suitable for maritime and inland waterway transport only – main carriage paid, the seller to provide the buyer, upon request, with the necessary information for procuring additional insurance.

CIF Cost, Insurance and Freight (. . . named port of destination) – suitable for maritime and inland waterway transport only – main carriage paid.

Figure 4.1 Incoterm 2000 group analysis.

Group D

DAF Delivered at Frontier (. . . named place) – suitable for all modes of transport – delivered at frontier point.

DDU Delivered Duty Unpaid (. . . named place of destination) – suitable for all modes of transport – delivered at (. . . name place of destination).

DDP Delivered Duty Paid (. . . named place of destination) – suitable for all modes of transport – delivered at (. . . named place of destination).

DES Delivered Ex Ship (. . . named port of destination) – suitable for maritime and inland waterway transport only – delivered on board the vessel at the named port of destination.

DEQ Delivered Ex Quay (. . . named port of destination) – suitable for maritime and inland waterway transport only – delivered on the named quay (wharf) at the specified port of destination, the buyer to pay for costs after discharge.

E Term – is the term in which the buyer's obligation is at its maximum.

F Term – requires the seller to deliver the goods for carriage as instructed by the buyer.

C Term – requires the seller to contract for carriage on usual terms at his own expense.

D Term – requires the seller to be responsible for the arrival of the goods at the agreed place or point of destination at the border and within the country of import. The seller must bear all the risk and cost in bringing the goods thereto.

Figure 4.1 contd.

Incoterms 2000 can be divided into recommended usages by modes of transport as under: all modes (i.e. combined transport), EXW, FCA, CPT, CIP, DAF, DDP, DDU, and conventional port-to-port or maritime and inland waterway transport only FAS, FOB, CFR, CIF, DES, DEQ. The seller must ensure the correct terms are used. Consider a containerised contract applying FOB or CFR where the risk transfers from seller to buyer on loading onboard ship. On delivery damage is discovered. It is impossible to show where damage arose – before or after shipment. Under FOB/CFR, a dispute would ensue; under FCA/CPT, it would be clear that the risk would be with the buyer once the goods are in the hands of the combined transport operator for carriage. Incoterms 2000 reflects the changes and development of international distribution during the past decade, especially the development of combined transportation and associated documentation, together with electronic data interchange. In analysing each term the seller and buyer should identify the following aspects:

Seller

1   supplying good(s) in conformity with the contract;
2   licences and authorisations;
3   place of delivery (not delivery of goods);
4   carriage of goods contract and insurance;
5   documentation and notice to buyer;
6   transfer of risks;
7   transfer and division of costs;
8   checking, packages, marking;
9   other obligations.

Buyer

1   licences and authorisations;
2   notices, receipt of documents;
3   taking delivery;
4   transfer of risks;
5   transfer and division of costs;
6   other obligations.

The use of bills of lading is now becoming less common in the liner trade and is being replaced by non-negotiable documents such as sea waybills, liner waybills, freight receipts and combined or multi-modal transport documents (see page 79). Today the transmission of such documents is electronic (see pages 114 and 118). As we progress into this millennium with the expectation of more competitive pricing, the buyer/importer will demand a delivered Incoterms 2000 price quotation. This will allow the buyer to compare the quotations on a like-for-like basis from different originating countries, and will enable them to avoid having to calculate the distribution cost as an add-on to the Incoterms 2000.

Factors Determining Choice of Incoterms 2000

Personnel involved in negotiating the sales contract have a wide choice in selecting the cargo delivery term most acceptable to the sale. The prime consideration is to ensure that each party to the contract is clearly aware of their obligation to ensure the consignment is despatched without impeding the transit arrangements. The following factors are relevant in the evaluation of the choice of the cargo delivery term.

1   Basically, the buyer is the stronger party in such negotiations, especially as s/he has to fund the carriage directly through his/her payment to the carrier under FCA/FOB or indirectly through CIP/CIF to the seller.
2   The seller has the opportunity of controlling the transit arrangements together with cost when concluding the arrangement, and funds them directly with the carrier. S/he may, through other contracts, be able to get a discount through the volume of business generated to the trade or route.
3   An increasing number of developing world and Eastern European countries now follow a policy of directing all cargoes on to their national shipping line or airline and buy under EXW/FCA/FOB/CIF terms. For example, a government may require all imports to be bought on a FOB basis and all exports sold on CIF. This saves hard currency and develops their shipping and airline companies. It also reflects, in many situations, cargo preference laws enforced by the buyer's government as part of their trading policy.
4   The seller, under CIP/CIF terms, can maximise the national income from such a sale and thereby despatch the consignment on the seller's national shipping line or airline, and likewise obtain insurance cover through brokers.
5   In some circumstances neither the buyer nor the seller has any choice to make. This applies to some commodity trades where there are standard international contracts of sale that relate to specific Incoterms 2000.
6   Conversely, with regard to item 2 the buyer may wish to take charge of the transit arrangement and cost when concluding the arrangements and selects the carrier and

funds them directly with the transport operator(s). This may include EXW/FCA/ FOB terms and thereby facilitate the development of a logistics strategy.

Overall, the most decisive factors in determining the most acceptable Incoterms are experience of the trading market and the development of a good business relationship between seller and buyer on a long-term basis. Every effort should be made to sell under combined transport terms.

Trade Finance – Introduction

Trade finance has become a strong bargaining point in the conduct of international trade. Both the seller and buyer are keen to adopt positions in the negotiation strategy, which will reduce their financial risk and secure the best deal possible. The global supply chain manager in his/her endeavours to improve financial performance must continuously review the financial terms of the contract to seek/identify improvements and, if necessary, consult his/her bank. Overall, there are three areas: currency, credit terms and method of payment.

Currency

The seller may opt to use his/her own currency, thereby ensuring profit margins are maintained and any currency risk variation passes to the buyer. Conversely, the importer may decide only to accept quotations in his/her own currency, such as the Swiss franc, and pass any currency risk to the overseas seller based in the United States. Also, the

a	the Incoterms have tended to focus on the tangibles in the contract of sale and not the intangibles as found in computer software;
b	Incoterms embrace the contract of sale and relations between the buyer and seller. They only have an interface with the contracts of insurance, transport and finance and no prima facie legal specifications regarding the duties the parties may wish to include in the contract of sale;
c	Incoterms remain primarily intended for use where goods are sold for delivery across national boundaries;
d	revision needed to adapt to the terms of contemporary commercial practice;
e	substantive changes have been made in two areas: customs clearance and payment of duty obligations under FAS and DEQ (see page 48) and loading and unloading obligations under FCA (see page 48);
f	the terms are, wherever possible, the same expressions as those in the 1980 UN Convention on the Contracts for the International Sales of Goods;
g	the opportunity has been taken in the 'introduction' of ICC booklet No. 560 to clarify a number of terms featured in the 13 Incoterms. These include shipper, delivery, usual charges, ports, places, points, premises, ship, vessel, checking, inspection, no obligation, customs clearance and packaging;
h	a feature of the 1990 revision of Incoterms identified the clauses dealing with the seller's obligation to provide proof of delivery permitting a replacement of paper documentation by EDI messages, provided the parties had agreed to communicate electronically. The 2000 revision has endeavoured to improve upon the drafting and presentation of the Incoterms in order to facilitate their practical implementation.

Figure 4.2 Salient features emerging from incoterms 2000.

exporter, keen to get business, may quote in the buyer's currency and thereby enables the buyer to compare quotations with other suppliers based in other countries.

Further options exist with the seller and/or buyer opting for a third currency, such as the US dollar, thereby sharing the currency fluctuation risk. The introduction of the euro currency, currently among the 13 EU States, removed any currency risk variation within trading partners operative in the Euro-zone.

Whenever buying or selling goods in currencies other than their own, importers and exporters become exposed to currency risk from fluctuations in the exchange rate in the period between prices being agreed and payment being received. Management of the exposure is essential to minimise the potential risk and to maximise the profit from the underlying transactions. The technique of protecting against future exchange-rate movements is usually referred to as 'hedging'. It can be exercised by three methods: spot contracts, forward contracts and currency options. International supply chain managers are advised to consult their bank for guidance.

Exporters/importers dealing with LDCs and a number of other currencies do not have a convertible currency that can be traded in the world currency markets. Consequently, they trade in a convertible currency such as US dollars, yen, euro, Swiss franc, sterling, etc., and settlement/payment is made in local currency such as the baht against the US dollar in Malaysia.

Credit Terms

A further factor is the granting of credit. The granting of credit terms, which are growing longer as buyer pressure increases, means that the exporter is without his or her money for longer periods of time. This automatically reduces cash flow and creates a finance problem for the exporter who ultimately has to seek assistance from his/her bank. The task of exporting overseas has become a more complex operation, demanding higher professional standards – especially in the area of trade finance. Selling overseas requires a different financial strategy compared with selling in the domestic market. The supply chain is longer, contracts are more complex and payment arrangements more complex. The prime consideration is to ensure that payments are received on schedule and that the exporter safeguards his/her financial interest adequately. Much of the risk can be insured against (see page 46) or mitigated through the payments system (UCP 600 see page 52).

UCP 600 – Documentary Credits and Allied Documents

There are several methods by which the debtor may remit payment to his supplier: debtor's own cheque, bankers draft, mail transfer and telegraphic transfer. Apart from 'cash with order' the documentary credit provides the most satisfactory method of payment. It provides reassurance to both the importer and exporter. Overall, the documentary credit is an undertaking issued by a bank on behalf of the buyer (importer/applicant) to the seller (exporter/beneficiary) to pay for goods and/or services, provided that the seller presents documents that comply fully with the terms and conditions of the documentary credit. The documentary credit is often referred to as a DC, LC Letter of Credit, or Credit. All documentary credits should be handled according to the International Chambers of Commerce practice known as the 'Uniform Customs and Practice for Documentary Credits 2007 revision UCP 600'. It superseded the UCP 500 – 1993, and is the sixth revision of the rules since they were first promulgated in 1933. The UCP

600 objective is to create a set of contractual rules that would establish uniformity in that practice, so that practitioners would not have to cope with a plethora of often conflicting national regulations. The universal acceptance of the UCP by practitioners in countries with widely divergent economic and judicial systems is a testament to the rules' success. The UCP 600 was devised/updated by 25 member countries of the UCP consulting group, embracing 400 members of the ICC commission on Banking Technique and Practice and ICC national committees. Over 5,000 individual comments were considered before a consensus text was reached.

The UCP 600 contains important new provisions in the fields of transport, insurance and compliance. Moreover, it features a 'Definitions' article designed to clarify the meaning of key terms, a changed practice for giving a notice if refused and numerous other modifications. It also includes Version 1.1 of the e-UCP – the 12 articles of ICC's supplement to the UCP that govern presentation of documents in electronic form.

The UCP 600 contains 39 articles plus the e-UCP for documents in electronic form. Details are given below:

- 1 – Application of UCP; 2 – Definitions; 3 – Interpretations; 4 – Credits v contracts; 5 – Documents v goods, services or performance; 6 – Availability, expiry date and place for presentation; 7 – Issuing bank undertaking; 8 – Confirming bank undertaking; 9 – Advising of credits and amendments; 10 – Amendments; 11 – Teletransmitted and pre-advised credits and amendments; 12 – Nomination; 13 – Bank to bank reimbursement arrangements; 14 – Standard for examination of documents; 15 – Complying presentation; 16 – Discrepant documents, waiver and notice; 17 – Original documents and copies; 18 – Commercial invoice; 19 – Transport document covering at least two different modes of transport; 20 – Bill of lading; 21 – Non-negotiable sea waybill; 22 – Charter party bill of lading; 23 – Air transport document; 24 – Road, rail or inland waterway transport documents; 25 – Courier receipt, post receipt, or certificate of posting; 26 – 'On deck', 'Shippers load and Count', 'said by shipper to contain', and charges additional to freight; 27 – Clean transport document; 28 – Insurance document coverage; 29 – Extension of expiry date or last day for presentation; 30 – Tolerance in credit amount, quantity and unit prices; 31 – Partial drawings or shipments; 32 – Instalment drawings or shipments; 33 – Hours of presentation; 34 – Disclaimer on effectiveness of documents; 35 – Disclaimer on transmission and translation; 36 – Force majeure; 37 – Disclaimer for acts of an instructed party; 38 – Transferable credits; and 39 – Assignment of proceeds – Supplement to UCP 600 for Electronic Presentation – introduction.
- e1 – scope of the e-UCP; e2 – Relationship of the e-UCP to the UCP; e3 – Definitions; e4 – Format; e5 – Presentation; e6 – Examination; e7 – Notice of refusal; e8 – Originals and copies; e9 – Date of issuance; e10 – Transport; e11 – Corruption of an electronic record after presentation; and additional disclaimer of liability for presentation of electronic records under e-UCP.

The international supply chain manager (3PLs and 4PLs) must be familiar with the UCP 600 and the following publications are strongly recommended:

a   Documentary Credits 2007 revision – UCP 600;
b   Commentary on UCP 600 No. 680;
c   International Standard Banking Practice for the examination of Documents under Documentary Credits ('ISBP') – No. 681.

The ICC's specialised list of publications covers a range of topics including international banking, international trade reference and terms (Incoterms), law and arbitration, counterfeiting and fraud, model commercial contracts and environmental issues. Many of the publications are available in several languages and are available from ICC National Committees, which exist in over 80 countries. Details are available on www.iccwbo.org. Publications are available in both traditional and electronic formats from the ICC Business Bookstore at www.iccbooks.com.

The ICC is based in Paris and was founded in 1919. Today, it groups thousands of member companies and associations from over 130 countries. Its objective is to promote trade and investment across frontiers and help business operations meet the challenges and opportunities of globalisation.

Market Development Strategy with Global Logistics Focus

Global logistics today is providing the right product at the right place at the right cost at the right time. The fusion of all these elements is a complex and demanding task and the importance of the logistics role cannot be overstressed. This is more so as globalisation continues to grow and the role of the 3PL and 4PL take the lead on a more vigorous scale.

Developing overseas markets is a key factor in the global logistics operation. This is especially so today as the supply chain becomes longer and the customer requires a wider choice of higher quality and price-sensitive products; moreover, taste, style and technology changes, which reinforces the need to have a high turnover of stock and keep obsolescence risk at a minimum level.

The following are the salient points in deciding in which areas/regions to export the product:

a   The company objectives as found in the business plan;
b   Legal and political constraints. This extends to agency agreements, channels of distribution, patent registration, licensing, joint ventures, tariff barriers, franchises, repatriation of funds, taxation, employment law and exchange control;
c   Political and economic stability particularly on inwards investment;
d   Culture – the culture of the company towards international portfolio development, especially logistics literacy and computer competence;
e   The product – degree of adaptation and competitiveness and impact on product life cycle;
f   The exporters' experience in the market, the level of competition both short and long term, and the exporter reputation in the marketplace;
g   Open or closed markets featuring non-tariff and tariff barriers, and credit rating;
h   Markets category classification – is it a key market or cluster market complex;
i   Member of any economic bloc or customs union and the accruing benefits;
j   Urgency or speed of entry to the market available such as licence or a franchise.

The exporter/logistics operator must be a strategist and be able to interpret and understand fully the importer/buyer needs and aspirations – in particular, to develop synergy with the overseas procurement officer, through continuous dialogue.

Areas in which the procurement officer will focus include the following: product requirements/developments/payment terms, flexibility of product availability, credit rating of exporter, calibre/professionalism of supplier personnel, commitment to the buyer, and overall competitiveness of the product, especially in value-added terms. Additionally, the exporter must be computer-literate, culturally and logistically focused and share the expectations of the role/function of the buyer. A key area for the procurement officer's strategy is quality control, compliance with international/national product standards and, now, price areas such as product guarantee, spares availability and maintenance/servicing arrangements. It is important for the exporter to identify why the supplier chose their product and in so doing develop the selection criteria to the benefit of both parties. Whatever the reason for the procurement officer's decision to buy the product, which may be price, design, availability, durability in non-price areas, etc., the exporter must strive to develop these areas. Overseas clients/markets buy goods for different reasons and place a different emphasis on the product role in the industrial or consumer market environment. For example, the industrial unit may be focused more on production output, durability and spares/maintenance and less on design and price. The exporter and importer/procurement must harmonise their strategies to the benefit of both parties. Ideally, the exporter must develop synergy with the buyer/importer.

Overall, the global logistic operator must be aware of the range of methods in which to conduct trade, the merits of each and areas in which greater efficiency can be realised. The method of exporting may be chosen for a particular reason and in a particular circumstance. The logistic operator must be aware of the rationale of the decision and the circumstance in which the decision was made. Such circumstances are continuously changing and the logistic operator must review regularly the solution to determine whether change is necessary and the benefit accruing.

There are two methods of exporting – indirect and direct. Indirect is the process of selling goods overseas through a third party, thereby relinquishing control of the selling process of the goods. This has the advantage to the exporter of obviating any need to have an extensive internationally focused organisation, because usually no contact is made with the overseas buyer. Examples include local buying office, piggy bank operations, an export house and trading houses.

Direct exporting is the process whereby the exporter becomes fully involved on a proactive basis. This generates a proactive situation compared with indirect exporting, which is reactive. Hence, the exporter becomes fully involved in the seven 'Ps' of the marketing mix – product, place, promotion, price, process, people and physical aspects, on an international basis. Examples of direct exporting include agents, distributors, joint ventures, licensing, consortia, franchising, free trade zones, government procurement, leasing, strategic alliances, mergers and acquisitions, management contracts and wholly owned subsidiaries. Business to business (B2B) and business to consumer (B2C) (see page 36) feature in this direct exporting category.

It cannot be stressed too strongly that global logistic operators/3PLs/4PLs are fully conversant with the ingredients of both direct and indirect exporting. It must be noted that buyers are continuously reviewing their suppliers in the interest of cost reduction, technology and efficiency, especially in rationalisation of suppliers. The global logistics operator has a distinctive role in the development of the rationalisation process.

Business to Business (B2B) and Business to Consumer (B2C) – Value-Added Benefit

Global logistics is all about efficiency in a high-tech environment. The global logistic operator must be conversant with the enormous increase in the B2B and B2C business, much facilitated by e-commerce international. To the exporter, it is a very efficient way to develop the international portfolio, and in particular eliminates the intermediary with significant cost savings and accelerates the decision-making process. Moreover, it develops empathy between the two parties and favours strongly a logistic- and computer-focused approach. It favours both the MNIs and SMEs.

The B2B e-commerce market is well established and enables international sales/logistic terms to concentrate on selling, which requires face-to-face interaction and the back office on e-commerce sales. It is a low-cost method of exporting and avoids multiple copies of catalogues. Such B2B emerges when the exporter/importer have a good relationship and complete synergy.

The B2C is distinguished from the B2B by the nature of the customer and how that customer uses the product. In business marketing, international customers are organisations such as businesses, government bodies and institutions such as hospitals. The B2C market is often conducted through e-commerce, such as cars and accessories, home appliances and accessories, books, financial services, tourism, transport and food products. It is very popular in the EU single market.

The logistics operator, both for B2B and B2C, must maintain and develop a good website and have well-trained and professional personnel handling enquiries. It must be serviced 24 hours daily to handle global enquiries in various time zones. The website must be targeted to focus on individual markets and in the language of the buyer. It is often prudent to feature in distant markets a local contact, such as agent/distribution/franchisee, who can demonstrate the product to the buyer.

It is important to bear in mind that consumer and business markets differ in the nature of markets, market demand, importer behaviour, exporter/importer relationships, buying power, and market environment influences such as legal, technical, cultural, political, exchange control and economic; also check country/company credit rating (see page 52).

Identifying Priorities

The 3PL and 4PLs are very fast growing markets; to put it into perspective, leading company Unilever uses 100 3PLs in its global operations and spends between €1 billion and €1.5 billion on warehousing and transport. It is one of the world's biggest manufacturers of FMCG for a consumer global market of 150 million people. The European brand represents 38 per cent of the €15 billion business. Unilever focus on benchmarking and encourage more dialogue from the 3PLs to understand the business and develop best practice. In the selection process key questions include: How can they add value to the business and not follow a route of reporting problems rather than develop an innovative culture of solving them through consultation? The key to 3PLs and 4PLs is to understand fully the business in which they operate, and how best they can improve it, embracing all elements of the supply chain and in particular those in which they are engaged with their client – the shipper.

A recent survey (2007) conducted by Containerization International related to a shipper survey and identified a range of priorities – in particular reliability of the supply chain.

Reliability focused on port delay bottlenecks, both for inbound and outbound cargoes. This is the result of a surge of seasonal traffic, especially in containers. A possible solution is to divert sailings – but often impracticable – or examine a hub port with a feeder service. The major trade is Asia to Europe. Often, such delays are outside the control of ocean carriers, non-vessel owning common carrier (NVOCCs) and 3PLs/freight forwarders. Potential improvements in reliability in key services embrace supply chain visibility, documentation and exception reporting, plus how shippers can better utilise 3PLs (and carriers) and provide value-added services. In this regard shippers favoured outsourcing the whole supply chain under a 4PL scenario. Exception reporting also was mentioned where agreed milestones had not been achieved. Major improvements were being realised with RFID (see page 108) developments on an individual container basis as well as collaborate projects between 3PLs and major shippers through an IT-based system.

A footwear company entrusted NYK Logistics with an all-embracing logistic operation, including purchase order management. A US-based shipper of healthcare products measured port to port, port to door, or shipper to door transit times as an important gauge of reliability and a useful tool for managing issues. Other improvements sought were IT track and trace systems.

A German chemicals and pharmaceutical shipper indicated managing their own operations is a competitive advantage with cost savings and ultimate selling prices. The company undertakes regular benchmarking to ensure the 3PLs maintain high-quality standards and realise competitive rates.

Currently there are 10,000 companies in the C-TPAT (see page 108) programme. Shippers featured in the C-TPAT programme confirmed a major benefit emerged in terms of accelerated clearance for imports to the US, but stressed additional work was involved to comply with the US Customs and Border Protection 24-hour rule.

It is important that 3PLs/4PLs seek to attain the best practice and keep up to date on changing conditions/regulations/technology/trade conditions in the global marketplace. The foregoing features the priorities that the shipper expects from the 3PL/4PL so that they can concentrate on other areas of their business outside core logistics.

Useful Sources of Information

Bolero <www.bolero.net/company/corporate_overview.html>

Commentary on UCP 600: Article-by-Article Analysis by the UCP 600 Drafting Group (2007), ICC Publication No. 680, ICC Publications: Paris

Containerization International <www.ci-online.co.uk>

Financial Times <news.ft.com/ft-reports>

Incoterms 2000, ICC Booklet No. 600. Paris: ICC Publications <wwww.iccwbo.org/incoterms/id3038/index.html>

Robert Parson (2007) 'UCP 600 – A new lease of life for documentary credits?', Clyde & Co: London <www.clydeco.com/knowledge/articles/ucp-600-a-new-lease-of-life-of-documentary-credits-part-1.cfm>

Chapter 5

Constituents of the International Purchasing/Procurement System

Introduction

Successful businesses have a strategic plan and focus as reflected in their business plan. It is facilitated by the availability of cyberspace resources, which enable the buyer to keep up to date with product development/differentiation and availability.

International purchasing is the process of obtaining a product/goods or service, which is available in a market or markets, access to which involves crossing international boundaries. Such international sourcing is desirable to enable the company to be managed in a competitive manner and operate successfully in a global market. The prime rationale of adopting an international purchasing strategy rather than using an indigenous supplier is to enhance the value-added benefit of the product or service to the consumer. Overall, the decision is tied to the product life cycle; it may be a price factor, quality, technology, availability, innovation, standards, design or fashion. Hence, global sourcing is not simply a buying function; it is the process of obtaining a product/service in line with consumer needs and technology, thereby enhancing the attraction, the profile, the quality or the value-added benefit.

Moreover, it embraces the complexities of multiple outsourcing, which often involves inbound and outbound logistics. This embraces the process of component suppliers – inbound – providing the goods for assembly in the outsourced assembly plant for distribution globally in the outbound logistics operation. An example is a car manufacturing plant, Dyson electrical goods, or the Distripark Rotterdam, involving spice supplies from various countries, which are mixed to client's specification and packaged for distribution throughout EU to various supermarkets – the outbound operation.

International Purchasing Systems Constituents/Strategy and its Interface with the Management of the Global Supply Chain

International purchasing embracing strategic supply chain management involves many disciplines, including logistics, marketing, product evaluation, international distribution, negotiation, linguistic skills and culture awareness of international environment, technical skills in the product specification, supplier audits, design, standards, trade finance operating in the buyer's, seller's or a third currency, terms of terms as featured in Incoterms 2000 and UCP 600, import regulations and constraints, the international trade legal environment and the documentation associated with finance, carriers, insurance and customs. Skills are required in costing the sources of overseas products/services, which not only embrace the price at the factory gate, but also carriage, insurance, import duty, booking charges, taxation, packaging, agent's commission and a hedging cost to counter any currency fluctuation. Overall, the whole international supply chain needs to be managed and continuously improved. Moreover, a strategic focus is needed with adequate planning.

The international purchasing strategy interrelated with the global supply chain embraces the following methodology:

a   Identifying through market research, in-house discussion and other sources, including legislation, the product/service specification and standards together with the volume and the quality required;

b   Researching the most suitable suppliers using all means available including trade directories, trade associations, trade exhibitions, logistic operators and cyberspace (i.e. the Internet);

c   Selecting the 3PL or 4PL (see page 70). This requires special skills to obtain an efficient 3PL or 4PL to deliver an efficient global supply chain;

d   Formulating a negotiating plan with the preferred supplier, which covers the product specification and complies with international/national standards, prices, availability, terms of sale – Incoterms 2000 – International Payment arrangements (letter of credit, open account, documentary collections) name of carrier/3PL, insurance, export/import documents and delivery date;

e   Activating the contract within the buyer global supply chain network relative to the date, place of delivery, quantity, funding arrangements with the buyer's issuing bank (see page 51) and processing import and customs documentation in accordance with the contract of sale, Incoterms 2000, UCP 600 and documentary collections;

f   Managing the global supply chain in accordance with the delivery date, involving the collection of the goods by the 3PL from the supplier's premises, perhaps in the form of a container to an ICD or seaport; clearance through customs at the importer's ICD or seaport premises; loading the container onto the vessel for its destination seaport and subsequent transhipment involving the 4PL at the container hub (see page 79) into a feeder service; unloading at the seaport for despatch to customs clearance and raising import duty if any at the seaport, ICD, or buyer's premises. Some importers, to avoid any import duty until the goods are withdrawn from the premises, arrange for the 4PL to place them in an FTZ (see page 83) or bonded warehouse (see page 87). Also, maintaining liaison with the issuing bank regarding payment arrangements and loan provision. It is likely the 3PL will take control of the goods from the time of the contract acceptance to delivery of the goods;

g   Tracking the cargo throughout the transit using online computer access – a facility available from the 3PL/4PL;

h   Taking delivery of the goods and undertaking any product evaluation – transit delays, damage claims, payment arrangements including currency, import customs clearance, etc. This may take place several weeks/days later if placed in an FTZ or bonded warehouse and withdrawn not as a complete consignment, but in limited quantities as required by the buyer. It may be processed and re-exported as found in the Port of Rotterdam Distriparks (see page 126);

i   Developing an after-care strategy, whereby the product is continuously reviewed for any subsequent orders or necessary modifications, and for regular suppliers initiating continuous dialogue and establishing empathy with the supplier;

j   To monitor the benchmark performance (see page 90) and analysis/review of the global supply chain and 3PL/4PL with a view to realising an added-value performance/objective. Transparency with the 3PL/4PL is essential to ensure there is complete integration between supplier/buyer and 3PL/4PL with all elements of the global supply chain to eliminate inefficiencies.

Global supply chain strategic management embraces a range of items that we will now examine.

i Positioning the firm in the supply chain. This embraces the degree to which the company wishes to rely on 'in-house' production resources and outsource activities. Outsourcing enables the company to take advantage of the latest technology and cost advantage, thereby adding value to the product. Also, it raises the profile of the company in the marketplace and produces a more competitive product. Small family businesses tend to be reluctant to outsource their production until a new generation of management is installed or competition outmanoeuvres them.

ii Product design strategies. Product design embraces a range of considerations as emphasised when negotiating the contract. The prime focus is on customer needs and technology reflecting competitiveness, cost and legal constraints (see page 98). However, does the company require 'in-house' or 'outsourced' design – with the latter benefits as found in the case study of the Indian automotive design/supply industry (see page 137)? CAD and CAE is common practice. Product design processes will reflect implications on packaging, storage, warehousing, transportation, import duty and infrastructure.

iii Environment of supply chain. Customers sourcing goods from less developed countries will find the supply chain very much under-developed and both expensive and slow compared with the logistic economies/analysis of fully developed economies such as North America (see page 133) and the EU (see page 126). Benchmarking (see page 90) and best practices provide a marked comparison between the developed world and developing countries. The supply chain environment will include political aspects, labour markets, customer profile, finance/cash flow, international regulations compliance/conventions, supplier profile, taxation, transportation, technology, EDI, software, cyber face, and the structure of the supply chain and degree of transparency. The foregoing list requires a strategic analysis in the company corporate strategic objectives, which will embrace several countries in the supply chain network.

iv It is very important that the marketing and logistics sectors work closely together to accomplish the company global supply chain strategic focus. The decision-making must be harmonised through careful objective analysis and working with the 3PL/4PL. Failure to design/construct a competitive supply chain results in a less competitive/attractive product to the consumer.

v Trade-offs. The marketing department is often faced with a near supply source with a sophisticated supply chain or a distant market involving extended lead times – longer supply chain times, but lower overall cost. It embraces managing the mobile asset (see page 18) – global supply chain. 'Trade-offs' can be extended to a range of scenarios and the decision-making must be based on priorities, technology, cost, quality, design and so on. Labour force skills are an important factor in the ability to change and keep up with twenty-first century technology. For example, Switzerland is renowned for its precision engineering, Italy for its creative design, Germany for its high-tech heavy engineering shipbuilding, such as cruise vessels, tankers and gas carriers, while China has emerged as a low-cost consumer product market with a trend towards industrial products, serving the mass market in Europe and North America.

vi Project management. An increasing number of capital projects are being developed as we progress through the twenty-first century. It may be an airport, seaport, railway, hospital, new town, highway, and so on. This involves a project team, which includes buyers for each sector. It features design formulation, product testing and market evaluation. Overall, much of the work is subcontracted. The logistic supply chain operation is very complex with extensive planning of a sequential nature and coordination by the project team. The key factor in the supply chain is reliability and transparency. Computer technology plays a major role in the project management. The project team is likely to include value engineering, value analysis and merchandising, and its task is to critically examine product design on a value/cost basis.

vii Structural planning. The strategic responsibility rests with the operations departments, which focus on the supply chain infrastructure (item iii). This embraces not only the environment route followed by the global supply chain passing through numerous countries, but access and exit points. It embraces: method of transportation, that is, containerisation, warehouse profile/management, use of FTZ/ICDs/economic zones/CFS, etc.; method of finance – including payment arrangements, alliance with other companies, selection of 3PLs/4PLs, value-added, componentised items versus finished product, insurance, quality control inventories and human resource management. IT and transparency throughout the supply chain are key factors.

viii Planning and control. An essential ingredient with global supply chain management strategy is an effective planning and control system. It focuses on procurement, warehouse systems, stock control, productivity, market forecast, resources/asset management, stock replenishment systems, inventory management, cycle inventory, operational performance of 3PLs/4PLs and finance/cash flow. A key area is purchasing and supply, correlated to demand/market conditions. The situation in the global supply market is more complex, particularly with the short product life cycle in fast-moving products. The need to dispose of the existing stock prior to the arrival of the new model requires good planning technique to discount old stock and build up new supplies of the new model. Extended lead times from China to North America/Europe present a logistic challenge. Often, the new model may be phased in by market such as the European brand to be followed by the US/Canada. New models require careful planning to accommodate them in the global supply chain infrastructure embracing 3PLs/4PLs.

Moreover, it involves extensive marketing, a product launch plan, adequate new stock and a good backup service including after-sales. The global supply chain may need to be redesigned to reflect a change in multi-suppliers, both inbound and outbound, which will result in a change in the 3PL and 4PL's software.

A strategic planning example arises in the global food chain, whereby a former bottled product shipped on pallets is moved in container tanks and the bottling/labelling is undertaken in the destination country, such as the Distripark in Rotterdam. This involves a complete redesign of the global supply chain involving significant investment by the supplier in production/handling/processing plant – maybe several hundred miles from the seaport – to the distributor embracing tank storage units. Also the carrier/container operator will need to have available the infrastructure. In the event, it is likely other shippers have container tank cargo.

A redesigned global supply chain arose when the New Zealand lamb shipments changed from the bulk shipment in refrigerated carriers to the containerised shipments. Planning and investments were required both in New Zealand and the European seaports, and the ongoing distribution by container to the food chain distribution cold storage warehouse. A similar criterion applies from South Africa, involving citrus fruit being shipped in containers rather than in purpose-built fruit carriers. The radical change from bulk shipments to containerised movement yielded the following in terms of the global food chain management: a spread of the shipment over a 12-month period in the smaller containerised volume movement rather than the bulk cargo shipment in reefer carriers; cargo can be distributed direct to the buyer's cold warehouse without double handling at the departure destination seaports – road/port handling departure to ship arrival, ship to quay warehouse sorting – onward carriage by road/rail/in refrigerated units; quicker service; lower freight cost; complete IT transparency in transit; much improved global supply chain management; and finally the avoidance of peaks and troughs throughout the supply chain, as the consumer can correlate the demand throughout the 12 months with the supplier accommodating the food in their cold storage warehouse. Overall, this strategy reduces lead time through the more frequent container service, improves inventory management, avoids discounting due to a product oversupply and improves the buyer's cash flow. It demonstrates the global logistics role in the need to focus on the much-improved global supply chain management. Overall, it places the overproduction risk with the supplier and avoids the buyer having to dispose of surplus food supplies.

ix Human resource management (HRM) is a key factor in the strategic supply chain management. Personnel must be committed to improve the value-added performance and integrate with all the sectors throughout the chain. Overall, the personnel must be forward-thinking and work within the supply chain infrastructure. Good multifunctional personnel who understand the progressive environment of global supply chain management are essential. A lateral/horizontal structure is required, fully integrated, especially the interface between the marketing and logistics personnel.

x The location of factories' distribution centre in the seller's/buyer's country/region is a critical factor in the success of a global supply chain. Examples of strategically located factories/distribution centres arise in the EU, where cross-border trading is permitted among the 27 Member States, with no border controls. It is further facilitated by the 13 Member States in the Eurozone, operating with a common currency – the euro. Factors influencing the strategic location of factories/distribution centres are numerous and include: reduced lead time to customer – not applicable in a distant market such as the Far East serving the EU and North America; centralised logistic flow to realise optimisation of cost; lower production cost/more competitive pricing; global information system; lower freight cost and e-commerce environment (see page 117). Outsourcing does embrace a strategic 'trade-off' in rationalising sourcing, production and distribution across national boundaries. Hence the need for a central decision-making structure for logistics is established. A further factor with the retailer sourcing products from the centralised global factor is the prerequisite to reflect local consumer needs. This embraces adding value to the product such as oriental furniture being imported into the Rotterdam Distriparks. The trader subsequently encourages buyer/supermarket/department stores to identify any 'add-ons' to the furniture such as cushions, reflecting local taste. A similar criterion exists in the global car market, whereby the distributor in the destination country/region will install a trailer bar and improved upholstery reflecting localised design and taste. Such a strategy encourages localised customised needs and is cost-effective as it reduces import duty.

To analyse the foregoing it is important to recognise the following: (a) the strategy must be well thought out and planned, embracing several stages of development with focus on a team-oriented approach to gain maximum competitive advantage in the marketplace; full advantage should be taken of e-commerce in communication research, procurement; (b) the 3PLs and 4PLs must be forward-looking, adding value to the global supply chain with the latest software offering fully transparency access at all times; (c) strategic planning must embrace three areas: cost, differentiation and customer focus; (d) in a global strategy as distinct from a localised strategy there are a range of challenges in the design and operation of the global supply chain: asset productivity, lead time, flexibility, inventory management, high-tech facilities, port/airport distribution hubs, response rate, quality control, freight cost, import duty, reliability, infrastructure, vendor management, customer service, 3PLs, 4PLs, e-commerce, impact on competitive pricing in the market-place, warehouse management, taxation, management productivity, costing and billing systems, bonded warehouse management, RFID/RDT technology, and so on.

Negotiating the Contract

E-commerce, globalisation, competition and computerisation are the four major engines driving change in the twenty-first century. The development of an increasingly compli-cated and diversified supply chain, as featured in chapter 2, demands a flexible and responsive approach (see page 2). Hence, communication between the buyer and seller today relies on excellent communication systems, not only for the online accessibility of discrete information, but also for direct global communication using video clip messages, and online visual conferencing aided by increasingly sophisticated web cameras and mobile phone technology. The ability to communicate better, faster, more efficiently and economically – whether by voice or data – is a major stimulant in a fast-growing inter-national trade. It encourages the buyer, in particular, to source overseas by easing market entry, access, and communication. Overall a well-thought-out plan involving an input from all parties is desirable.

A key factor of international buying entrepreneurial skills is contract negotiation. It involves many elements of which the principle one is adequate planning and market research to ensure that the product specification is acceptable to the end user and fully conforms to all the relevant national and international standards – in particular, compli-ance with the supply chain management standard ISO (see page 74). Moreover, the terms of the contract and monitoring its performance are key areas in global supply chain management. We will now examine the key ingredients for the logistics operator to focus on in contract negotiation.

A wide range of considerations are involved in the product specification embracing the following:

a   Commercial aspects – driven by market research and industrial research to allow an empathetic strategy with the consumer or end user to be developed. It reflects the added benefit the product brings to the user. Other elements include the design, colour and the users' environment, cultural needs and buying power. Consumer design tends to be a mass fast-moving market while the industrial sector focuses on technical performance and reliability with a much longer life cycle, spanning many years. Productivity and performance are key areas and capital cost is less significant while day-to-day operating costs are crucial.

b   Technical aspects – of products are a priority in product choice, both in consumer and industrial sectors. High-tech products reflect market leadership, and the prudent buyer would be advised to look into future investment in product development. Quality is a key factor in product specification, including legal and technical considerations. Foodstuffs are a massive market, much of which is shipped in controlled temperature ISO containers (see page 74) or trucks to maintain quality. Product testing at the time of shipment and following arrival are key audit strategies in supply chain management. The pre-shipment inspection (see page 117) should be adopted.

c   Legal aspects – compliance with legal specification is paramount and no deviation is acceptable in product specification. Legalisation is tending to increase as more countries achieve developed status. The ISO takes the lead in this area (see page 74), but particular markets, such as Japan, the US and the EU, are very concerned with legal specifications. Suppliers should not be utilised if they cannot produce evidence of compliance with the appropriate legal specification embracing an approval certificate. This applies not only to the product specification, but also the supplier's total quality management (see page 63). Health and safety form part of the legal environment. This embraces a wide range of areas, including industrial design and use of specific materials, health certificates for agricultural and animal products, and product specification determines the level of import duty. Careful customs planning is an area where import duty can be reduced to ensure the correct Harmonized System code is used. This is an area where the logistics operator and supply chain manager must give special attention, especially to reduce cost. The patents limit market penetration, and it is important that the appropriate patent registration has been granted.

d   Transportation – the international buyer must be very familiar with the transport arrangements on routing, transit time, freight, insurance, packaging, stowage areas, together with any constraints. The latter points can influence the product specification such as whether the goods are shipped as componentised break bulk or as a complete unit. Moreover, the supply chain manager should continuously focus on improving the utilisation of the cubic capacity of the container, thereby – through the reduction of broken stowage – increasing, for example, by up to 5 per cent the number of units shipped at no extra freight cost. It is likely that 3PLs and 4PLs will be employed and the benefits and compatibility of the throughout supply chain transit must be continuously evaluated.

e   Product standardisation. We live in an era of standardisation, which has been driven by market development, cost–benefit relationship, legal requirements, competition, product support system, physical environment, market conditions, buying power, media, culture, green environmental issues, and economic blocs and customs. Logistics operators must be aware that markets are becoming more homogenous – more common consumer requirements – and more globalised, which through increased competition is driven by lower unit cost and ultimately a reduced product range with emphasis on standardisation and the evolution of the global core product, which can be customised locally for individual markets.

f   Product formulation. The process of buying services overseas or outsourcing remains a growth market and is examined on pages 150–2. Outsourcing involves people, process and physical aspects, all of which must be reflected in the selection criteria of the supplier and contract formulation.

g   National and International Standards. Adequate research must ensure the correct specification is formulated to reflect in the contract the relevant national and international standards such as BSI, ISO and EU regulations.

h   Sourcing of products. Product sourcing may be at international, regional or global level. It requires in-depth analysis and focus on the contract formulation.

i   Source and location. Choosing an acceptable overseas market is a crucial decision to be taken by the procurement executive. It requires evaluation, not only from the product specification, but also from the logistic standpoint and availability of 3PLs and 4PLs and the supply chain management. Location is a key factor, especially in the country infrastructure and computerised literate market. Flexibility, quality control and reliability are some of the many factors that arise in the effective supply chain management. Risk assessment should be undertaken.

j   Tendering. The task of tendering represents an important element in contract selection and is defined as 'an offer to sell at the price indicated and can be converted into a contract by acceptance in the form of the buyer's order'. The buyer must bear in mind a range of considerations, including the compliance with the quality management assurance, and have the appropriate accreditation (BSI, LRQA, ISO9000, EN 29000).

k   Supplier audit. This embraces analysing a supplier's creditability and related quotation. This embraces production capacity, professional skilled labour resources, high-tech equipment, delivery timescale, transportation arrangements, total quality management, accreditation, product quality, compliance with national and international standards, any comparison with previous buyers and compliance with an international logistic plan, the method of payment (see page 52) and Incoterms used (see page 46). The ICC Model International Sale Contract is a guide for traders, importers and all parties involved.

l   The overseas market. A critical aspect in buying overseas is to visit the overseas market to identify or audit potential sellers. A strategic focus is required, incorporating a plan and stated objectives. Focus must be on culture, management commitment and an acceptable international logistics approach involving 3PLs and 4PLs.

m   Digital trade. This relates to the electronic transmission of all documents and data between various elements of the international supply chain. In September 1999, Bolero International devised and launched a new service – bolero-net. It involves an open commercial module, a unique legal framework and complete security. Electronic commerce opens up an economically more efficient way of running a business. Overall, it enables an international business to reduce operating costs while also raising the quality of its operations. The international logistic must be continuously researched to keep up to date and take advantage of the continuous digital trade revolution, and focus particularly on the supplier to respond to such development/innovation.

n   Negotiating skills. The process of concluding a purchase overseas involves many skills and each situation varies by product/service, culture, competition, language, management culture and attitudes, infrastructures and environment in the seller's country, export/import regulations, including digital trade development, protocol and political structure. Overall, the buyer must work towards an objective and the negotiation route to that objective will vary by product, service and country.

o   Terms and conditions of the contract. The terms and conditions feature Incoterms (see page 46), Uniform Customs and Practice for Documentary Credit ICC publication No. 600 (see page 52), covering payment and delivery arrangements. Incoterms feature method of delivery of the goods by the exporter and indicate what charges are included in the price, and also define the responsibilities of the parties to the contract of sale for the arrangement of insurance, shipping and packaging. The buyer is responsible for ensuring that the order is being processed in accordance with the contract terms and may appoint an agent to verify this at various stages of the manufacture until final despatch under the pre-shipment inspection arrangement. The logistics operator must become closely involved and eliminate intermediaries where possible. The profile of packaging will determine the stowage factor in the container.

p   Transport. The transport will feature one of the following: Air freight – embracing air waybill document and subject to Warsaw Convention 1929 or amended Warsaw Convention 1955, CIM International Rail Consignment Note embracing COTIF convention signed in Berne 1980, CMR International Road Haulage consignment note, combined transport embracing a range of rules not yet approved internationally, and Bill of Lading – sea transport embracing Hague Rules and Carriage of Goods by Sea Acts 1924, 1971 and 1992.

q   Costing the constituents. The overseas buyer's objective to purchase the product will reflect the company's strategic objective and embrace a wide range of costing elements. The logistics operator must be aware of the freight and product cost involved in the despatch of the finished product and componentised unit, and the benefits of FCL and LCL shipments and the Incoterms used. It may be EXW/FCA favouring the buyer, or CIP/CIF favouring the seller. The payment terms require close examination, especially in relation to cash flow, risk, timescale and currency. Study the ICC publication on documentary credits (UCP 600), documentary bills collection UCP 458 and other options embracing open account, bill of exchange and advance payment.

r   Tender receipts, analysis, evaluation and acceptance. These require close examination, especially any variations from the tender and constraints.

s   Quality procedures. These include pre-shipment inspection, testing any samples, and the buyer visiting the overseas production or manufacturing plant to check on quality control procedures/techniques/monitoring.

t   Dispute procedures. These feature arbitration and conciliation. The ICC issue guidelines and procedures.

u   Finally one must consider security, which is examined in Chapter 9.

To conclude, the logistics operator must devise a plan that ideally must be tested to ensure its objective is capable of being realised. A strategy of continuous evaluation must be adopted to reduce cost and improve efficiency.

Financing Global Supply Chains

Over the past 20 years, the development of the global infrastructure has been outstanding. Progress in infrastructure, communication and technology has been intrinsically linked to global flows of products and information. Adding the financial flow is the ultimate supply chain integration.

This fundamental change demands a new philosophy by the logistics community. Hitherto financial considerations are not part of the logistics function. It is another dimension of adding value and making the supply chain become more competitive. Measuring a supply chain performance usually embraces operational tools analysis, and it is quite rare that the cost of financing the capital is included in the calculation. This is surprising in an industry that is capital-intensive, placing so much reliance on equipment and assets.

For MNIs the cost of carrying an inventory can be extortionate. A multi-country and multi-echelon inventory can do a lot of damage to the cash flow as well as having the adverse impact of numerous taxes and customs duties.

Scrutiny of the MNI balance sheet is a key factor to identify and eliminate all removable cost, which is made easier with global visibility for the inventory. This approach drives financial controllers to control the financial aspects of the supply chain and energises new thinking in alternative methods of distribution.

The international movement of goods generates financial flows, which are subject to additional complications such as distance, culture, multiplication of intermediaries and ever-changing regulations. For the MNIs, this complexity is increasing with the number of countries, currencies and financial institutions the company is dealing with.

Many companies trade globally through subsidiaries that are using their own payment procedures and their local banks. With the development of compliance and security requirements this autonomy can be a source of risk.

A particularly sensitive area for companies is the US Sarbanes-Oxley Act. This requires a certain amount of internal controls by US treasury departments. Most financial directors are unhappy with decisions being made at a local level and require more visibility and require real-time data.

Financial controllers tend to centralise and standardise, which leads to the consolidation of a number of financial service providers the MNIs are using. In common with logistics operators, financial service providers are now developing a deep local knowledge.

Using several, logistics providers worldwide can limit the inventory visibility; then, using several banks in multiple countries can blur the vision of the global lending and cash-flow requirements to finance that inventory. The financial partner can prove invaluable in countries where the regulations on cash management are obscure or inexistent. Requirements for the global logistics and financial services providers are showing a lot of similarities.

Banks have traditionally always been intermediaries. They usually provide traditional financial products such as working capital lending and assets-backed security. Some products have been rejuvenated by technology while other banks with a global network can change a simple purchase order into a letter of credit (see page 52) for the local supplier, thus controlling both ends of the transaction and reducing the risk (UCP 600, see page 52).

There is an even greater form of this close-circuit transaction with global settlements, such as bolero.net messaging system. This embraces Bolero XML – a validated global cross-industry XML standards solution that allows all parties of a trade chain to seamlessly 'talk' to each other by automating their information exchange (see page 79). Hence buyers and sellers, when joining the Bolero Network, adopt a common set of rules, thus mitigating risks.

In that environment carriers hold an enviable position. Not only do they already know the buyer and seller, but they also control the goods through their tracking systems. Overall, the global carrier has a global presence, a portfolio of clients worldwide and an up-to-date knowledge of international trade services.

Hence the global carrier has a large range of products. The most common is cash-on-delivery (COD) with payments collected at the time of the release of the goods. With the extensive use of technology, funds can be transferred electronically and payments are settled by alert message. Some carriers run receivable management services for businesses offering longer payment terms to their customers, but still require a quick turnaround from invoice to cash. Logistic providers now issue letters of credit and again use their global IT capabilities to automate the process.

They can also deal with export financing. For a supplier it can take the form of a line of credit to cover the manufacturing cost of export orders. For the buyer it can be a way to finance imports at a rate more favourable than what is available on the domestic market.

Although credit guarantees are usually offered by government agencies capable of supporting risks that are too great to be covered by private enterprise, some carriers provide buyers with defaults and insolvency cover.

Like banks, they also provide asset-backed loans: while banks are traditionally lending against account receivables, real estate and equipment, carriers are also lending against inventory. This has been made possible by considerable investments in tracking technology and inventory visibility. This strategy is proving popular with companies with significant supply chain cycles as an option to finance such assets.

Trade finance today is becoming an integrated part of the global supply chain. It is taking full advantage of the new software systems offering transparency throughout all the elements of the global supply chain. Financing the trade cycle has become more sophisticated with which it is delivered. Every company's trade cycle is unique, although there will be elements (e.g. purchasing, manufacturing, shipping, credit, etc.) that are common to all. Each stage in a trade cycle places different demands on a company's finances, but a key component in determining the overall level of working capital required for any business is the time taken between the start of the cycle (i.e. ordering goods, components, or raw materials) and receipt of payment for corresponding sales of finished products.

Today, many trade banks provide advice to traders to ensure at each stage of the particular trade cycle that a structure can be put in place to provide working capital for the different stages in the cycle, and in consequence directly relate to the needs of the client business. As the bulk of international trade is undertaken on terms of 180 days or less, these facilities are an important consideration for any company involved in importing or exporting. Trade finance is built into the export price. Hence the quicker the transit the shorter the time the asset is in transit, and the quicker the payment, thereby reducing the working capital timescale.

Outsourcing (see page 150) is being driven by the logistic strategy with shorter and more cost-effective global supply chains with the result of more competitive pricing, both for near and distant markets. China, India and the Far East are examples. Product pricing is the key factor. Factors involved may be summarised as follows:

1 How far minimum cost and return on capital can be relative to what the market will pay.
2 The degree of fluctuation in exchange rates.
3 What credit terms are available in the market and whether the cost is borne by the buyer.
4 Inbound multi-country sourcing for manufacture, processing and outbound despatch to the overseas market. This presents an enormous challenge to the global logistics operator to reduce transit time in the trade cycle and thereby reduce the working capital requirement.

5   Aligned to item 4 there is distribution, local mark-up in the local currency, taxation, customs duties and a wide range of compliance issues, which arise through national governments and international agencies.

6   Sources of raw material and possible price changes.

To conclude, the logistics operator today recognises that the fusion of the product, information and financial flows is complete. The modern logistics professional now has to manage a three-dimensional supply chain.

Useful Sources of Information

Alan E. Branch (1998) *Shipping and Air Freight Documentation for Importers and Exporters*, 2nd edn, Witherby & Co Ltd: Livingstone

Alan E. Branch (2001) *International Purchasing and Management*, Cengage Learning Services Ltd: London

ICC Publications <www.iccbooks.com/Home/Terms.aspx>

Chapter 6

Selecting the International Logistics Operator

Introduction

Selection of the third-party logistics (3PL) operator and key factors in its development are critical areas in business today. The company engaging the logistics operator must at the outset have a logistic culture and accept changes in the organisation structure in the interest of efficiency and more vigorous competition in the global marketplace.

Criteria of Selecting the Third-Party Logistics Operator

Cost is the number one factor driving the selection of a 3PL. The need to drive significant cost reduction is still the key decision-making criteria. Cost and service are the two most prevalent factors responsible for using a 3PL provider. Other factors include the following:

a   Emphasis on improved supply chain management. The focus is on continuous evaluation;

b   Implementation of new information technologies – a growth subject to continuous innovation and cost efficiency in the SCM;

c   Collaborative partnerships. This is the key to improving the user–company 3PL performance;

d   Value-added services – the perceived benefit to be derived from the 3PL selected;

e   Provision of core services, inbound/outbound transportation and warehousing services (see page 87). Delivering core services is a key factor: this embraces outbound transportation, warehousing, customs clearance, brokerage, inland transportation and freight forwarding;

f   Opportunities to drive forward supply chain management (SCM) improvement: rates/freight negotiation; LLP/4PL services; materials management; inventory ownership; order entry/processing/customer service; customer and supplier compliance; and factoring (trade financing);

g   Global modular products with a particular focus on the single accountable entity such as an LLP or 4PL.

To increase effectiveness in the face of increased outsourcing, a strategic approach is required. There are many reasons for outsourcing, but the most common include accessing economies of scale, increasing flexibility, refocusing of business on 'core' activities, reducing overheads, simplifying organisations and adding value.

The first stage in the selection task is to consider the implications of distribution strategy for the achievement of business plan goals, including the effect on cost, quality and flexibility. This will probably involve an 'in-house' evaluation of the activities involved. The next step is to conduct a full costing exercise taking into account the nature of the service to be provided, the price of the services, the net revenue released by reducing the in-house resource and cost of switching. The final stage is to identify the number of viable suppliers in the market, bearing in mind that no two logistic companies are exactly the same. All have their own areas of specialisation. Particular attention should be given to: the professional qualifications of the directorate; membership of trade associations; the company's track records; the level of commitment, interest and experience in the area of logistics sought; and their contract terms, resources and client base. Adequate time should be devoted to supplier selection and meaningful discussions conducted with potential candidates. A plan must be formulated, costed and adhered to, with a realistic timescale.

The Key Factors in the Development of a Successful 3PL

The growth of 3PLs continues to be outstanding as companies – manufacturers, retailers, wholesalers and distributors – are turning over parts of their supply chain to firms that have their roots as commodity service providers. Firms that know ocean shipping, forwarding, warehousing or tracking are now handling and in some cases managing broad domestic and international logistic activities. It is all about outsourcing (see page 150).

Third-party logistics operators, regardless of their experience in outsourcing, face common challenges to prime their market and keep it primed.

The first consolidation is the 3PL mission statement – the 3PL's position in the marketplace, its objectives and strategic focus. It may be: an ocean carrier with a service option; a warehouse with a 3PL service; or a logistic service provider with a strong shipping, transport, warehouse, or forwarding capability. It is important to reconcile the company situation between how the company positions itself in the market and how the 3PL's clients perceive the company in the marketplace.

The second consideration is development of a strategy. Operational efficiency is doing the same or similar activities better than competitors. Management tools, such as benchmarking, partnering, re-engineering and change management, for example, are means that let companies reduce costs and achieve performance improvements. They are necessary to sustaining competitiveness, but they can also be temporary achievements, as competitors work to mimic programmes that work.

Strategy is basically how the 3PL differentiates itself in the marketplace. It's what makes the company unique and separates it from the competition. Positioning can reflect the customers' 3PL target, the type of service provided or the blend of customers and service. For example, a strategy can: define the 3PL's customer, identify competitors, and obtain both secondary and primary data; establish the market size, its composition size, trends and specific requirements. It is important to have empathy with the customers, the decision-making process, and those who are influencers and decision-makers in the company, together with the internal and external factors that contribute to the final decision. The 3PLs must establish from their customers how they are perceived in comparison with competitors. Continuous market research is required to determine the 3PL's changing customer needs, both new and existing. Marketing is very important to realise success. Marketing must fully integrate with a prime logistic focus.

The next area on which to focus is the strength and weakness of the company and how to exploit the strengths in terms of business development and remedy the weakness. This applies to all parts of the 3PL, regardless of whether it is a corporate office, division or field location or partner/alliance, and irrespective of whether it is domestic or international. The checklist features: the organisation structure – vertical, horizontal or matrix. Overall, the organisation should reflect the chain of command with no duplication of responsibilities. More importantly it should support the means of providing a dynamic, ongoing logistics service with successful results. 3PLs embrace the skills set to establish themselves as a supply chain service provider who can develop a tailored programme to meet the needs of each customer. Solution providers feature not only the container and more but also the palletised products. The successful 3PL operator focuses on the process: not primarily the container or pallet.

Many 3PLs tend initially to focus on investing in assets, warehouses and technology without knowing how these fit into 3PL solutions. Such an approach constructs answers without knowing the questions. The successful 3PL sells, designs and manages customised logistics in an international or domestic venue. This raises the issue whether existing personnel are capable of selling logistics and supply chain solutions to all importers and provide one-stop shopping. A strategy can be formulated for importers who bring in less than 500 containers per year; this is a different segment than the broad approach of targeting all importers or even all large importers.

Alternatively, a different strategy is needed for the focus on importers of less than 500 containers, which are engaged in distribution/wholesale to mass merchandisers and large retailers. The benefit of this strategy is that the 3PL can assemble the resources and approaches required for the selected market.

The third consideration is management, which separates the outstanding 3PLs from the also-rans. It requires leadership with a sustainable vision, especially in terms of processes, goals, innovation and methodology – in particular, entrepreneurialism. Such personnel develop a proactive rather than a reactive approach. The leaders see the logistics service as the prime consideration, and not the freight, warehouse, or other assets employed. They see the supply chain process, not the transactions. All this separates them from the executive caretakers who can flip-flop with management *de jure* approaches, indifference or quick fixes to growth, positioning and profits. Investors realise how critical outstanding management is to a company's success and likewise the progressive 3PL. Such executives can break the company from its commodity service origins into being a value service provider.

The fourth factor is market research. A well-thought-out marketing plan is a prerequisite. The 3PL must fully understand the market, its components, culture and major players. Moreover, the 3PL must recognise its place/position in the market together with the opportunities and also undertake the formulation of a market profile. A more holistic sales approach is needed for 3PLs than for commodity service providers. Commodity sales personnel tend to deal with the customer perspective of the need to manage costs, but the customer has additional accountabilities. Hence the need for 3PL sales personnel to address the customers' supply chain accountability scope. Basically the accountability scope is 90 per cent of the customer attention span as compared to the 10–25 per cent that freight or warehousing cost. Hence 3PLs must focus on the 90 per cent and not the 10–25 per cent to gain business.

The next area on which to focus is staff training. Staffing is often built with existing personnel who have sales and operations experience, but with the commodity service parent company. In consequence, most 3PLs regard training as an essential ingredient to success, coupled with continuous performance monitoring thereafter. Experience confirms less than 10 per cent of the sales can make the mindset change to sell logistics.

Hence the need to recruit non-shipping personnel to do the logistics selling at all management levels. This influences the decision makers to inject a logistic management culture into the organisation strategy and decision-making. It is essential to recruit personnel who have global supply chain knowledge and experience extolling good practice to sell and assist with designing and managing integrated logistics programmes.

A range of other areas 3PLs must focus on – inherent in any successfully run 3PL company – include process design capability, and focus on people, technology, budget, sales targets and advertising. The overseas network is a key objective for international 3PLs.

To conclude, the successful 3PL strategy must be to focus, not on today or tomorrow, but the day after. Hence the directorate must be forward-looking with an in-built strategy formulated in the business plan. The ongoing challenge for 3PLs is to successfully design, sell and manage a logistics solution with easily monitored metrics and accountability. There is regretfully a high failure rate of outsourcing (see page 150). Causes range from a rush to procure business and understanding the process and requirements to some 3PLs converting back into a commodity service. This conversion defeats the very purpose of the 3PL. Outsource service providers seek competitive advantage: they know that preserving competitive advantage is an ongoing challenge.

Contract Logistics

Contract logistics is a growth market. Dachser Far East Ltd is a leading logistics operator. A definition of contract logistics is that the customer is not limited to using Dachser transport networks, but also commissions Dachser to take care of warehousing, picking, packaging, display building or other individual services. It also implies that the parties involved enter into a building contract for at least 12 months and generate an annual turnover of at least 1 million euros through their joint activities. The diversity of its applications is limited only by the ingenuity of the staff working for the logistics provider and by the capacity of the networks that give physical shape to the services provided.

An example is Otis, which is the biggest manufacturer of elevators, escalators and moving sidewalks, employing 60,000 personnel to develop, manufacture, install and maintain the equipment. Dachser organises the global procurement of supplied parts, components and spares for escalators and elevators, and for on-time delivery right through to the production lines. It also stores – alongside supplied components – semi-finished goods, takes care of the short-term intermediate storage of complete escalators or components, and consolidates goods picked from the warehouse inventories for customers on a contract specific basis.

Otis has commissioned Dachser to carry out the global distribution – via land, sea, or air – of accessories and spare parts, of complete escalators and elevators, and of supplied parts in assembly. It delivers items to Otis engineers throughout Europe in accordance with fixed schedules, organises special transport services, and handles all the administrative tasks for the Otis despatch department.

Basically, Dachser's service embraces a complete package and has its own staff working on the customer's premises, and has taken responsibility for the majority of Otis's in-house logistics activities. These embrace: ramp handling and secure goods transport packaging and labelling; and it is continuously on call to deal with Otis's needs.

For the customers, the key factor is that the contract logistics provider can integrate their specific requirements into a standardised physical and IT network. It is very cost-effective. Moreover, it ensures freight capacity utilisation is higher, which in turn keeps overall process costs lower than they would be if the companies handled all these tasks themselves.

The final advantage of contract logistics services that form an integral part of logistics providers' freight network, is security. Such systems offer direct access. Capacities can be guaranteed, even when there is a bottleneck in the market. Such one-stop shopping provides a global cost advantage – unlike working with a large number of different freight partners. Overall, it keeps customer process costs to a minimum.

Another Dachser client is Chamberlain, a US-based world market leader in the development and production of garage and door openers, as well as other locking and opening systems. It requested Dachser to set up and run a logistics concept in China. This embraced establishing a significant amount of stock in China, a warehouse solution and development of a competitive distribution network. It also included a global vision and included a bonded service. Overall, it featured the necessary documentation with the authorities and institutions for all inbound and outbound cargo. It is the lead logistics provider in Europe. Dascher has a pan-European network.

Dachser's service portfolio embraces the following from a customised freight forwarding and fully integrated logistics service standpoint:

a   Airfreight: Customers may choose from the following airfreight options: express, economy, door-to-door, sea/air transport, European-wide distribution, charter, in- and outbound consolidation services;

b   Seafreight: A range of sea freight choices: independent choice of carrier, Europe-wide distribution, CFS warehousing, consolidation of buyers, project shipping, own weekly consolidation services to several destinations, worldwide full and consolidation container service (FCL/LCL);

c   Domestic freight: A domestic freight option for every eventuality: by train, truck, air or sea, customers may choose between express, time definite and economy services. Cash on delivery/money collection services are also arranged;

d   Warehousing and logistics: warehousing operations are in place and fully operational, servicing several major international customers, offering a full portfolio of services for all types of cargo, including, but not restricted to, the following: general cargoes, import-bonded storage (inside and outside the FTZ), export-customs-approved and dangerous goods. Also access to several modern facilities with state-of-the-art security and fire protection systems according to customer requirements and the required scope of service import and export trading services.

Dachser's leading partners include:

•   Airfreight partners: Air France, Cathay Pacific, Eva Air, Lufthansa, Martin Air;
•   Seafreight partners: APL, China Shipping, COCSO, Evergreen, Hanjin, Maersk, MOL, MSC, Senator Lines.

International Organization for Standardization – ISO
Supply Chain Management Selection

The ISO is a global network that: identifies what International Standards are required by business, government and society; develops them in partnership with the sectors that will put them to use; adopts them by transparent procedures based on national input; and delivers them to be implemented worldwide. It is a United Nations organisation, based in

Geneva. ISO standards distil an international consensus from the broadest possible base of stakeholder groups. Expert input comes from those closest to the needs for the standards and also to the results of implementing them. In this way, although voluntary, ISO standards are widely respected and accepted by public and private sectors internationally.

ISO – a non governmental organisation – is a federation of the national standard bodies of 149 countries – one per country – from all regions of the world, including developed, developing and transitional economies. Each ISO member is the principal standards organisation in its country. The members propose the new standards, participate in their development and provide support in collaboration with the ISO Central Secretariat for the 3,000 technical groups that actually develop the standards. ISO members appoint national delegations to standards committees. In all, there are some 50,000 experts contributing annually to the work of the organisation. When their work is published as an ISO International Standard, it may be adapted as a National standard by the ISO members and translated.

ISO has a portfolio of 15,036 (March 2005) standards that provide practical solutions and achieve benefits for almost every sector of business, industry and technology. They make up a complete offering for all three dimensions of sustainable development – economic, environmental and social.

ISO is a market leader in global supply chain management. With billions of dollars worth of goods moving at any time along global supply chains, the ISO/PAS 28000:2005 for security management systems is a major security initiative. It is designed to enable better monitoring of freight flows, to combat smuggling and to respond to the threat of piracy and terrorist attacks as well as to create a safe and secure international supply chain regime.

Supply chain embraces an overall process that results in goods being transported from the point of origin to final destination, and includes the movement of goods, the shipping data, and the associated processes as well as the series of dynamic relationships. It involves many entities such as producers of the goods, logistics management firms, consolidators, truckers, railroads, air carriers, marine terminal operators, ocean carriers, cargo/mode/customs agents, financial and information services, and buyers of the goods being shipped. For example, a company may employ more than one logistics firm, trucking companies may subcontract to operators, or other companies, and vessel-operating companies may divert the cargo to other carriers for various reasons.

Since supply chains are dynamic in nature, some organisations managing multiple supply chains may look to their service providers to meet related governmental or ISO supply chain security standards as a condition of being included in that supply chain in order to simplify security management.

As security hazards can enter the supply chain at any stage (see page 107), adequate control throughout is essential. Security is a joint responsibility of all the sectors in the supply chain and requires their combined efforts.

Hence, it is a key issue in supply chain management and the ISO has developed a code of practice. This embraces 'Best Practice for Custody in Supply Chain Security' and 'Security Management Systems for the Supply Chain' publications (see page 107). Additionally, ISO have published guidelines to assist industry for maritime port security reflecting the ISPS code for 1 July 2004.

A further area is the US Customs Trade Partnership against terrorism (C-TPAT) clause, December 2004, US. This includes Security Clauses for Time and Voyage chartering (see page 108).

ISO/Pas 28000:2005 Specification for security management systems for the supply chain outlines the requirements to enable an organisation to establish, implement, maintain and improve a security management system, including those aspects critical to security assurance of the supply chain. These aspects include, but are not limited to, financing, manufacturing, information management and the facilities for packing, storing and transferring goods between modes of transport and locations. It can be used in a broad range of organisations – small, medium and large – in the manufacturing, service, storage and transportation sectors at any stage of the production chain. Its availability reassures business partners that security is taken seriously within the organisations they deal with. Overall, ISO offers a systematic approach to security management in global supply chains systems standards – ISO 9001:2000 and ISO 14001:2004 – including the Plan-Do-Check-Act cycle and requirement for continued improvement, as well as the risk management item of ISO 14001:2004.

While ISO/PAS 28000 can be implemented on its own, it is designed to be fully compatible with ISO 9001:2000 and ISO 14001:2004 and companies already using these management system standards may be able to use them as a foundation for developing the security management system of ISO/PAS 28000. To help users to do so, ISO/PAS 28000 includes a table showing the correspondence of its requirements with those of ISO 9001:2000 and ISO 14001:2004.

Currently, ISO/PAS 28000:2005 is one of several developments underway for intermodal supply chain security being undertaken by ISO/TC8. This includes ISO/PAS 28001 best practices for custody in supply chain security, which enables industry to meet best practices as outlined by the World Customs Organization. Additionally, ISO/PAS 28004 embraces security management systems for the supply chain. It outlines the general guidelines on principles, systems and supporting techniques, which will assist users of ISO 28000. It will reference ISO 19011:2002, guidelines for quality and/or environmental management systems auditing and future ISO/IEC 17021 conformity assessment – requirements for bodies providing audit and certification of management systems.

ISO/PAS 28000 is the output of ISO technical committee ISO/TC8 Ships and Marine technology in collaboration with other technical committee chairs. Fourteen countries participated in its development, together with several international organisations and regional bodies. These include BIMCO, IMO, APH, ICS, WCO and IACS.

The auditing and certification of supply chain security management systems is contained in ISO/PAS 28003. It provides the requirements for ensuring that the bodies that carry out certification of these systems perform their work competently and reliably. The aim is to give confidence to customers who require suppliers like air, road, rail and sea transporters to implement security management systems and to have them independently audited and certified. Overall, it provides both principles and requirements. The principle behind all supply chain security regulations is to ensure that cargo and manifests reach their destination unmodified.

An important area in which ISO has remained focused is the selection process of supplier and possible responsibility for purchasing decisions. The ISO 9001:2000 is the supply chain tool and is an international standard that gives requirements for an organisation's 'quality management system'. Suppliers refer to it as 'ISO 9001 certified' or 'ISO 9000 – compliant QMS'. In supply chain terms it embraces a wide range of topics. These include the supplier top management commitment to quality, its customer focus, adequacy of resources, employee competence, process management (for production, service delivery and relevant administrative and supply processes), quality planning, product design, review of incoming orders, purchasing, monitoring and measurement of its processes and products, calibration of measuring equipment, processes to resolve customer complaints, corrective/preventive actions and a requirement for the supplier to monitor customer perceptions about the quality of the goods and services it provides.

The ISO 9001:2000 does not specify requirements for the goods or services that are being purchased. This is the responsibility of the customer to be explicit in the needs and expectations of the product. However, it is reasonable to refer to the product specifications, drawings, national or international product standards, suppliers' catalogues, or other documents as appropriate. Overall, conformity with ISO 9001:2000 results in the supplier having a systematic approach to quality management and is managing its business to ensure the clients' needs are clearly understood, agreed and fulfilled. It is not a substitute for a declaration or statement of product conformity.

Supplier selection is a critical area in supply chain management. ISO 9001:2000 addresses the following requirements in the purchasing process: requirements regarding the purchasing information so suppliers clearly understand their customers' needs and the opportunities in which suppliers' products can be verified as meeting the customer specification. Customers are encouraged to consult their own technical staff to ensure all the stated requirements and the applicable regulatory requirements are met. Overall, under ISO 9001:2000 the QMS can be met by conformity with four areas: suppliers' declaration of conformity; second-party assessment, for example by the customer or another customer; third-party assessment – often referred to as certification or registration – embracing a certification body or registrar; and accreditation by nationally or internationally recognised accreditation bodies. To conclude, ISO 9001:2000 is a useful basis for organisations to demonstrate that they are managing their business so as to achieve consistent quality goods and service in the supply chain management selection process.

A new published document is the ISO 22000 series, giving the requirements for the bodies that carry out auditing and certification of the food safety management systems (FSMS). ISO technical specification ISO/TS 22003:2007 provides information, criteria and guidance for carrying out ISO 22000:2005 auditing and certification. It will be useful for certification bodies, the accreditation bodies that approve them, suppliers wishing to have their FSMS certified, their customer and food sector regulators.

Certification to ISO 22000:2005, food safety management systems – requirements for any organisation in the food chain – is not a requirement of that standard, which can be implemented solely for the benefits it provides. However, where certification is required by customers, or by regulators, or is judged desirable as a marketing differentiator, ISO/TS 22003:2007 will help to build confidence in such certification throughout the food supply chain.

Comprising 10 clauses, two annexes and a bibliography, ISO/TS 22003 covers topics such as resource requirements, competence of management and personnel (including auditors and person involved in decisions related to certification), process requirements and requirements for certification bodies. It closely follows the requirements established by ISO 17021:2006: Conformity assessment – requirements for bodies providing audit and certification of management systems, which places rigorous requirements for competence and impartiality on the bodies that offer audit and certification to management system standards.

ISO/TS 22003 is the latest document in the ISO series for food safety management systems, which harmonises good food safety practice worldwide. It was launched in 2005 with ISO 22000, backed by an international consensus among experts from government and industry.

ISO 22000 can be applied to organisations ranging from feed producers and primary producers through food manufacture, transport and storage operators, and subcontractors to retail and food service outlets. Related organisations such as producers of equipment, packaging material, cleaning agents, additives and ingredients are also affected by the prospective standard. The standard was followed by technical specification ISO/TS 22004:2005: Food safety management systems – guidance on the application of ISO 22000:2005, which gives advice for all types of organisation within the food supply chain on how to implement an FSMS. ISO/TS 22003:2007 – requirements for bodies providing audit and certification for food safety management systems was developed by ISO technical committee ISO/TC 34 food products in collaboration with ISO/CASO: Committee on conformity assessment.

Six Core Products – Supply Chain Management – Warehousing – Customs Clearance – Air Freight – Consolidation – Project Cargo

The global logistics operator company concentrates on six core products: supply chain management; warehousing; customs clearance; air freight; consolidation; and project cargo. It will improve supply chain visibility by developing tailored processes and tracking systems. This will lead to improved buying processes and decision-making, reduced stock levels, and improved reaction times in delivering to end users. Overall, it will reduce supply chain cost, thus cutting lead times, creating fast-flow procedures, and introducing upstream controls.

To amplify the foregoing, a leading Asian company engaged on sourcing, borderless trading and virtual manufacturing and supply chain management, identifies seven core principles that underpin the company. These are detailed on page 130.

Useful Sources of Information

Dachser Far East Ltd <www.dachser.hk>
ISO (International Organization for Standardization) <www.iso.org>

Chapter 7

International Transport

Introduction

Transport is at the core of the logistic global operation. Often it is multi-modal, embracing other forms of transport. The efficiency of the global supply chain is very much focused on the transport network used. Overall, it is very complex and increasingly so, as multi-sourcing is widely practised, especially in assembly plants relying on inbound and outbound component sourcing. More emphasis is being placed on overland distribution of road, rail and canal, embracing combined transport from a supplier to consumer supply chain. In some cases we have the air bridge, which adds a new dimension to the logistic operation globally.

The two most notable drivers of changes in the international logistics services market are globalisation and technological development. Broadly, globalisation has resulted in increased trade, which has necessitated the need for efficient and cost-effective logistics services networks. This in turn has given rise to changes in the structure of the global logistics industry, including third- and fourth-party logistics (3PL and 4PL) as well as the outsourcing of logistics services. Technology as a driver has resulted in a twofold impact. On the one hand, technology has resulted in the provision of fast and accurate logistics services, while on the other hand, technology has resulted in changes to transport services, which is a key input into the logistics sector. Two significant results of these changes are the containerisation of cargo shipping and the use of wide-bodied aircraft by the logistics services provider. These changes in particular have on the whole enabled large turnovers in terms of volume of goods, time and cost efficiency.

While the global market for specialist services was valued at USD400 billion in 2007, there is a large difference in the size and scale of logistics services operations in individual countries. This divide is most evident when one compares the scale and level of sophistication of logistics service operations in developed and developing countries (see page 2). Further, developed countries remain the major importers and exporters of logistics services, whereas developing countries, with the evolving exception of larger developing countries like China and India, lag further behind. It is these differing levels of development of the logistics services sector that raises varying challenges and opportunities for different countries and makes a one-size-fits-all approach an unworkable approach.

Trade-Offs Inherent in International Logistics – Multi-Modalism

As we progress through the twenty-first century, the modern global business demands a highly sophisticated and adaptable multi-modal transport structure/organisation with a genuine worldwide door-to-door and just-in-time (JIT) logistics capability with an emphasis on partnership with the customer. Hence, the organisation must be consumer-driven in the competitive global market with a strong emphasis on synergy between carrier and shipper. The total multi-modal transport product must be logistically driven and market-led to provide an acceptable service/schedule to the consumer, the shipper. The globalisation of the world economy and the resulting increase in international trade, have had, and will continue to have, significant implications for transportation networks worldwide. It is an ever-changing scene.

The globalisation of trade has resulted in dramatic changes in domestic freight carriers that support international commerce – for example, increased trade with China (see page 130) and the Pacific Rim (see page 131) has led to the development of enhanced East–West transportation infrastructure. NAFTA is requiring similar development of North–South corridors. The expansion of trade agreements to include Latin American countries is having significant impacts on transportation needs in the Appalachian region. The emergence of the West Coast as the primary entrance point for the Pacific Rim trade has placed early pressures on the development of major East–West corridors such as I-80 (interstate 80), I-40 (interstate 40) and key transcontinental corridors. The surge in Latin American trade in recent years has put a new emphasis on emerging North–South trade lanes that penetrate the ARC (Applied Research Corporation (Singapore)) Region. The increase in global trade coupled with other developments including the proposed widening of the Panama Canal and the establishment of tranship-ment points in strategic locations such as the Bahamas suggest that North–South lanes, as well as East–Coast ports, will continue to see dramatic increases in the volume of goods handled. A similar analysis applies to the growth and expansion of hub ports globally reliant on multi-modalism (see page 79).

Overall, for a logistics operation to be successful, on a global scale, two main criteria must be satisfied:

a   There needs to be an integrated network of professionals throughout all the countries concerned to ensure the smooth passage of goods.
b   There has to be a high level of specialist expertise and knowledge relating to the multitude of laws, conventions and regulations (see pages 9–10) that weave a complex web across international trade.

The trend over the past two decades has been for international companies to rationalise their businesses by integrating production, sales and marketing across frontiers. Likewise, their suppliers have followed suit and in the logistics industry there has been a strong move towards creating international networks, either through merger or acquisition, or through confederations of independent professionals.

Consequently, there is no establishment pattern of international logistics networks. Each global logistics company will have its own particular type of network with its own strengths, suitable for some types of customer and not others. A crucial part of the special expertise required is knowledge of international laws and codes (pages 10–11).

The logistics operator in evaluating the 'trade-offs' inherent in international logistics must first examine multi-modalism – combined transport – and its special features. It is closely aligned to containerisation. Basically, it is the development of the transit system beyond the sea leg on a port-to-port basis, to the overland infrastructure or air freight.

The international entrepreneur will designate production in country A, assemble it in country B and source its component units from countries C, D and E. It is broadly an extensive logistics operation in which computers play a decisive part in its operation and control through electronic data interchange and RFID. Hence the overall operation is completely integrated, involving carriers, suppliers/manufacturers and the consignor and consignee. The role of 3PLs and 4PLs is very extensive in multi-modalism. Today, the more extensive the global multi-modal network becomes, the greater the acceleration of world trade growth. The multi-modal structure offers low-cost global distribution which, coupled with fast transits involving dedicated services, brings markets closer together and bridges the gap between the rich and the poor nations. Basically, it results in the concept of the total product being applied to transportation on a global scale.

The key to the operation of multi-modalism is the non-vessel owning carrier (NVOC) or non-vessel owning common carrier (NVOCC). This may result in a container (FCL or LCL) movement or trailer transit. In such a situation, carriers issue bills of lading for the carriage of goods on ships that they neither own nor operate.

An example of a logistics operator/freight forwarder offers a groupage service using a nominated shipping line and infrastructure. The logistics operator offers his own tariff for the service he buys from the shipping line at a box rate. The logistics operator provides a range of in-house facilities such as warehouses, customs, packaging, collection, delivery and RFID. This type of operation is particularly evident in the Far East, the US, part of Africa and European trades.

In examining a 'trade-off' to evaluate multi-modalism with other options the following factors are relevant:

a   The service is reliable, frequent and competitively priced. Goods arrive within a scheduled programme involving various transport modes and carriers operating in different countries.

b   In many companies it features as a global network either as a supply or retail chain. The former may comprise an assembly/process plant serving a local market while the latter involves the retailer buying the product in an overseas market. The retailer may be a shop, manufacturer, consumer, etc.

c   Many companies operate their global schedules on the 'JIT' basis (see page 94), requiring dedicated and integrated schedules within the shippers warehouses and distribution arrangements. Many companies regard it as a distribution arm of their business with online computer and RFID access. This embraces the EDI system, which strongly favours multi-modalism as a global distribution system.

d   The service is tailor-made to the trade/commodities it serves, involving high-tech purpose-built equipment. The product may be refrigerated, fragile cargo or high-tech electrical goods.

e   It has a high profile, which is a good marketing ploy in the promotion of a company's business.

f   Companies are looking for offshore manufacturing and sourcing outlets for their components and bulk cargo needs. Countries with an established multi-modal network are especially well placed in such a selection process.

g   The documentation requirements are minimal with the combined transport bill of lading involving one through rate and a common code of conditions.

h   More and more companies are focusing on international distribution as an important element of their international business. Such companies identify two profit centres: the manufacture/supply of the product and the channel of distribution from the supply point to the overseas destination.

i   Companies using the multi-modal network as a global supply chain are very con-
     scious of transit times and the capital/assets/cargo tied up in transit. Quicker transit
     times bring the sourcing and assembly plants situated in different countries closer
     together, thus reducing the lead-time to source the goods, reduction in capital tied up
     in transit, and fall in working capital to run the business.

j   A key factor is the level of facilities provided by the NVOCC at the terminal ware-
     house. Many are high-tech, utilising the RFID bar code sorting system, and have
     purpose-built facilities for specialist cargoes as found in distriparks and districentres.
     These are found in major hub ports (see page 126) and inland waterway ports such as
     Duisburg. The ports of Singapore (see page 130), Rotterdam (see page 126) and
     Dubai (see page 126) are very much in the lead with the trading port concept offering
     districentres, distriparks and, in Rotterdam, European Distribution Centres linked
     to a range of multi-modal outlets.

Aligned to the foregoing, international entrepreneurs must continuously search the web
to keep up to date on the expanding multi-modal network, especially port development
focused on high-tech container ship development (8,000 TEUs–12,000 TEUs) and the
related inland infrastructure developments. The modern port is a trading port and
similar remarks apply to hub airports such as Frankfurt.

The following points apply:

a   Air/rail/sea/canal/port operators are working more closely together to keep pace and
     facilitate trade development. Examples include the sea/air bridge from Singapore
     and Dubai and the sea/rail land bridge in North America.

b   Governments are taking more interest in the development in their nations' eco-
     nomies by encouraging a global trade strategy and providing the infrastructure to
     facilitate this objective. China is forging ahead to trade expansion and has seven
     seaports in the leading 20 ports.

c   The development of distriparks, districentres, International Distribution Centres,
     and free trade zones (FTZs) continues to grow.

d   The documentation involving the carrier's liability and code of practice relative to
     multi-modalism is now in place through the auspices of the International Chamber
     of Commerce (see page 52) and other international bodies.

e   World markets are rapidly changing and the Far East is the fastest growing market
     globally. Its infrastructure is continuously being improved and it is an established
     industrial zone. Many companies use it as a low-tech sourcing resource adopting
     multi-modalism as the global distribution system.

f   Containerisation technology continues to improve and the market in recent years
     has shifted from a product-driven to a consumer-led strategy, whereby the shipper is
     the dominant factor in container design and development. Today, there are over
     40 container types. Palletisation is extremely popular today as a cargo unit distribu-
     tion method, embracing specially designed containers such as the SeaCell container.

g   Most mega-container operators have customised logistics departments to advise
     their clients on providing the most cost-efficient method of distribution and the
     optimal route.

h   The enlargement of the EU to 27 Member States has resulted in a harmonised cus-
     toms union, which to the entrepreneur is a single market with no trade barriers. The
     same obtains in the North American Free Trade Area (NAFTA) covering Canada,
     Mexico and the United States. Such trading areas strongly favour multi-modalism

and remove international boundaries as impediments to market-driven logistics distribution centres.

i   Fast-moving consumer goods (FMCG) markets such as those for foodstuffs and consumer products require sophisticated logistics distribution networks. These involve highly sophisticated global logistics operations and effective supply chain management. This speeds transit times, reduces inventory cost in terms of stock, provides a service to the consumer, and overall means quicker movement through the supply chain to the consumer.

j   EDI coupled with the growth of RFID has brought a new era in global logistics. It manifests itself in multi-modalism. EDI has no international boundaries or time zones and provides ultimate control over performance monitoring of the goods. RFID/bar codes are now used in most global distribution networks to route and segregate cargoes together with many other disciplines.

The strategy to adopt in any trade-off regarding multi-modalism is essentially market-led and high-tech. It is an ongoing strategy and an exciting one as the global logistics multi-modal network is being continuously remodelled and expanded. Given below are areas that require special attention:

a   Logistics operators and supply chain managers must continuously study the market to discern trends and opportunities for more efficient supply chains. The lead-time to introduce changes is often short and flexibility and reliability are key factors.

b   Trading blocs such as ASEAN, the EU and NAFTA continuously review both their internal and external market multi-modal systems.

c   The subcontinent, especially India and China, together with South Africa, are developing global distribution networks embracing rail networks and seaport modernization and the provision of FTZ.

d   The airport and seaport – especially the latter – are key players in the development of multi-modalism, particularly the hub airport and seaport.

Key Factors in a Transport Mode(s) Trade-Off

There is no panacea/formula to adopt in any trade-off comparing one transport mode with another and the impact on shipper. Each must be considered on its merits and in the main reflects the market infrastructure and the shipping/logistics operator/supply chain manager objective and resources. It is a changing scene and the availability/competence of the 3PLs/4PLs are key factors.

There is a range of transport-oriented trade-offs embracing sea v air, frequency v cost, speed v cost, reliability v cost, inventory management/speed/cost, value-added benefit v cost, value of cargo v mode of transport, FMCG speed v cost, components v finish product cost, frequency v warehouse cost and relocation of industrial plant v cost. Overall, there is the interrelationship of cargo/speed/frequency/reliability/cost/quality focused on transport mode. In LDCs compared with fully developed countries, inland transport costs are disproportionately high, relative to the cargo product value (see page 79).

Speed

Speed is important to the shipper who desires to market his/her goods against an accurate arrival date and to eliminate banking charges for opening credits. This can be achieved by selecting the fastest service available and thereby obtaining the minimum interval between the time the goods are ordered/despatched and the date of delivery at their destination. Speed is particularly important to manufacturers of consumer goods as it avoids expense and the risk of obsolescence to the retailer carrying large stocks. In the case of certain commodities and especially fresh fruit and semi-frozen products and fashionable goods, a regular and fast delivery is vital to successful trading. The need for speed is perhaps most felt in the long-distance supply chains/trades where voyage time may be appreciably reduced and the shipper given the benefit of an early delivery and frequent stock replenishment. Air freight is the market leader in the speed analysis and favours fashionable garments, perishable products and those of an urgent delivery. Examples of cargoes favouring air freight include high-street fashionable high-value garments, flowers from Kenya, computer equipment, citrus from various markets such as Africa, medical supplies and Scottish salmon to Japanese restaurants and hoteliers.

Speed is an important trade-off and is related to cost. In the consumer market and project management, speed is critical, and today naval architects are striving to improve ship design and marine engineers are developing new propulsion technology. The result is large vessels such as 8,000/10,000 TEUs are exploiting the economies of scale in operating and building cost and electric propulsion systems.

Speed is not so important in the world tramp trades where generally lower-value cargoes are being carried and where many trades are moving under programmed stockpile arrangements. In this category are included coal, mineral ore, timber, bulk grain and other cargoes, which normally move in shiploads and have a relatively low value in comparison with higher value consumer and industrial goods: these demand a low transport cost. Examples are iron ore from Venezuela and Australia to China for the Chinese steel industry.

A 'trade-off' of change is the decline of the bulk cargo reefer carrier and fruit carrier. This is due to the abandonment of seasonal shipments in favour of the year-round containerised operation. The rationale behind such a development is logistically driven, embracing the producer, the retailer and consumer. Producers no longer ship at the time of their seasonal availability, but grade and store the fruit, meat, etc. in cold storage and respond to shipment demand in accord with the retailer/consumer demand over the computer network.

Frequency

A 'trade-off', which emerged in late 2007 and points to the future, is frequency of service versus speed and cost. This arises with mega-container operators with 10,000 TEU capacity fleet, which are experiencing high fuel consumption cost with new tonnage to maintain the speeds of the smaller capacity ships they displaced. Consequently, the larger vessels are operating at lower speeds than their predecessor, but providing additional vessels, thereby increasing the service frequency and reducing the lead time for the shipper.

Frequency of service is a key factor in the global logistics operation and especially important in the international supply chain management. It is most important when goods can only be sold in small quantities at frequent intervals. This is very important with fashionable goods, especially with high-value garments such as retailers of ladies' garments with a limited stock. A feature of air freight is frequency of service and speed, which favours such a criteria.

A salient trade-off involving frequency of service favours replenishment of low stock levels. It reduces the lead time and obviates the need to have high stock levels with extended lead-time replacement and its attendant risk of obsolescence. Low stock levels inherent in frequency of service replenishment contribute to a reduced risk of selling off obsolescent stock at discounted prices, thereby eroding levels of profitability. It also reduces/eliminates warehouse cost.

Inventory management trade-off embraces speed and cost. This embraces in the global supply chain the automotive carriers carrying 7,000 cars from China to Europe and North America. It is a reflection of the transfer of car production from Europe/North America to China. The trade-off is low production cost/low distribution cost/high-tech infrastructure/reliability of service/frequency of service. Major global car producers now follow this strategy, which is logistically driven and quicker than the supply chain cycle from the producer to the buyer, thereby reducing the capital tied up in transit/improving cash flow/reducing asset management cost (see page 131).

Frequency of service versus warehouse cost is a key factor in the retail business. The distribution centres and their strategic location relative to the consumer are key factors.

FMCG is a market that has a trade-off between speed and cost. Consumers demand a wide-ranging product choice. This requires lower stock levels with faster frequent replenishment cycles and competitive reliable distribution cost. In the food business, palletisation features strongly in cross-docking to speed transit times.

The indivisible load is a market that has grown in recent years, embracing a transformer or engineer plant with a total weight of up to 250 tonnes. It requires special arrangements and is a major logistics operation, involving extensive pre-planning. It is strongly associated with project installation management (see page 78). The decision to ship the indivisible load is usually a technical one: cutting lower overall transport cost; quicker transit; much reduced site assembly cost; less risk of damage in transit; lower insurance premiums; less technical aid, that is, staff resources required by the buyer as there is no extensive site assembly work; equipment tested and fully tested operationally in the factory before despatch; no costly site assembly work; less risk of malfunctioning equipment arising; earlier commissioning of the equipment which in turn results in the quicker productive use of the equipment with profitability benefits to the buyer. Overall, the trade-off is chartering a vessel/aircraft or using an existing schedule service with special lifting equipment and evaluating the cost between various options. Much depends on the programme for the product outlined by the customer. A key point is the terminal location with facilities to handle heavy lifts and access to the client site. Cost is usually not the major consideration, but convenience, quality and reliability of service are critical.

Aligned to the indivisible load is the out-of-gauge consignment. This embraces a yacht, railway rolling stock, heavy engineering equipment, escalators, etc. The trade-off is between transport mode, speed, cost and convenience of service.

A market that has grown is CKD – completely knocked down. This is practised widely as the goods arrive componentised to an assembly plant. It is practised widely in the automotive industry and consumer products. The goods are sourced from specialised suppliers and transported to an assembly/manufacturing plant, usually involving crossing international borders.

The free trade zone (FTZ) is a trade of having a distribution centre/assembly/processing plant or dispatching the cargo to the importer direct. Over 950 FTZs exist and sites are usually located in the port environs and are free of customs examination and duty until leaving the area. This enables companies to import products/components for manufacture, assembly, processing, labelling and distribution to neighbouring markets or despatch to more distant markets crossing international boundaries by sea, air, canal, or overland. Examples are Rotterdam (see page 126), Hamburg (see page 126), Singapore (see page 130) and Dubai (see page 126).

Packing

Packing is a key area in transport trade-offs. Goods sent by air, containerisation and palletisation require less packing. A wide variety exist: shrink packing for palletised cargo secured to the pallet; flat wrapping for furniture such as kitchen and dining-room wooden chairs; plastic containers that are heavy duty crates, which are stackable and nestable boxes and have a size range from 400 mm by 300 mm up to 1,200 mm by 3,000 mm; heavy-duty reusable stackable plastic trays for fruit in containers or road vehicles, and finally the widely used carton. A range of factors need to be considered: risk assessment, cost, value of cargo, mode of transport, insurance premium cover and dimensions/configuration of cargo, frequency of handling cargo and method. Ideally, it is sensible to have professional packers evaluate a transit test and have regard to the stowage aspect to realise the best loadability in the transport unit. Skilful packing can increase container capacity utilisation by up to 15 per cent. A stowage plan will aid effective use of cargo space. Regulations do exist regarding packing specification as found in dangerous (see page 10) classified cargo by all transport modes.

Insurance

Packing and insurance are not always identified in the supply chain management focus on areas of potential improvement of cost saving. When goods are transported from one country to another they pass through different legal regimes governing the contract. To reduce the uncertainties that might arise from conflicting legal systems a number of international conventions have been devised, which regulate the carriage of goods across frontiers and limit the liability of the carriers. These include: Hague-Visby Rules – sea transport (see page 9); CMR convention – road transport (see page 9); COTIF convention – rail transport (see page 9); and Warsaw convention – air transport (see page 9). Each convention deals with: responsibility of the carrier; basis of carriers' liability; limits of financial liability; carriers' responsibility for subcontractors; documentary requirements; consignors' liabilities; special provisions concerning dangerous goods; and time limits for claims and limitation periods.

The key to insurance cover is the term of scale as found in the Incoterms 2000 (see page 46). This is a negotiating area between the seller and buyer. Insurance premiums are based on a variety of factors such as risk, transport mode, carriers' liability, nature of cargo, value of cargo and case history of cargo claims. A cost analysis is required, which must be continuous, by the 3PLs and 4PLs.

Value-added benefit embraces the perceived benefit the shipper gains from the logistics operation strategy adopted. The trade-offs can be measured in financial, marketing and customer-focus terms. A significant factor today is that the efficiency of the global supply chain cannot be measured by an examination of the balance sheet, but an in-depth examination of the ingredients of the supply chain; hence the need to have transparency throughout the chain.

Warehousing

Managing an inventory can require the use of storage facilities to ensure a smooth level of supply to customers. Today, the modern supply chain eliminates the need for a warehouse. However, the use of warehouses does bring a range of benefits embracing it: it enables economies of scale by permitting long production runs; it allows companies to build up stocks in anticipation of seasonal or new product-demand; it can improve customer service by allowing the rapid replacement of faulty goods; it facilitates break bulk and other assembly operations where large orders are separated out into different batches before onward shipment to customers; and it provides a secure and a suitable environment protecting goods from damage deterioration and theft.

A further factor is the trade-off between warehouse provision and cost. This is realised through outsourcing by companies to logistics operators, not only to save capital cost of investment in building, but also in order to access the specialised knowledge and handling techniques that they can provide. A key factor is location, which must be strategic.

Inventory management is a key factor in the warehousing management.

IT and E-Commerce

Computer power has revolutionised the world of logistics by speeding the flow of accurate information across the whole supply chain. As e-commerce develops strongly, this access to information continues to have a profound effect on global supply chains and distribution in general. An important skill of a logistics professional is being able to manage the massive flow of information. There is always the danger of overload or duplication, so a modern logistics organisation has to invest continuously in software, hardware and personnel training.

The trade-off with IT and e-commerce embraces the following rationale:

a   Operational planning software can facilitate routine tasks such as order processing, load selection, stowage plan – all transport modes, cargo tracking and warehouse management/stock control;
b   Tactical planning embraces reworking distribution systems or timings to achieve specific objectives or respond to strategic objectives;
c   Strategic planning computer programmes can yield enormous advantage to facilitate strategic decision-making such as supply chain routing, distribution centres/warehouse location and a range of options available.

Information technology offers numerous trade opportunities. The salient ones are detailed as follows:

a   'Off-the-shelf' systems – often produced by software companies specialising in the logistic industry – by handling routine events and records;
b   'Bespoke' systems tailored to a specific company's requirements;
c   EDI linking two or more computer systems to promote information to each other automatically. This permits an external logistics supplier to become an integral part of a manufacturer's or retailer's operation;
    (Associated with IT and e-commerce is RFID examined on pages 108–13.)
d   The Internet has become an integral part of the logistics and supply chain network. It provides accurate and up-to-date information. It is interactive, permitting

enquiries, orders and payments to be made (see page 52) at low cost globally. More-over, it permits cargo tracking.

E-commerce has changed the dynamics of the supply chain and distribution in funda-mental ways. The salient points are detailed below:

a   Marketing and selling can be undertaken globally. Shippers/exporters/importers who do not have a website are seriously disadvantaged in developing their business.
b   High levels of returns create the need for efficient 'reverse logistics'.
c   It develops a new era of warehouse and delivery systems.
d   Overall, it develops a quick response rate to enquiries/delivery, all contributing to optimum stock levels.

Project Installation Management

Project installation management is associated with indivisible loads, examined on page 85. However, installation management relates to the field of installations, which we will now examine. An action plan is essential and key areas area as follows:

a   What are the critical dates? Research confirms that a failure to comply in this area results in revenue loss and severe disruption. This requires coordination with the suppliers and a thorough checklist.
b   A site survey is desirable to determine points of access and identify key areas. The opportunity to meet the site general manager is important, especially to discuss any critical areas likely to impair completion of the project within the timescale.
c   The third point is to establish the person to sign off formally the installation of the project.

The project execution must be timed with precision. The arrival of the installation must be planned with the arrival of the product delivery. This is not a problem when the logistics company is also carrying out the installation, but can be an issue when two com-panies are involved. The area of installation must be prepared in advance. Depending on the type of installation, it may be necessary to arrange for goods to arrive at staged internals.

   Health and safety requirements must be taken into account. A risk assessment should be carried out as part of the site survey. Moreover, before installation takes place, detailed briefings on the method to be used should be given to the installation team and to the customer. The degree of planning should be commensurate with the category of installation. There are broadly three types of installation:

   i The large-scale installation will tend to be contracted directly with the customer and this type requires all the resources of the planning methods and communications.
   ii The next category embraces the need for small reconfigurations or 'top-ups' where much of the planning that has gone on before can be used again with suitable additions.
   iii For small companies there will be a need for a more direct dialogue with the end user to discuss issues such as access.

The complexity of project installations is very accentuated in a global market. It involves different cultures and a longer supply chain – often multi-modal. Access to the site may be more vulnerable and traffic regulations different, such as weight restrictions on bridges, limited width and availability of lifting equipment. This especially applies to LDCs and developing countries with a poor infrastructure. Computers play a dominant role in the preparation, research planning and execution of the project, especially analysis and checkpoints.

Choosing the logistics company is critical and requires careful analysis. Study pages 70–78, which fully evaluate the criteria.

There are many pitfalls to avoid and the more serious are as follows: failure of other contracts being ready; access to the site and parking restrictions; inadequate space to carry out installation; and arrival of damaged goods. Adequate planning and contingency plans can eliminate/minimise such problems.

Finally, two further areas for the logistics operator on which to focus: in the area of pre-installation, do on-site contractors have ID; adequacy of health and safety obligations; details of other contractors working on-site and any conflict in operations; availability of any lifts and will the installation site be clear of any obstructions. Ideally a 'method statement' should be formulated to outline the installation processes on-site.

The second area is the checklist: appoint a project manager; undertake site survey; formulate conclusive site installation plan; installation team to be thoroughly briefed; timescale of site installation to be precise; adequate site access; ensure specialised equipment available; adequate experienced manpower available; undertake post-installation check to ensure site left to customer satisfaction; disposal of packaging in accordance with local conditions; and check the installation is fully operational.

Global installation embracing extensive supply chains can include multiple sourcing, usually from different countries. It is a complex operation with adequate pre-planning essential.

Chapter 8

Operations Management

Benchmarking – Supply Chain

A benchmark may be defined as the predetermined level/standard. This may embrace price, quality, design, efficiency and cost-effectiveness. It is against the benchmark that all comparisons are made. The base line of a product/service is cost.

Benchmarking embraces the process measurement into a cross-functional relationship. It incorporates all the elements in the global supply chain and has focus on the product specification, the operational performance, and the management practices and software solutions. Moreover, it has a strong interface with planning to ensure the prescribed standards are formulated vigorously at the outset with the global supply chain management. Overall, it must provide standard descriptions of the relevant management processes, a framework of the relationships among the standard processes, standard process performance metrics and standard alignment to features and functionality. Basically, it is the framework in which the company must operate, especially within all the ingredients of supply chain management. The key factor is to realise customer satisfaction.

Benchmarking in the supply chain is related to three major elements: the supplier, the distributor and the interface between the supplier and distributor. The prime consideration in setting the benchmark is to realise customer satisfaction. This embraces the time cycle, the cost and asset utilisation. The point to consider is that the core values of the customer are ones of continuous change and the supplier must move with the market and consumer preferences continuously; hence the need to develop empathy with the customer, or range of customers.

An examination of the benchmarking evaluation of the supplier/distribution embraces the following: product design, price, consumer culture which varies by LDC, and developed markets, quality control, consumer acceptance, market research, cost control, degree of technology, option/commitment to outsource, supplier/distributor resources/management to embrace change through innovation/technology, staff training and motivation, compliance with national and international trade regulations. Benchmarking globally is complex and to focus/develop some of the foregoing includes the following: cycle time, cost embracing budgets and international currencies, asset utilisation throughout the supply chain component links, security and quality control.

When tenders are invited the specification will identify specific standards such as automobile emission (see page 137), fire resistant furniture (see page 74), BSI/ISO technical standards for industrial equipment, phytosanitary (plant health) certificates and food products – texture/size/production environment.

Moreover, to monitor benchmark standards the buyer will often organise pre-shipment inspection arrangements involving a ship classification such as Bureau Veritas

Lloyds Register, Quality Assurance (LRQA), or Societe Generale de Surveillance (SGS). This involves examination of the goods at place of manufacture – if necessary at each stage of the manufacturing process – and assembly to ensure full compliance with export contract terms. Also, the cargo is examined prior to shipment, such as being placed in the container or on the ship or aircraft. If everything is in order the SGS will issue a clean report of findings (CRF) to their principal to activate payment arrangements. If the consignment is in default, a non-negotiable report of findings (NNRF) will be issued by SGS and payment of the goods will not be activated.

Benchmarking embraces the supplier and distributor. A strategic focus must be maintained at all times. Overall, there is the impact on the business, to keep ahead of the competitors. The second aspect is the response rate. A key factor in supplier selection in a global supply chain is the ability of the supplier to increase production to respond rate. A key factor in supplier selection in a global supply chain is the ability of the supplier to increase production to respond to the buyer consumer surge in demand, such as seasonal variations. It may be garments in a supermarket, Christmas food products and white kitchen furniture. A further aspect is the economic consideration. This embraces efficient use of the assets (see page 2).

Benchmarking embraces adding value, thereby increasing the perceived benefits to the shipper/buyer/consumer. This includes reducing the lead time to source the product, effective cost control, quick transit time, product outsourcing, JIT strategies and total quality management. The latter embraces not only inspections in the logistic process, but also takes action on inadequate performance.

Benchmarking embraces setting standards and has a strong interface with the global supply chain. It also embraces developing the best practice as examined in B2B and B2C (see page 55).

Global Supply Chain Management

Global supply chain management embraces the logistics operator's task to ensure that goods of a saleable quality are manufactured and transported safely and cost-effectively and are delivered on time with the continuous tax to 'add value'. This features three aspects, particularly:

a   Vendor management involving the processing of customers' orders direct to their suppliers and monitoring the production process;
b   Information featuring receipt of customers' order via EDI download (this leads to 24-hour monitoring and reporting of status and cost down to item level);
c   Communication, permitting customers to receive advance notice of shipments, which are scheduled via international email links.

The key benefits are reduced inventory levels, improved visibility of all costs to item level, improved delivery on time and clearer responsibility. The global supply chain is very complex, including numerous elements that we will examine later (see figure 1.1, see page 3).

Effective global supply chain management generates competitive advantage in the marketplace and achieves cost reduction. Moreover, it introduces a logistics management culture in the company, which in turn raises the quality of the service, which can be further improved by adding value to the service through a variety of options. The key is its adaptation and transparency, whereby all parties in the supply chain have complete integrity through the continuous exchange of data. For the global supply chain to be successful, it must satisfy two main criteria.

First, there needs to be an integrated network of professionals throughout all the countries concerned to ensure the smooth passage of goods. Secondly, there has to be a high level of specialist expertise and knowledge relating to the multitude of laws, conventions and regulations which weave a complex web across international trade.

We will now examine three areas of significance in the global supply chain: delivery and customs clearance, distribution management, and import logistics and distribution.

i   Delivery and customs clearance arises in an example of a leading drinks company with over 50 brands worldwide. The objective is to receive and handle stock and to arrange transport and overseas shipment. The four main features of the service include:

   a   Inventory management featuring direct data exchange to provide online reporting;

   b   Order picking embracing maximising deliveries of export shipments direct to the end customer;

   c   Quality control including checking on arrival, arranging, relabelling and repacking as required;

   d   Security, the adoption of sophisticated arrangements suitable for a high value commodity.

The key results include delivery only when market demand dictates, secure and cost-effective storage and efficient onward distribution services involving a 4PL.

ii Distribution arrangements. An example is the requirement of a major sportswear company that imports merchandise from suppliers in the Far East. The objective is to improve upstream process controls and maximise direct delivery to high-street stores in Europe. It embraces three main elements in the service, which include the following:

   a   Quality control embracing collecting goods from suppliers and ensuring compliance with specified quality standards (see SGS – LRQA – see page 91).

   b   Consolidation and delivery, embracing sorting labelling and packaging goods according to end-customer and/or requirements and providing delivery direct to the customer.

   c   Information, embracing full integration via EDI between the customer purchase order system, their financial and distribution systems, and the global supply chain management system. The ultimate results were improved supplier quality standards, reduced warehousing (see page 81) and handling cost (see page 79) and shortened order cycle times.

iii Import logistics and outbound distribution. An example arises involving an electronics manufacturer that sources components in the Far East for manufacture in Europe. The objective is to manage the inbound supply of components to exacting production schedules and distribute the finished products across Europe. It embraces three main features as follows:

   a   Supply chain management embracing the despatch of orders, the monitoring of production, consolidation and delivery on time to the manufacturing plant;

b   Information embracing tracking progress in the supply chain so that customers can accommodate changes to the production plan;

c   Consolidation/distribution, featuring maximising container usage to cut costs and distribution 'on time' to retailers.

The key results are proactive control of delivery schedules and reduced shipment costs from the consolidation and integration of inward and outward distribution.

To develop the foregoing three key areas the global logistics company has concentrated on six core products within the context of global supply chain management. This has embraced not only supply chain management per se, but also warehousing, customs clearance, air freight, consolidation and project cargo. It will improve supply chain visibility by developing tailored processes and tracking systems. This will lead to improved buying processes and decision-making, reduced stock levels and improved reaction times in delivering to end users. Overall, it will reduce supply chain cost, thus cutting lead times, creating fast-flow procedures and introducing upstream controls.

An Asian company operating in the Chinese market engaged in sourcing, borderless trading and virtual manufacturing, and supply chain management, identifies seven core principles as follows:

a   The customer must be at the centre and responsive to market demand.
b   Focus on core competency and outsource new-code activities and develop a position in the supply chain.
c   Develop a low-risk and profit-sharing relationship with business partners.
d   Design, implement, evaluate and adjust the workflow, physical goods flow and cash flow in the supply chain.
e   Adopt information technology to optimise the operation of the supply chain.
f   Shorten product lead time and delivery cycles.
g   Lower cost on sourcing, warehousing and transportation.

In comparison with the Asian company, another global operator has identified the following key areas sought by customers:

a   Strategic solutions to the problems of long-distance product sourcing and movement. This is achieved by matching the client's business needs to the latest techniques and expertise to formulate solutions to the problems of long-distance product sourcing and movement. An example is the European-based department stores buying a range of consumer products from the Far East. Key factors are quality control, coping with variations in consumer demand and distributing supplies in a cost-effective manner;
b   Companies that can provide capabilities interfaced across a range of different transport modes including sea, road, rail, canal and air as found in multi-modalism;
c   Improvements in quality of service to end customers. This basically centres on customer asset management – ensuring the goods arrive in a quality condition to a prescribed schedule with zero failure rate;
d   Improvements in profits realised through all the marketing and financial benefits to the user inherent in the global logistics system embraced in the supply chain management;
e   Management of 'trade-offs' within the supply chain;
f   A fully outsourced logistics management service.

Users of the service include automotive manufacturers, high-street retailers, wines and spirit producers, footwear, fashion garments, sports goods, and electronic manufacturers.

Effective global supply chain management embraces identifying the customer's needs, defining the customer's services objectives, and designing the global supply chain. This involves development of a supply chain structure, ideally with direct delivery from the manufacturer to the consumer/purchaser.

This embraces the development of the economies of scale; the exploitation of materials and labour with focus on their competitiveness; maximising benefits in investments and resources including infrastructure through outsourcing on a global scale; enhancing and defending competitive advantage; focusing on a degree of standardisation on customer needs and tastes in different counties such as an EU brand through the CE accreditation and cluster markets concepts; operating within the economic, political and legal constraints in trading blocs and other countries; and developing a purchasing (see page 58) and supply chain management strategy.

Supply Chain Cycle Time Management Reduction

A key factor in the twenty-first century global logistics environment is to focus on reducing the supply chain cycle time and thereby reduce the lead time from the time the purchase order is placed with the suppliers to the final placement in the supermarket or customer warehouse. It involves many ingredients in the composition of the supply chain, which we will now examine. Overall, it is related to global supply chain management. The company is a 3PL, manufacturer, wholesaler, distributor, retailer, importer, exporter, supplier, customer, logistics service provider, freight forwarder or any other category of firm in the supply chain management. A major key to success is reduction in the supply chain cycle time or, to use another term, time compression.

Increasing velocity, rapid response to changing market conditions, minimising time – and sustaining that velocity – are the reasons for collaboration, integration, supply chain transparency, and other endeavours to accelerate the movement of product and information.

There are numerous financial and non-financial cycle time metrics, for example: on-time customer order delivery, manufacturer to order complete, cash conversion cycle and days sales outstanding. A good one should be measure of the length of time for a process, especially one that crosses the organisation. The cycle time should be important to the company. It should recognise crucial key points that add value and competitive advantage for the company.

A key area in the process that crosses the organisation is 'days-in-inventory', which measures the number of days that inventory is held. For manufacturers this would include raw materials, and work in process.

Days-in-inventory is an important part of the cash conversion cycle. Reducing inventory levels and days-in-inventory improves profits and frees up much needed capital. This pleases shareholders and the company directorate, especially as any interest charge falls as overdraft falls. This measure is often calculated as inventory (cost of goods sold/365 days). This method of calculation can be misleading and can understate the total inventory in the supply chain. Basically, it represents capital – the value of the goods – in transit. A reduction in inventory reduces the working capital to run the company. Overall, it excludes inventory that is on order and is being manufactured at suppliers, and inventory that is in transit. This is an omission that results in an understatement of the real days-in-inventory and the cash conversion cycle.

In our analysis we will include the time from placement of purchase orders with suppliers until delivery. Adding to this is the inbound portion of the calculation for internal controls and risk assessment. Regardless of the technical issue of when title transfers, there is the company commitment and need for the material being ordered and shipped. This embraces the purchase order at supplier time and the in-transit time, which will yield a better analysis and understanding of the factors driving the inventory levels, days and turns, which all contribute to the product lifecycle management. This new cycle time is the total inventory days in the supply chain and it is consistent with the length and definition of a supply chain. Overall, the supply chain cycle runs from the purchase order placed with the suppliers through to final arrival of the goods with the customer/buyer. Hence the analyst can measure the real total time for the inventory, including the inbound element where the clock actually starts to tick on the inventory.

Evidence exists that manufacturers and wholesalers have more than 60 days of inventory and retailers 90 days of inventory tied up. These times do not include the entire inbound inventory in the supply chain. Real supply chain inventory is likely to be 25 per cent higher. This is a very significant amount of capital, especially when it is funded on a bank loan/overdraft attracting interest charges.

Reducing the supply chain cycle time requires an analytical approach. This requires continuous monitoring to identify areas/elements where scope exists to execute improvements. Some may be very radical and others relatively minor. Innovation can be a key factor. Transparency and technology throughout the supply chain is paramount. A plan is desirable and a sequence could be as follows:

a   The first stage is to measure the present process. Identify factors that increase the cycle time and implement changes. This also requires seeing that there is an interconnection and interdependence of events and actions throughout the supply chain. Few events and actions have a singular cause and effect: there are often domino effects.

b   Recognition. There are basics to address: a supply chain is complex, made up of many suppliers located worldwide, each of which has its own supply chain. Hence there are chains with chains. The purpose of all this activity is to place the product timely and correctly in stores or at customer facilities. Essentially, it must be designed, directed and managed as a process, not as a series of order and shipping transactions. Pushing bad logistics processes and practice up or down the supply chain impedes time.

c   Product and information/data should flow unimpeded. Operational effectiveness depends on process, technology and people that cross internally within the company and externally with suppliers and customers.
    The process should be assessed for gaps and redundancies. Measure the time required in each action and the reason for the action. Study continuously any organisational dysfunction that can creep in and add unnecessary time.

d   Work with a cross-functional team. This will improve the quality of the assessment and prevent invalid assumptions that can flaw the effort.

e   Inventory is created as a buffer for uncertainty. Basically, uncertainty increases, almost exponentially, as the time required to position it correctly increases. Hence inventory increases as time increases.

f   Time is not on any financial statement, but its effect is. Inventory is not on the monthly/quarterly profit and loss (P&L) account, but on the annual balance sheet. The aspect to consider is, it may be difficult to gain commitment to reduce cycle time because it is not readily identified and measured either on the P&L account or balance sheet.

g   Trade-offs do exist between time and inventory and cost. These need continuous evaluation.

h   Global sourcing adds to time and to inventory that must be carried out because of it. Global transit time can be reduced using airlines rather than sea, but it is a trade-off between time and higher air freight charges (see page 79).

i   External factors exist that impact on time and may be beyond control to be reduced. This may be customs and security examination/controls when crossing international border or entering a seaport.

j   Logistics infrastructure in sourcing countries is another factor that adds time, cost, and impedes the flow of the product from suppliers' facilities to ports and airports. In less developed countries – particularly in Africa – infrastructure is generally poor, costs high and transit time (see page 130) much extended, compared with the developed markets of North America and Europe.

k   Supply chains can work on a pull or push approach (see page 101). The pull approach relies on customer demand 'to pull' through a logistics system. In contrast 'the push' or proactive approach uses inventory replenishment to anticipate future demand.

l   Managing vendor performance. This is a critical area to reduce the supply chain cycle time. Suppliers at the supply chain source have a profound impact on the supply chain in regard to time, inventory and costs. This goes far beyond pricing and placing purchase orders. Visibility of purchase order is a key area. This embraces suppliers' efficiency regarding transit time, embracing each step in the chain, from the vendor's plant to delivery at the warehouse, store, or customer.

m   Integration up and down the supply chain, but external and internal integration is mandatory. Non-integration adds to the supply chain time and the lack of responsiveness and dead spots in the cycle time.

Integration demands forecasting or other inventory planning with suppliers to for- mulate their plans. Integrate purchase orders into transport load planning. Everyone in the supply chain should be working from the same data, information and system or platform. Manufacturers must integrate through the production process. Trans- ferring data up and down the chain is not enough. Data is not information. To collect, analyse and forward data takes time. Suppliers and service providers then re-enter the data into their systems. In turn they do this to their suppliers. All this adds to the cycle time. Conversely, integration reduces time and increases accuracy.

It must be recognised that integration may not be readily and easily possible with all parties in the supply chain. Focus primarily on key suppliers and service providers that are key to the volume or critical products, parts or needs. To have key suppliers integrate with their key suppliers manifests itself in benefit terms through the supply pipeline.

n   Collaboration with key suppliers and service providers is another area that realises time compression. Work together as partners and be open to transparency of data. Sending procedures and demanding compliance with requirements is not collabor- ation. Work to align the process between both parties so that it flows smoothly and with minimal time.

o   Inventory analysis. Establish how the inventory moves and where inventory sits or is transferred for opportunities to move it more quickly and with fewer handlings. Improvements can be realised with the following two key areas:

i The warehouse distribution network, where warehouses are located as to time from stores or customer or suppliers, impacts supply chain cycle time by becoming fixed repositories based on needs that may be historical and outdated.

ii The multi-tier inbound logistics approach. What modes, carriers, service and parts are used can reduce transit time, and increase inventory and cash conversion velocities.

Inventory in transit is not inventory available for sale. Develop a comparison for inventory items 'A' and some items 'B' as compared to many 'B' items and 'C' items. A comparison may be product sourcing from a range of countries, each at varying price levels, but different transit times, distance freight charges and infrastructure.

p Endeavour to bypass the distribution network where possible. Examples include shipping inbound containers direct to store or customer; using a transfer facility at port(s)/airport(s) such as FTZ, ICD (see page 79) to permit quick unloading to containers and transfer directly to the specified destinations; and allocating inventory in transit and cross-docking containers at a distribution centre. All the foregoing provides time reduction opportunities.

q Technology, its use and development. Technology is a key factor to achieving time compression in supply chains. Overall, it is a necessity – a process enabler. However, technology in isolation will not realise much needed improvements. It must be used across the supply chain enterprise both external and internal. Overall, it is the ingredient to gain much needed supply chain visibility. Such visibility is needed for multi-tier inbound operations to bypass the distribution network programmes. The following are the critical areas:

i Global suppliers and transport providers cannot be readily managed with emails. Technology is needed.

ii Supply chain complexity and scope may require more than software to be used for effective control.

iii Portals provide useful tracking information and shipment visibility.

iv Tracking purchase orders and contents of an inbound container has great value compared with just tracking a certain number. Most major container operators (see page 120) offer this facility with an online access. Visibility into the container sets the stage for significant abilities to reduce time and inventory.

v Converting sales – point of sales – data into replenishment orders on warehouses, and in turn purchase orders on suppliers, is critical.

vi Supply chain execution technology may be the most valuable of the technology applications. It is vital to integration and collaboration.

vii Ease of connectivity. This embraces web-enabled interfaces and mobile access.

viii Maximum supply chain process coverage. This includes order/procurement management, transportation, distribution, warehousing, vendor, finance and finally directing and managing the process and reducing time and inventory.

ix Event management and exception management capabilities should be part of the technology used. This empowers control of the process.

To conclude our analysis, to reduce the supply chain cycle time achieves primarily three objectives: to improve the competitiveness of the product in the global market; to decrease the days of inventory held; and reduce the cash conversion cycle. This results in capital inventory reduction, and any related interest/bank charges. Additionally, such capital can be used for other uses. All parties must continuously strive to improve the supply chain through a strategy of time compression.

Logistics Result Evolution Strategy

Logistics has become in the twenty-first century a fast-moving management tool with continuous focus on productivity and performance monitoring. Failure to have a competitive global logistics focus in a business results in business decline with accelerating rapidity. Hence the need to have in place a structure/environment to monitor and respond to inadequacies within the global logistics environment and supply chain.

Companies must acknowledge the high cost of logistics in total overhead costs in sales activities and a percentage of the selling price. It embraces administration, inbound and manufacturing, and outbound/fulfilments logistics.

The second point is the accelerating velocity of the global supply chain performance. Border cycle times are becoming quicker, response to changes and exceptions faster, and real-time flow of supply chain information is generating a greater focus on supply chain execution as a primary source of corporate success. It reflects consumers' demand for products in fast-moving markets. This is exemplified in the automobile market, supplying cars from Korea and China, to EU/US, the food chain market from near and distant markets to consumers/supermarkets in EU/US, and the consumer markets of clothes/household goods from China/India/Turkey to EU/US. This has been greatly facilitated through digital trading and continuous investment in containers and infrastructure, including remodelling of services. The automobile supply chain performance has much improved through the modern fleet of automobile carriers on scheduled services with a capacity of up to 10,000 cars, serving key automobile hub ports in Europe and the US.

Aligned to the previous point is the role of global logistics as a source of customer satisfaction and company differentiation. Consumers in the developed world tend to become increasingly impatient to wait for their chosen product delivery and switch to other suppliers. This results in a loss of sales. Corporate companies with a strong global logistics/supply chain network tend to feature it in their marketing strategy/promotional material.

Emerging from the three foregoing principles is the need to focus on the approach to realise these objectives.

The first and foremost is to feature the global supply chain in the business plan. This will allocate resources and investment and have a director at board level to monitor ongoing performance. In many companies it will embrace managing change.

The next task is to quantify the end to end of the global logistics. This will embrace analysis of the global supply chain, crossing international boundaries/cultures and incorporating 3PLs and 4PLs. It embraces measuring results to corporate objectives – a formidable task. Two problems tend to emerge: lack of experience/expertise in value analysis, and high cost and time of external consulting studies. This generates the need for a process and methodology that provides the expertise and experience of traditional consulting, but delivering this detailed insight into the opportunities for unlocking logistics value within much tighter cost and time constraints. Logistics is a highly leveraged function for value creation. Even small improvements in logistics processes can drive major increases in revenue and profits.

There is a wide range of sources of logistics value in the global supply chain and the salient ones are as follows:

i Operating cost – transportation/freight charges – packaging, customs duty, handling cost seaport/airport, customs clearance, insurance, distribution, labour cost, warehouse charges, administrative cost, inventory and technology/software;

ii Working capital reduction – reduced inventory, deferred payment of import duty through bonded warehouse (see page 78), customs planning (see page 78), trading currency planning, reducing safety stocks and network inventory levels, zero failure rate in order processing payment, factoring (see page 52), accelerating payment cycle (see page 66), and rationalisation of suppliers and supply countries;

iii Return on assets – the investment in the logistics and global supply chain network continues to rise. It embraces logistics systems, distribution centres, materials handling, transportation and communication. Capitalisation can be reduced through leasing/hiring and outsourcing. Also, through merger and acquisition, joint ventures and operational alliances. A continuous review of distribution centres with a rationalisation focus does yield financial benefit with higher throughput and optimisation of resources. In the EU for example, with a single market and no cross-border customs constraints, the distribution cost base can vary by country, reflecting labour and taxation levels. One distribution centre can serve several countries. Such a strategy requires a cost benefit analysis with focus on the catchment area, the infrastructure and the global supply chain network access. A good example are the districentres, based at the Port of Rotterdam (see page 126). Any system devised on the return on assets must be intrinsic and pragmatic;

iv Revenue and market share growth – logistics is driven by efficiency with continuous focus on the inbound and outbound operations, and responsiveness to market/consumer demands. Management tends to focus on revenue production to improve market share with emphasis on product throughout, thereby exploiting the economies of scale in the supply chain. Efficiency can result in lower prices, thereby outmanoeuvring competitors and raising revenue and profit levels. This strategy is very significant in fast-moving markets with emphasis on minimum inventory levels. The 'time to volume' of many products is being aggressively accelerated. Logistics capabilities are critical for supporting new product launches that can meet demand, which are increasing in large volumes very early in the release cycle.

Aligned to the foregoing is flexibility (see page 79) and velocity (see page 83). Companies that proactively work with customers to meet new requirements and synchronise logistics operators will drive down total supply chain costs, increase revenue and gain market share. A proactive strategy is required. A similar strategy is required to deal with velocity, which is related to flexibility (speed of process of change) and execution of cycle times;

v Creating logistics value – this embraces a wide range of areas and is subject to continuous change and evolvement in a global market. Market research is the vehicle to keep up to date, especially through trade associations, journals and networking. Innovation is a key area through creative thinking and brainstorming. Overall, it embraces all elements/segments of the global supply chain. Areas on which to focus embrace distribution centre operations, transportation management, labour productivity, global infrastructure, changing international trade regulations including customs, supply chain visibility, real-time control and integrated logistics – (see Table 8.1);

vi Logistics score-carding and performance measurement. This is essential when a company embarks on new logistics technology initiatives. Such analysis should

Table 8.1 Analysis of salient sources of logistics value

Key Areas	Traditional Value Sources			Emerging Value Sources		
	Operating expense reduction	Working capital reduction	Improved return on assets	Top line growth	Flexibility	Velocity
D C Operations	a	b	b	a	a	a
Transportation management	a	b	b	b	b	b
Productivity management	a	c	b	c	c	c
Global visibility	b	a	b	a	a	a
Integrated logistics	a	a	b	a	a	a

Source: Reproduced courtesy of Red Prairie Corporation.

Notes
a Highest value impact
b Medium value impact
c Lower value impact

embrace functional area, current performance/metric, expected performance/metric, time frame, and value from improvement. This information must be determined prior to launching the project and would include all necessary improvement areas and metrics to support the goals and cost justification of the project. These need to be sequenced as specific process changes and software capabilities are phased in. To allow immediate analysis and reaction, operational metrics should be captured in one of today's robust, online logistics score-carding systems;

vii Sustaining results – this is a common failure among companies arising from detractions from vendors, consultants and company personnel. It arises for many reasons including: lack of continuity from the vendor's sales and consulting teams to its implementation personnel; project pressure, which often results in a switch from operational results to project schedule and cost as the primary objectives; and turnover of the project of functional managers less informed/committed/focused on high level results expectations. Hence the need to have implementation/project teams – both internal to the company and from the vendor and consultant standpoint – to start their work with a precise understanding on the expected results for the project. This strategic approach with full commitment at all levels is essential to realise and maintain the specified goals with a continuous review to add value throughout all levels of the project. Transparency is a key factor;

viii Auditing – as alluded to in the previous analysis, the continuous monitoring of the logistic improvement is essential. It is an essential ingredient of the projects and must be inherent in company culture. Areas of failure to meet operational objectives embrace: a poorly designed process; software has not been configured appropriately to meet the process and project goals; and failure to follow the process as designed during earlier phases of the project.

A plan to develop a comprehensive product line is found in Table 8.2.

Table 8.2 Product line plan

Source	Make	Delivery
Inbound logistics – reduce inbound transportation costs 10–30%	Manufacturing logistics – real-time flow of raw materials, WIP and finished goods inventory	Order fulfilment on time, every time, least possible cost, zero failure rate
Supplier collaboration – realise seamless inbound product flow and information	Inventory management – total control and accountability of network inventory	Outbound transportation – reduce outbound transportation cost 10–30%
		Productivity management – increase labour productivity and throughput 10–25%

Source: Reproduced courtesy of Red Prairie Corporation.

Demand-Driven Supply Network

As we progress through the twenty-first century a tectonic shift emerged in the supply chain management. The factory push economy (see page 29) of the twentieth century that made the US a world powerhouse has given way to a retailer-focused pull economy where customer demand is the dominant force in shaping supply chain operations.

This has been greatly facilitated by the global development of the infrastructure, embracing communications and transportation – most notably the Internet and containerised shipping – the latter embracing multi-modalism. The opening of China and, more recently India, as both a supply base and huge potential market has stimulated it. The resulting globalisation of supply and demand has substantially increased the complexity and variability of supply chain operations. To support the shift, traditional supply chain practices must be supported by a new approach where responding quickly and profitably to customer demand is the guiding principle as found in the demand-driven supply network (DDSN).

DDSN is a term coined by AMR Research to define the practice of designing supply chains, or networks, around the imperatives of sensing, shaping and responding to customer demand. According to AMR, companies fully deploying DDSN have 15 per cent less inventory, a 17 per cent better perfect order performance, and 35 per cent shorter cash to cash cycle time. Additionally, DDSN leaders have 10 per cent higher revenue, and 5 per cent to 7 per cent better profit margins than their competitors.

Despite these impressive results there often arises a missing link in the DSSN framework, which can increase savings and profit margins. Many analysts focus on the supply side of the equation, but omit examining manufacturing and inventory management – a reflection on a vestige of the factory-based mentality. Their theory is that basing manufacturing and inventory planning on customer demand through disciplines like sales and operations planning will better tailor supply to demand, producing higher revenues at lower cost. What is absent is the connection between customer demand and the supply of human resources needed to execute distribution functions. Since labour represents 50 to 70 per cent of the distribution operations cost for most companies, better aligning supply and demand for this variable resource through demand-based planning and scheduling can significantly impact bottom-line results.

We will now examine key areas of the DDSN with focus on integrating the workforce planning to create a demand-driven workforce for improved efficiency, customer service, quality and safety.

a   The customer demand is essential as exemplified by the world's largest company Wal-Mart in their buying power with manufacturers such as Procter & Gamble, Unilever and Kimberly Clark. No longer can large manufacturers develop new products, create demand through sophisticated marketing programmes, and formulate price strategy and delivery schedules to maximise the value/success of their manufacturing and distribution operations. Mega-retailers such as Wal-Mart and Tesco create demand through their customer base and dictate price through extensive retail operations as well as requiring additional services such as store-ready pallets, special packaging and labelling and other value-added services. Hence 'pull' has replaced 'push' as the dominant supply chain dynamic, shrinking the latitude suppliers have to manage production and distribution, and putting a premium on efficiency and agility.

Another factor in the marketplace is the impact suppliers have on consumers. To satisfy varying and changeable consumer tastes, products have greatly proliferated. This product explosion has commoditised products, shortening product lifecycles and elevating the importance of new product development. More products with shorter lifecycles and the uncertainty of new product development initiative success have greatly complicated distribution planning and operations for both suppliers and retailers. A major contributing factor is the globalization of markets and personalisation of supply and demand. For example, a buyer with a PC located in Frankfurt, Johannesburg, or Sydney can order a product made in China online from a supplier in Cleveland, US. This globalisation of both supply and demand has resulted in the world being a consumer- and supplier-based environment, generating complex communications and supply chain network. It has been facilitated by technologies such as the Internet, satellite communications and containerised shipments, which have contributed to the complexity and variability of supply chain operations. An analysis of the foregoing generates a focus on the only viable option: to build more agile, adaptable supply networks aligned to an ever-changing customer demand, as exemplified in the DDSN.

A key factor in executing DDSN strategies is the agility and adaptability of the distribution workforce to execute the plan. This embraces two separate disciplines: workforce management and labour management, which must be fully integrated through the auspices of sales and operations planning to create a single demand sensing execution capability, found in the demand-driven workforce (see Figure 8.3).

b   In earlier years two separate workforce systems have developed to meet differing manufacturing and distribution operations. To meet the needs of the factory-based push model of the twentieth century, workforce management systems were created to take input from manufacturing execution systems and order management systems to produce workforce plans and schedules. These were sometimes augmented with time and attendance systems to ensure workers were available to fulfil the schedules. More recently, these systems have been adapted to meet the scheduling needs of highly variable retail operations. During the same time frame a parallel set of workforce systems have been developed for distribution labour management. These solutions employ industrial engineering principles to design the optimal way to perform distribution tasks and to develop engineered standards on which to measure performance. They then use performance monitoring and reporting software to evaluate results. The engineered standards also form the basis for modelling near-term workforce staffing requirements.

Regretfully, these two types of systems, coming from different disciplines and having different objectives, have never been integrated to leverage their respective strengths to form a single view of workforce performance management. Moreover, neither system has previously been tied into the sales and operations planning process to match supply and demand for this variable and expensive resource.

A significant benefit of labour management is the development of engineered standards for specific distribution operations. These standards are developed by evaluating subprocesses or tasks with industrial engineering discipline, such as precisely where to place a tote or position a fork-lift truck to minimise pick-up time. The engineering model provides the discrete baseline data for estimating everything from schedules and work plans to assessing the impact of changes in warehouse layout, process or slotting configuration (see Figure 8.1).

This detailed baseline data is ideal to predict future resource needs, but the absence of integration prevents the schedule optimisation capabilities of workforce management from leveraging the engineering model of labour management; combined they can provide a more detailed and accurate plan for resource scheduling and allocation across the operation. Research confirms business processes in the supply chain gain in complexity and there is a paramount need to manage the effect on labour resources.

c   Planning is an essential ingredient in today's global environment, which is complex and variable. The supply chain is subject to continuous change from mega-retailers, product proliferation with shorter lifecycles, and increased emphasis on new product initiatives with focus on customer demand data, which is regularly updated and available in real time to support operational planning needs.

Sales and operational planning has been defined as the translation of upstream

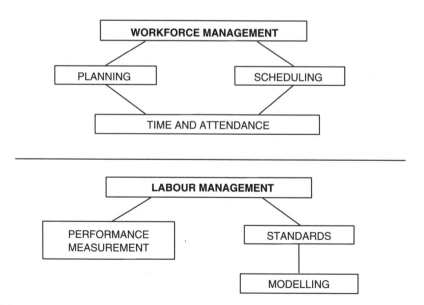

Figure 8.1 Workforce systems.

Source: Reproduced courtesy of Red Prairie Corporation.

demand data into an actionable operational plan and that rapid product commoditisation, shorter product lifecycles, high product mix and higher product volatility are all putting pressure on margins and accelerating the importance of
planning. Hence the need to integrate the planning and scheduling of workforce
management with the engineering model of labour management and tie the resulting
capability into the sales and operational planning process. The first step is to
merge the workforce planning with labour management. This is realised through a
new class of labour management termed workforce performance management,
which mirrors and supports the integrated workforce performance management
process.

Workforce performance management (see Figure 8.2) embraces the following:
(i) applying industrial engineering principles to create an environment under which
the workforce can be most productive; (ii) adopt the engineering model plus
demand signals plan to allocate human resources across distribution operations; (iii)
track time and attendance information to provide a total picture of on-site performance from the time they clock in until they clock out; (iv) employ real-time
performance measurement technology to monitor and evaluate performance against
standards; and (v) provide rewards, incentives or discipline, based on the foregoing
results.

The fact that workforce performance management (see Figure 8.2) has evolved
into a single integrated business process provides a sound foundation for integrating
the two types of business applications – workforce and labour management – to
create an integrated workforce performance management process. Moreover, it
allows the deep engineering model and data standards of labour management to be
leveraged for more accurate workforce planning and scheduling.

d   The demand-driven workforce (see Figure 8.3) has a planning focus on Standards
and Communications Protocols (S&CP) processes with a view to balancing estimated
demand with supply. This embraces interpreting estimated sales into a manufacturing plan, which feeds into the manufacturing system. The problem arises with the
supply chain execution system, such as warehouse transportation, and labour man-
agements do not receive this forecast and have little to no visibility of the planned
flow of inventory into the warehouse from either outside suppliers or manufacturers,

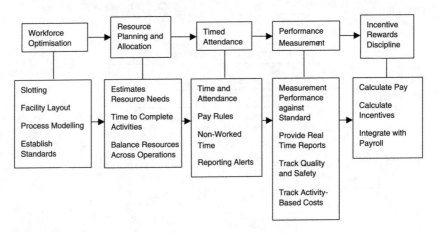

Figure 8.2 Workforce performance management: An integrated process.

Source: Reproduced courtesy of Red Prairie Corporation.

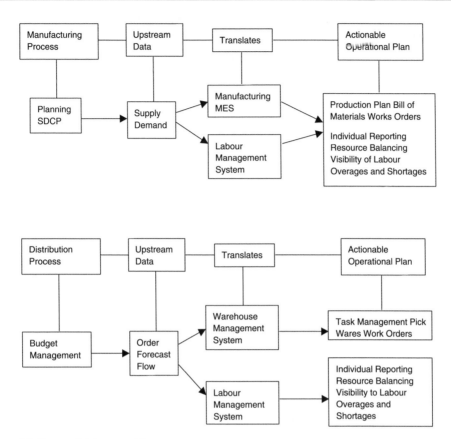

Figure 8.3 Demand-driven workforce.

Source: Reproduced courtesy of Red Prairie Corporation.

of to plans for new product introductions, special promotions or other forecasted changes in demand. Without such data the operations management is unable efficiently to plan for and allocate the human resources to fulfil this fluctuating demand. Hence with no clear visibility into what is coming into the warehouse or distribution centre, operations managers must be reactive and plan for the worst scenario. Without such data, operations managers may be required. Hence, the challenge is to plan and allocate the workforce to a meaningful upstream demand data and then translate such data into an actionable operation plan. This involves an understanding of the relationship between operational activities and required labour resources. Long-term demand can be used for staffing plans to adjust workforce size to fluctuating needs. Shorter term demand can be used to identify required skillsets and create work schedules. Research confirms that by deploying labour management systems, productivity increases by 20 per cent for warehouse operations. Thus, an agile, adaptive demand-driven workforce enables DDSN to be more agile, adaptive and profitable in responding to customer demand. Moreover, it generates the best practice in the engineering model process.

To conclude, China has driven the pull economy and the DDSN is an essential ingredient to meet this challenge. However, in addition to the DDSN criteria, focus must be on the distribution workforce where immense savings can be realised and efficiency achieved.

Useful Sources of Information

Red Prairie Corporation <redprairie.com>

Chapter 9

Security Global Supply Chain

Introduction

An area of growth in the early part of the twenty-first century has been security in international trade. It applies to all elements of the supply chain and the US is very much in the lead in its development. Logistics personnel designing the transit operation and the supply chain managers must have full regard to the ISPS Code, CSI and C-TPAT constraints and the RFID. It is a complex area, especially with regard to the interface between ship and port and customs clearance.

ISPS Code

The international agencies are in the lead regarding security and the International Maritime Organization (IMO) works very closely with the ISO. The International Ship and Port Facility Security Code (ISPS Code) was adopted at the IMO conference in December 2002. The aim of the ISPS Code, effective from 1 July 2004 and adopted by 100 countries is to establish an international framework for cooperation between contracting governments, government agencies, local administrations and shipping and port industries to detect security threats and take preventive measures against security incidents affecting ships or port facilities used in international trade, and to establish relevant roles and responsibilities at the national and international level. The basic aim is to enhance maritime security on board ships and at ship/port interface areas. These objectives are realised by the designation of appropriate personnel on each ship, in each port facility and each ship-owning company to make assessments and to put into effect the security plan that will be approved for each ship and port facility.

The ISPS Code identifies details of measures embracing both shipboard and port security plans. National administrations are required to set the security levels and ensure the security level information is provided to ships entitled to fly their flag. Prior to entering a port, or while in port within the territory of the contracting government to the Safety Of Life At Sea (SOLAS) Convention, a ship shall comply with the requirements for the security level set by that contracting government, if that security level is higher than the security level set by the administration for that ship.

The ISPS Code outlines requirements that shipowners can only meet with, for example, charterers and any sub-charterers. Moreover, delays and expenses may be incurred in connection with security measures taken by local port authorities or other relevant authorities according to the ISPS Code, the burden of which must be borne by the owners or charterer or shared between them. A similar criterion applies to liner/containerised shipments. The ISPS Code does not stipulate new duties for the port agents, but they must be prepared to assist arriving ships and their respective ship security officers with a number of security-related issues.

The logistics operator must recognise that the stringent measures under the ISPS Code result in a great deal more paperwork and stringent searches of cargo and stores and unaccompanied baggage boarding the ship.

CSI and C-TPAT

The Container Security Initiative (CSI) checks out the integrity of the container from the original point of 'stuffing' through the complex system of transportation, including the ship, to its final destination.

The CSI goals are to establish the criteria for identifying high-risk containers, to pre-screen containers before they are shipped to the United States, to use non-intrusive technology to pre-screen high-risk containers, and to develop smart and secure containers. It was devised by the US customs in consultation with a number of major trade partners on the implementation of two schemes: the CSI and the Customs Trade Partnership against Terrorism (C-TPAT). The IMO in cooperation with the World Customs Organization (WCO) are striving to introduce more security in the ship and the CSI continues to be extended to other countries. C-TPAT guarantees US importers various levels of expedited customs clearance and goals handling, based on supply chain security measures implemented by the importers.

Radio Frequency Identification (RFID)

Emerging from the terrorist attacks in September 2001 on the United States, the need to improve security at US ports and the containers passing through them has become paramount. A number of schemes were introduced such as CSI and C-TPAT, but one that has gained momentum on a global scale is radio frequency identification (RFID). It not only improves security, but also is a major contributor to supply chain management, especially in the container field as a new global standard for a RFID-based container tracking system.

Measures encapsulated in the Security and Accountability for Every (SAFE) Port Act of 2006 have brought major opportunities for providers of radio frequency identification (RFID) systems, which are, increasingly, being used to track marine containers and other types of cargo through the supply chain.

In the US, customers of RFID solution providers are not only benefiting from significantly increased supply chain visibility and security, they also expect to see the cost of such systems come down, partly due to an increase in the number of system vendors and suppliers.

Shippers are also benefiting from the ability of RFID technology to monitor the condition of goods in transit more efficiently. Variables such as temperature and the amount of light and humidity inside containers can be measured as they move through the supply chain – a major benefit for companies shipping sensitive goods, such as pharmaceuticals and foodstuffs.

This technology is becoming more widely used, due to the rapidly expanding RFID infrastructure and development of the first commercially endorsed global standard for electronic cargo seals (known as e-seals or tags).

ISO 18185, published in May by the International Organization for Standardization, incorporate the intellectual property of Mountain View (CA)-based Savi Technology, a major supplier of RFID systems for the tracking of cargo, and, since 2006, a subsidiary of Lockheed Martin.

Its e-seal is attached to a container when it is loaded at the shipper's premises. The seal includes detailed data on the items in the container.

The seals are located at various points in the supply chain, such as port terminals, customs clearance areas, trucking facilities and free trade zones.

Savi Technology has agreements with terminal operators and port authorities for the establishment of RFID readers at ports in the US, Asia and Europe. Participants include Hutchinson Port Holdings (HPH), the Virginia, South Carolina and Georgia port authorities, TraPac Inc, Modern Terminals (in Hong Kong) and Port of Rotterdam. This has enabled Savi to start tracking containers in the trans-Pacific (including Shanghai-Savannah), Far East–Europe and transatlantic trades.

Shippers can monitor the progress of their shipments in detail via the Internet, as the system links the shipment data with the e-seal number.

The new global standard is based on the existing mechanical seal standard (SO 17712). By 2012, all US-bound containers must be scanned at the port of loading.

Hence, RFID is a growth market in supply chain management. It is fast displacing the long-established Electronic Product Code (EPC) system, which hitherto has been the panacea for all supply chain requirements. Current indications suggest there is a significant disparity in RFID standards and global network proposals between the East and the West.

To realise a truly global support there is unquestionably a need for global numbering systems and support technology, which can accommodate the legacy systems including both EPC and the ubiquitous ID. In view of this disparity and these developments, it could be that supply chain stakeholders are not getting a fully inclusive picture of the potential for RFID and may become disillusioned about network infrastructures where there is no discernable migration strategy from existing systems to those envisaged.

However, to facilitate a truly global structure for supply chain management requires a numbering system and associated technology that can be adopted by all. There is a need for a global numbering system, supported and funded by national governments, administration by an international body (with EAN.UCC being a prime contender), but made freely available to supply chain stakeholders to facilitate global open systems identification. Such a system would accommodate the legacy of other numbering systems such as EAN.UCC and EPC and provide a migration path to a fully adopted global solution. There is also a need for infrastructure proposals that are integrated, achievable in practical terms and positioned within an appropriate migration strategy.

The growth of RFID is further evidence that SCM is a fast-moving market; to reflect the global RFID market, the ISO have introduced standard (see page 108) ISO 18000-6.

A growing number of global companies are introducing RFID to become more efficient in the management of the global supply chain management. The methodology for a company to adopt an RFID strategy is complex and diverse. The first task is to produce a well-thought-out strategy based on thorough research. Many have a pilot exercise with experienced consultants and by joining EPC global. The research should focus on the global supply chain and cost savings, increased revenue production and throughput. An investment analysis should be conducted to identify the return on capital investment. RFID technology is changing continuously and the investment option selected must focus on adding value to the company business. Companies are encouraged to visit competitors who have RFID and establish the problems and the benefits. The ideal solution is to recruit an executive experienced in RFID logistics.

Planning is an essential ingredient in the development of RFID. It must be customer-driven and each element costed/identified. Moreover it must have empathy with the marketplace and key performance indicators (KPIs) identified. This embraces volume, flexibility, risk areas, staff training. Moreover, the technical focus is paramount: orientation and alternation, environment testing, tag placement, and reader/antennae placement.

Product testing – often termed transit test – is a key element in the adoption of RFID. It enables the logistics operator to identify problem areas in consultation with the beneficiaries. Contingency plans must be formulated to counter shortcomings in the system. Moreover, emphasis must be placed on future product changes in size, weight, configuration and nature of packaging. This includes dangerous cargoes such as chemicals. A salient point is tag readability on a conveyor moving at 150 feet per minute.

The penultimate consideration is evaluating the pilot phase, which may be multi-focused in the ultimate global supply chain, embracing containerised shipments, road haulage palletised cargo, or air freight. The global supply chain may involve several transport modes – called multi-modalism – each in different stages of high-tech development such as road/ship/rail, or road/air/freight/road, and also 3PLs and 4PLs. This embraces various countries embracing different languages and stages of logistical culture/development. This includes testing software equipment and processes. Transparency is essential throughout all the elements of the global supply chain.

The final stage must have a financial input, especially the return on investment (ROI). A financial appreciation is needed, which could feature a discounted cash flow spread over 3–5 years. A risk assessment is needed and strong marketing input. Use the KPIs to gauge success and measure performance against predicted results at each stage. Overall, the analysis must be measured against the business plan. Two further important points on which to focus on are: the presence of any radio frequency (RF) technology using the ultra-high frequency (UHF) bond can cause prohibitive interference, which must be overcome; the second point is the need to have an experienced logistics executive at each stage of the global supply chain network.

The RFID strategy/commitment must emerge from the company directorate to reflect a forward-thinking company. A strong empathy with the end user is essential. Many companies employ consultants and a leading one is Red Prairie – www.redprairie.com.

An example of the rapid growth of the RFID to improve visibility and security in the supply chain arises in the US – a country with the most advanced global and high-tech logistics network. Save Technology have devised a new global standard for an RFID-based container tracking system – while Horizon Services plan to expand its deployment of RFID across the US.

It is significant to note that Wal-Mart's decision to mandate passive RFID tags to its suppliers emerged from the US Department of Defence making the same demands on their own supply chain.

For a company such as Wal-Mart, which has USD28 billion in assets, the advantage of adopting RFID includes working more efficiently with fewer warehouse personnel, while soft cost savings emerge where inventory is at any given movement. In the period 2004/5 since its introduction, Wal-Mart has received 7,000 RFID tagged pallets and more than 200,000 tagged crates and has read 1m–5m EPCs. Wal-Mart's experience identified readability of 100 per cent for the wholly equipped pallet; for pallets tagged individually the rate falls to 90 per cent, and if the tagged cases transported on conveyor belts through the warehouse pass the reading equipment individually, the success rate is around 95 per cent. However, for mixed pallets packed for the stores in distribution centres, the result is 66 per cent.

In June, the first RFID-based information network was launched in South America. Savi Networks has contracted with Bogota-based Emprevi, which provides logistics and security services to shippers, to provide visibility for goods moving between manufacturing facilities and ports in Colombia

Also in 2007, Savi Networks started working with major shippers and 3PLs in North America, Europe and Asia. These include: the Metro Group, one of the world's largest retailers, tracking shipments between Asia and Europe; Western Digital, with the Secure Free Zone project, in which e-seals are applied to trucks in Thailand; and Unipart Logistics, which tracks Jaguar car parts moving between the UK and the US.

The implementation of RFID systems by shippers is expected to increase further in the near future, due to Savi Technology announcing (in August) that it had licensed its intellectual property, incorporating ISO 18185, to six other RFID suppliers across the US, Europe and Asia.

Meanwhile, US domestic ocean carrier Horizon Lines is the first shipping line to have implemented a door-to-door RFID tracking solution, while several international carriers, including APL, have undertaken ocean freight RFID.

The main benefits to shippers of RFID-based systems, which incorporate e-seals (or tags) on containers, read by devices located at various points in the supply chain (encapsulated in ISO 18185), are as follows:

a   E-seals provide an added level of deterrence unavailable with mechanical seals. The latter require a physical inspection to identify security breaches. E-seals simplify this process by providing a wireless and automated alarm and tracking feature. However, e-seals do not prevent theft via a hole being cut in the container's side or its doors being removed.

b   ISO 18185 incorporates two radio frequencies to make the RFID system compatible with different industries and cover the requirements of all segments of the supply chain. These are active UHF (433MHz) and microwave (2.45GHz). This so-called 'active-based' RFID system features a longer range than 'passive' systems, which are restricted to deployment in small sections of the supply chain. For example, passive systems meet Wal-Mart's requirements for all its shipments from US-based suppliers to its US distribution centres to be RFID-enabled. Active systems have the added advantage of allowing omni-directional communication for increased flexibility.

c   Cargo is still predominantly tracked today using antiquated electronic data interchange (EDI) or fax-based methods, which are error-prone and unreliable. When attached to a container, an RFID e-seal provides a wire-less, automated alert to port officials, customs inspectors, ocean carriers and shippers that the seal has been tampered with, negating the requirement for a manual inspection.

According to consultant ABI Research, the cost of RFID devices is expected to decrease rapidly in the next few years. This is largely due to the increase in RFID system suppliers with the advent of ISO 18185.

Many active RFID solutions include tags costing USD50–100. But single-use e-seals, designed to be the cheapest active RFID devices available, today cost about USD20. According to vendors and users, the 'target suggested retail price is approximately USD10 in volume'.

In addition, shippers have to pay the system suppliers – the largest being Savi Technology and General Electric (which markets its non-ISO-based Commerce-Guard system) – a service fee, usually on a per transaction basis.

At a conference in the Asia–Pacific region in 2007, embracing Malaysia, Singapore, Indonesia and Thailand, the uptake of the RFID revealed a figure of 61 per cent in the coming years. However, a number of constraints exist: the need for more education and strategy; it is an expensive investment for low-value products; some 80 per cent of end users are not using RFID technology due to high set-up costs; warehouse management (66 per cent) and bar coding (62 per cent) are still the prevalent technologies used in facilitating the logistics process; half the operators have no transport planning or fleet management systems; and technologies such as ERP software and GPS-based vehicle tracking systems are being used by 35–40 per cent of companies. Currently, 14 per cent of the product value is the average cost currently incurred in the Asian countries. In Indonesia, there was a need for warehouse management and fleet management in the warehouse outsourcing and goods distribution environments. Warehouse, fleet, vendor management systems proliferate among Thailand's customs clearance services, regional distribution businesses and automotive hubs. Additionally, high security demands in the hi-tech sector, perishables, dangerous goods handling, reverse logistics and regional distribution in Singapore opened companies up for RFID, advanced planning and scheduling solutions.

Finally, the ISO working group in 2007 identified a range of RFID applications in supply chain management. The benefits included to track products in movement, including loss prevention, inventory control and in-transit visibility.

ISO focus on supply chain designates an overall process that results in goods being transported from the point of origin to final destination and includes the movement of the goods, the shipping data, and the associated processes, including the dynamic links between the different participants. These include many entities, such as producers of the goods, logistics management firms, consolidators, trackers, railroads, air carriers, marine terminal operators, ocean carriers, cargo/mode/customs agents, financial and information services, and buyers of the goods being shipped.

Some 20 years ago the data entry was manual; this was followed by bar-code technology; today, we are entering a new era of RFID. The bar codes can be scanned one at a time, while RFID enables potentially hundreds of tagged items to be read within a second. Further – depending upon the materials, tags can be embedded within the product packaging and read without ever having to open the transport unit. Since multiple items can be read – both within the package and the package itself – it becomes necessary to distinguish which of the two levels of packaging are being read. Today, RFID systems enable reading of all tags: product tags, transport unit tags or any combination of packaging levels.

Basically, an individual product may have numerous levels of packaging: the product package, transport units, returnable transport item and to the freight container. This is evident in the automotive industry receiving dock, embracing a 40-foot container of car seats, small returnable containers filled with fasteners, shipping labels affixed to unitised pallets, product packaging for janitorial supplies, and product tags on individual axles and transmissions. To require unique reading equipment for each product type would be completely unworkable. Consequently, the technologies employed throughout the chain of large returnable containers, small returnable containers, shipping containers, product packaging and product tagging must certainly be non-interfering and preferably interoperable. Hence, a freight container – an article of transport equipment – must feature the following: a permanent character and strong enough to be suitable for repeat use; specially designed to facilitate the carriage of goods by one or more modes of transport, without intermediate reloading; fitted with devices permitting its ready handling, particularly its transfer from one mode of transport to another; so designed as to be easy to fill and empty, and having an internal volume of at least $1m^3$ ($35°3Ft^3$).

RFID standards have five basic categories:

a   Technology. How we encode characters into the bars and spaces of bar-code (symbology) techniques for using radio waves to encode information (RFID), and technologies where personal identification can be placed in a 'smart card' – integrated circuit (IC) card.

b   Data content. Techniques called 'semantics' where specific abbreviations, tags, or identifiers can provide knowledge as to the type of data that follows, such as where an 'S' might mean a 'serial number' while a 'P' might mean a 'product code'. These data elements and their semantics might then be joined with other elements of data into a longer message that could be coded into a specific technology. The means by which this combination occurs is the 'syntax' of the message.

c   Conformance. This embraces the processes by which a specific device can provide assurance that its technology and data content follow the rules. Such processes might include: print quality for optically readable media; to test specification; and means to assure compliance to established air interface standards for wireless IT.

d   Network. The process by which various types of objects can communicate with one another.

e   Application standards. Where the technology, data content, conformance and network come together to solve user requirements in an application, such as the tracking of freight containers, returnable transport items, transport units, product packages, products and electronic container seals.

Finally there are challenges embracing the introduction and development of the RFID system. For example, certain packaging materials and package contents have the effect of erratically reflecting, absorbing or otherwise detuning radio waves. In such cases, what might have been a single application at the beginning of a project becomes more complex and may require a definite technology while permitting specific alternatives with trading partner agreements.

Useful Sources of Information

Containerization International <www.ci-online.co.uk>
IMO (International Maritime Organization) <www.imo.org>
ISO (International Organization for Standardization) <www.iso.org>
Red Prairie Corporation <redprairie.com>

Chapter 10

Specialised Software in the Supply Chain Process

Background – Need for Specialised Systems

Almost every company involved in the international movement of its products makes use of corporate computer software for its general operations. The software may take the form of Financial, Manufacturing (Marginal Revenue Product), sales order processing (SOP), purchase order processing (POP), warehouse management system (WMS) or all-encompassing enterprise resource planning (ERP) systems, employed singly or in combination.

However, because of the intricacies and variations in the data and documentary requirements of international trade, these systems, which have been designed primarily for domestic market operations, can rarely deal satisfactorily with situations involving the export of goods. As a result, specific arrangements usually have to be made in order to deal with the complexities of shipping arrangements and export documentation.

Many exporters employ specialised export software to deal with this problem. Products available range from basic programs providing just a method of manually keying-in data into on-screen forms to the more highly automated systems with rules and procedures and specialised shipping-related data maintenance facilities, of which Exportmaster is an example. Exportmaster ShipShape concentrates principally on documentation, while Exportmaster Professional also encompasses quotation, pricing and costing functions. Both are developed by Exportmaster Systems Limited and are used by manufacturers, retailers, exporting intermediaries, forwarders and logistics providers.

Exporters not employing specialised software handle their documentation and related activities 'off-system' by way of word-processing documents and spreadsheets, using templates where possible. Others still use manual typewriters and even handwritten entries for difficult items.

Failure to use a specialised system leads to the following risks and problems:

- Data has to be keyed first into the company's processing system and then separately into the export documents. It may also need to be rekeyed or copied and pasted between individual documents. Re-entry of data is inevitably a time-consuming and wasteful process.
- Whenever rekeying or re-entering data is undertaken, errors can arise. Errors, whether of omission or commission, cause serious problems at ports of arrival, rejection of letters of credit and financial discrepancies. Documentary errors are probably the most frequent and significant cause of compliance offences.
- Documents produced by individual input or by a variety of systems and in

unstructured environments such as word processing almost inevitably suffer from inconsistency of format. This not only projects an unprofessional image, but also risks problems in interpretation by officials expecting to see data presented in standard international layouts.

- Where information is simply entered as text in documents, rather than as data in a proper system, it is not available for management reporting operations.
- The user of manual methods indicates that there is no formal process to cause the correct documents to be produced or related tasks to be executed. The correct completion of a shipment consequently depends solely upon the knowledge and attention of individuals.
- Exporters who produce their export documents using word processing or spreadsheets suffer from the problem that no historical data is stored in a genuinely extractable format, because the content of the documents is no more than text. They are therefore unable to specify reports analysing export-specific historical performance or work-in-progress by customer, product, territory and period, other than what might be generally available at domestic-market level in their corporate system.

Functions and Objectives of a Specialised International Trade System

The major objectives in the deployment of a specialised export system may be defined as follows:

- To further integrate corporate systems and eliminate manual operations;
- To eliminate rekeying and other repetitive activity;
- To reduce potential for errors;
- To speed up and control the shipping process;
- To present a professional image in documentation;
- To permit production of export-related management reports;
- To reduce vulnerability to the knowledge of individuals or their absence;
- To enhance customer service.

The main areas of functionality that are not properly addressed by corporate software systems are:

- The maintenance of specialised export data;
- The formats of export documentation;
- The complex procedures relating to export transactions;
- Destination-related compliance issues.

Pre-Order – Enquiries, Quotations and Order Capture

While many exporters will use their specialised system solely for shipping purposes, others will wish to make use of pre-order functionality. Although their corporate systems may well have facilities for the generation of quotations, these may not correspond to export document formats and their pricing may not take account of the export sales and distribution costs associated with the level of Incoterms in use on a transaction. Furthermore, overseas customers may need to receive a pro forma invoice in the correct export and country-specific format for the purposes of opening a letter of credit, obtaining an import licence or complying with other local requirements. As well as calculating

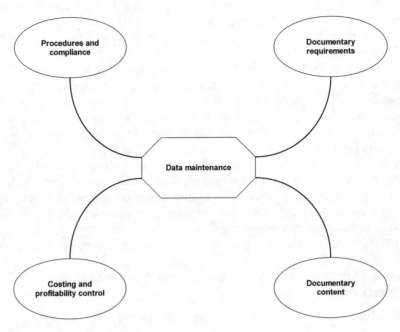

Figure 10.1 Export system functionality.

the export prices and issuing quotations and pro formas, Exportmaster can also extend the data input function back up the chain to the customer's original submission of an enquiry or order. The customer can be presented with a product listing (for instance, in the form of a spreadsheet) against which s/he simply needs to enter quantities for the items required. This can be uploaded electronically into Exportmaster for generation of the relevant pre-order documents and then further uploaded into the corporate system via an electronic interface or submission of an EDI (electronic data interchange) document.

Export-Specific Data

Except for the simplest of export transactions, a company's corporate system will tend not to have access to the type of data necessary for completing a set of export documents. Since it is clearly undesirable for operational staff to have to enter all the missing data items manually against each shipment, it is imperative for the export system to hold the export-specific data for territories, customers, products and transaction types in a way that makes it available to transactions as they are being processed.

Exportmaster can maintain standing data relating to various relevant areas:

- Territories;
- Customers;
- Products;
- Customs commodity codes (tariff codes);
- Hazardous cargo classifications;
- Countries of origin;
- Freight rates and other sales and distribution expenses.

Maintenance of this standard data reduces dramatically the amount of intervention needed by the individual user when handling a transaction.

Shipment Procedures

Rules and procedures can be set up within the system. They can apply to a whole area of operations or to a single customer. Typically a set of procedures will define which documents are to be produced and at what stage, activities to be undertaken (such as legalisation or certification), checks to be carried out and notifications to be issued.

When the user double-clicks a line in the procedural system, it updates its status to 'Done' and, where appropriate, actually carries out the function, such as printing a document or transferring data to another system.

The status control system allows the user to step through the activities as shown in Figure 10.2. Lines requiring action are colour-coded and have the status *'Do now'*. Action lines in the system may be simple checklist prompts, control lines managing the activity flow, document triggers or automatic system activity triggers. *Action Reports* (see Figure 10.3) are also available and can be organised either by shipment reference or by activity.

Action reports can be printed out, faxed or emailed and their contents can be determined by deadline date if necessary.

Letter of Credit and General Compliance

Export transactions require a greater level of editability than their domestic-market equivalents. This can be the result of complex shipping arrangements, but is most likely

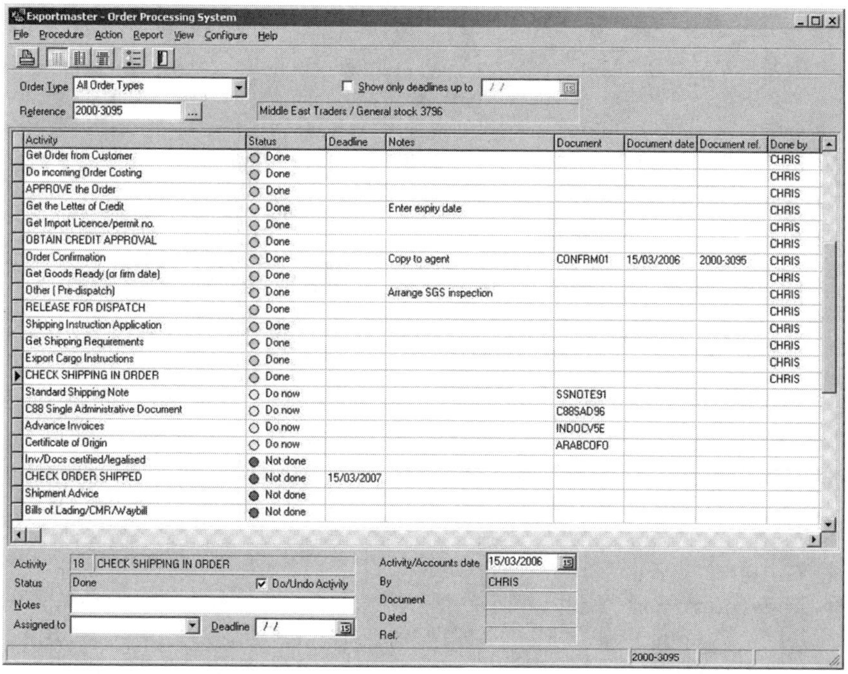

Figure 10.2 A typical Exportmaster shipment procedure.

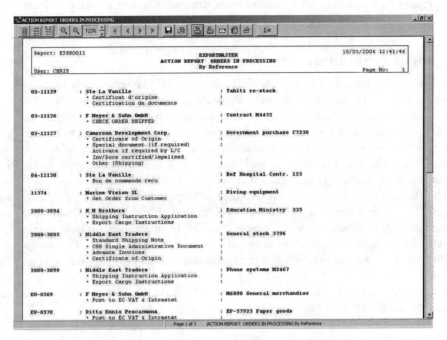

Figure 10.3 An Exportmaster Action Report grouped by shipment reference.

to be driven by the demands of instruments such as letters of credit, bank guarantees and special authorisations, which demand that the data contained in a document should correspond exactly with what is contained in the instrument. This can of course be totally different from the text and descriptions normally employed by the exporter. In order to deal with these requirements, the user edits the basic data in an export transaction (something not normally permitted in corporate systems) so that it corresponds with the requirement. Thereafter, any document printed in connection with that transaction will automatically incorporate the correct amended version of the data.

The Software-Driven Process

Figure 10.4 illustrates a typical process employing the Exportmaster system. Not all of the functions shown will be relevant to all shippers. Users will employ only those modules that are appropriate to their particular situation.

Data Capture

The term *data capture* is used to describe the method whereby the information about a transaction is acquired by the system, usually by one of the following methods:

- Manual entry by the user;
- Electronic download of data across a network from a corporate processing system;
- Reading a computer file that has been supplied by a third-party service provider;
- Reading a spreadsheet in an agreed format emailed by a principal or third party;
- Electronic download from a website.

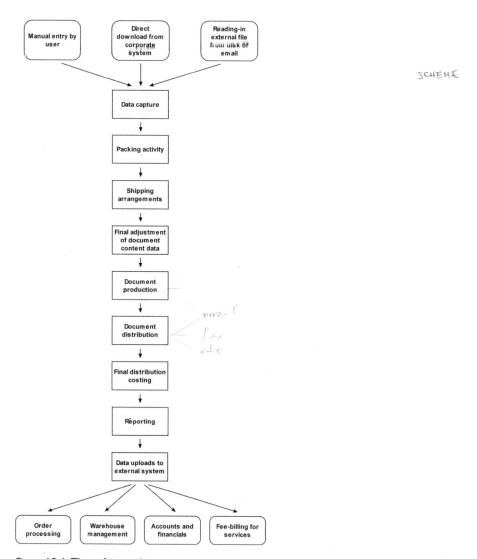

Figure 10.4 The software-driven process.

Whichever of these methods is employed, the export-related standing data already stored in Exportmaster against the customer, territory or products will be automatically merged with the newly entered data without intervention by the user.

Packing Operations

As well as customers, many authorities and financial institutions require the exporter to submit detailed packing lists. Within Exportmaster, packing operations can be carried out on-screen with visual representations of units of packing facilitating the process. Multiple-level packing is supported so a product could be packed into an inner carton, the inner into an outer carton, the outer onto a pallet and the pallet into a container. The resulting data configurations permit the production of packing lists which show what is packed in each outer, packing allocation lists which show against a product what quantity has been packed into which outer, and case or pallet documents that detail the contents of a particular packing unit (which may be required, for example, in connection with the shipment of hazardous cargo).

Shipping Arrangements

The procedural system prompts and monitors the area of shipping instructions and arrangements and, especially where letters of credit are involved, works to ensure that deadlines are met. Deadlined items that are approaching their due date are brought proactively to the attention of the user.

Dispatch-Time Data

Except in the case of the simplest transactions for the most straightforward destinations, most shipments will require some measure of data editing prior to production of the final shipping documentation. The editing may involve new data or amendments to the standard data. These are some examples of data changes that might be needed prior to shipment:

- Addition of data not available when the shipment is created, for example, name of vessel, berth of loading, flight number, etc.;
- Requirements of an unusual shipment with special handling or shipment requirements;
- Amendments to text to comply with a letter of credit;
- Last-minute alterations to a despatch (e.g. where a container is being filled and quantities have to be adjusted to match the quantity that it was possible to load).

An advantage of a system that is data-driven (as opposed to word processing) is that, once an amendment has been effected (for example a change in product description to comply with the terms of a letter of credit), that alteration will be automatically reflected in any document subsequently produced for the transaction in question.

Data can be edited either through the data fields themselves (Figure 10.5) or through the medium of an appropriate document (Figure 10.6).

Document Completion and Production

Most export systems come already equipped with a range of standard international export documents, including the SITPRO/UN forms range. In the case of Exportmaster, there is also a facility for the design of custom documents by the user. There is therefore no limitation upon the types of document that the system can produce, other than those imposed by the types of printer in use. The most common documentary output is as follows:

- Invoices (commercial and consular) and their derivatives;
- Packing lists;
- Shipping notes, instructions and advices and other despatch documents;
- Certificates of origin;
- Movement certificates;
- Transport documents;
- Insurance documents;

Shipping Record Operations - Exportmaster - [Consignment: 2000-3095]

File Consignment Consignee Customer Shell Overlay Configure View Help

Shipping Method Sea

Invoice | Transport Docs | Origin Docs | Banking Docs | Customs Docs

INVOICE DOCUMENT DETAILS (cont.)

Mark/Numbers/Container no.   Number and description of goods

MET	5 pallets
3796	Paper goods on shrink-wrapped pallets
DUBAI	strapped with vinyl tape
UAE	
1-5	

Total cube (m3)   20.07

Total packed weight (kg)   3187

Total gross weight (kg)   2787

Total net weight (kg)   2415

Main declaration

We hereby certify that the goods in this invoice are
of United Kingdom origin and that the prices and
values stated are true and in accordance with our
books

Place of issue   Croydon

Date of issue   / /

Figure 10.5 Editing through data fields.

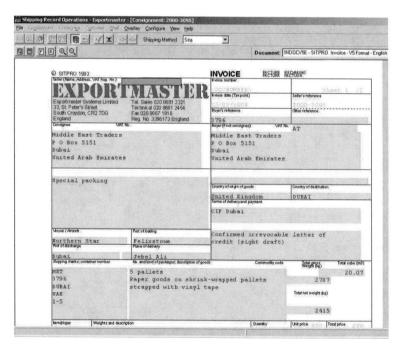

Figure 10.6 Editing via a document view.

- Bank collection documents;
- Shipping marks and other labels;
- Letters (standard and semi-standard) often relating to documentary enclosures;
- Customs declarations;
- Hazardous goods declarations;
- Customised certificates of quality assurance, conformity, etc.;
- Quotations and pro forma invoices.

Many export documents involve the use of forms. Traditionally, these used to be supplied as pre-printed stationery and Exportmaster can fill in these pre-printed versions where they are still in use, but the software is equipped with a digitised range of stand-ard forms, including the SITPRO/UN-approved set, which it can reproduce on plain paper during the printing process. All of the forms can be viewed on-screen with their contents before printing, so that they can be more easily checked and adjusted if necessary.

Within the context of an export system the word *document* has a wider meaning than it does elsewhere. It is not to be confused with the *form*, which is simply one component of the document. The term *document* can of course mean the piece of paper or its equiva-lent, which finally results from the printing or production process, but it can also refer to the *document design* that generates the output. The *document design* is a configuration of text, data, layout, rules and conditions, which will generate the desired output, which may be printed, stored or electronically transmitted. The most important properties that can be controlled by a document design are as follows:

- The size and orientation (portrait/landscape) of the document;
- The number of copies normally required;
- Whether any printing is required on the reverse of the sheet;

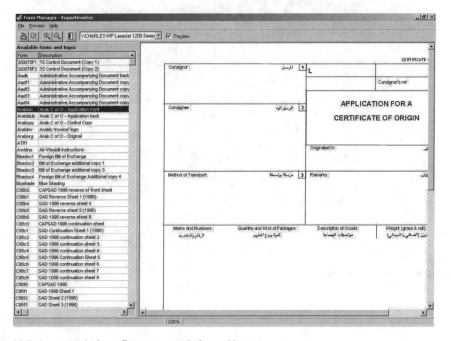

Figure 10.7 An example from Exportmaster's forms library.

- Items of *fixed text*. *Fixed text* is text that will always be the same on a document, regardless of which shipment is being processed. Example: ' *Total Value*';
- Items of *data*. These are items, such as header text, products, and so forth, that are specific to a particular shipment and that will therefore vary from shipment to shipment. Example: '*Shipped under Import Licence 579234*';
- The *positions* in which fixed text and data items are to appear;
- The *fonts* and *style attributes* for the fixed text and data items;
- The *order* in which line items (product lines) are to be *sorted*. Line items are sometimes sorted into tariff code order for example;
- Whether the line items are to be *subtotalled* and at what level, for example commodity code, country of origin or product group;
- Whether anything is to be included in or excluded from a particular sheet in a *multi-part set*;
- Whether any *scripted conditional rule* is to be applied and in what circumstances. Example: a document might include a special clause only when a particular product appeared among the line items on a shipment;
- The *default method of output* for the document, which might be:
  - printing on paper;
  - emailing;
  - faxing;
  - storing as a PDF file;
  - electronic transmission (UNeDocs, e-Biz-XML, etc.).

Any documents can be produced at any time on demand. However, in practice action lines will generate most in the procedural system. Documents may be printed (locally or remotely over a network), faxed, stored in PDF format, or emailed. Email is rapidly becoming the preferred method of receipt for documents where presentation of the genuine original is not imperative. With the use of scripting, documents can be transformed into other formats (EDI or XML for instance) for electronic transmission to other systems. Electronic transmission of one kind or another is expected before long to become the norm rather than the exception. A current example is the replacement of the C88 (SAD) paper document by electronic submissions to the UK customs authorities under the New Export System (NES).

Statutory Reporting

An export system can be of considerable assistance in meeting statutory and other governmental reporting and declaration requirements. Customs declarations are an obvious example although a forwarding intermediary often carries these out on behalf of the exporter.

EU exporters shipping significant quantities of goods to member countries of the European Union are required to submit regular Intrastat statistical reports and associated VAT declarations (the EC Sales List (ESL)). These can be time-consuming to collate manually. Exportmaster can generate and validate these reports automatically as a by-product of the normal documentation process. The reports can be output in printed form or as electronic files for transmission to the customs authorities via email or an EDI network.

Profitability Analysis

Calculating the profitability of an export consignment is a complex process because of the sheer number of different cost components involved and the variety of methods of calculation, for example, *per kilo, per cubic metre, per container, per shipment*, and so forth.

Exportmaster has a system of costing models that can be designed for different scenarios. They can deal with shipments on a 'before and after' basis, whereby estimated costs and margins can be compared with 'actuals' once shipment has taken place. Unlike a spreadsheet a costing can draw data dynamically from the shipment itself and from the standing databases. Its results are available for use in management reports. They allow identification of true net profit after all export expenses right down to the level of individual products per customer or destination.

A shipment costing can deal with terms through from Ex-Works (EXW) to delivered duty paid (DDP) while marketing product-pricing costings can include on-costs right through to the consumer price on the supermarket shelf in the country of destination if required.

Summary

The early part of this chapter pointed out the problems associated with more traditional methods of producing export documents and managing the shipping process. It also explained the benefits of using an integrated export system with as great a degree of automation as is practically achievable. Regardless of the relative weight of those problems and benefits, it is clear that there will be considerable and growing pressure on exporters to adopt dedicated export-specific software systems as they become compelled, sometimes by law, to keep pace with the introduction of electronic submission and

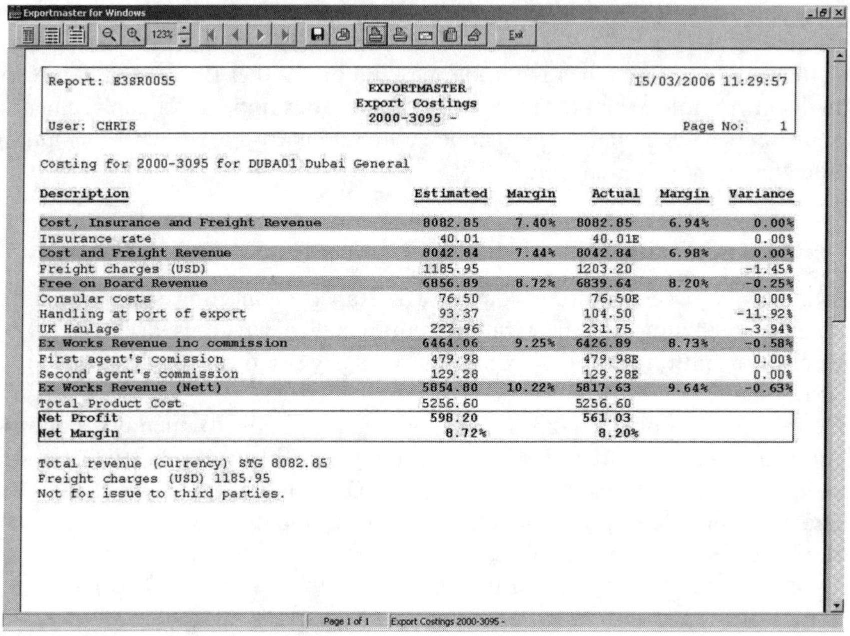

Figure 10.8 An Exportmaster costing showing a CIF transaction.

data-exchange systems. Personnel in the logistics and exporting sectors are therefore increasingly expected to familiarise themselves with software systems, the use of which is now becoming the standard method of operation.

Useful Sources of Information

International Master Systems Ltd (Export Management and Documentation Software) <www.exportmaster.co.uk>

Chapter 11

Global Trade Scene

Introduction

The global logistics operator must be conversant with the global trade scene to ensure strategically that they keep pace with changes and opportunities.

A book written by Alan Greenspan, which was published in 2007 by the Penguin Press, identifies the areas and changes that have emerged during his chairmanship of the US Federal Reserve Board during the period 1987–2006. The book is entitled *The Age of Turbulence*. It traces the changing global scene with particular emphasis on the challenges running the US economy and its interface with the global economy – in particular, future trends and the shift to the reliance on China and the Far East as a manufacturing base, and the growth of technology and the changing structure of the global capital markets. Overall, it focuses on the structure of the world economy up to 2030. Significantly, one can identify the growing importance of global logistics and international supply chain management in the changing scene on longer supply chains spanning numerous cultures and differing economic structures and infrastructures. It is an exciting period of global logistics development.

Global Trade Scene

Today, the world is a single integrated marketplace where supply chain efficiency has become a competitive necessity. Manufacturers and retailers have sought cost savings and service improvements to enhance their competitiveness by supplying larger markets with fewer production and distribution centres.

The international entrepreneurial task is to evaluate opportunities continuously on a global basis. An area in need of examination is the continuous growth of economic blocs/trade associations, whose prime objective is to function as a single market, ideally with cross-border controls and free of customs examinations, once the goods have entered the market from a third country. Overall, there are 10 major trading blocs.

We will now examine the major trading areas of the world, particularly from a global logistics and supply chain strategic environment.

European Union – Logistic and Supply Chain Strategic Environment

On 1 May 2004, 10 new Member States joined the EU: Cyprus, the Czech Republic, Estonia, Hungary, Latvia, Lithuania, Malta, Poland, Slovakia and Slovenia. Eight of them are former Central and Eastern European markets, which bring 74 million new consumers into the EU. On 1 January 2007, Bulgaria and Romania joined the EU. The 27 Member States have a population of approximately 500 million and have become the largest single market for trade and investment in the world – larger, even than the US and Japan combined. It is the ideal market for a pan-European distribution strategy, logistically driven on a single market basis. It has the added benefit of a 13-member country Eurozone, permitting no currency risks when trading in the pan-Eurozone (see page 52).

The single market features may be summarised as follows:

a   European standards involving the development of the 'Euro Brand' product in all 27 States (see page 51);
b   Liberalisation of public purchasing with contracts being awarded on merit and not on nationalistic products;
c   Liberalisation of open markets in information technology and telecommunications;
d   Liberalisation of financial services, embracing insurance, banking and investment securities, and so forth, thereby permitting freedom of capital transfer throughout the community;
e   Liberalisation of transport services, involving deregulation of shipping, air transport, and road haulage;
f   Acceptance of professional qualifications gained in one state and recognised in the remaining states, thereby permitting freedom of labour mobility among the professions;
g   Abolition of state subsidies, unfair competition and restrictive agreements, and abuses among companies within the market;
h   Adoption of one trade patent throughout the EU;
i   Elimination of physical barriers to trade, thereby permitting freedom of movement of goods and people across borders;
j   A total of 13 members in the Eurozone using a common currency – the euro. Countries in the Eurozone include Austria, Belgium, Finland, France, Germany, Greece, Ireland, Luxembourg, the Netherlands, Portugal, Spain and Slovenia.

The EU market access strategy can help logistics operators and supply chain managers:

a   Provide basic information to business on conditions for exporting to and investing in key third-country markets via the Market Access Database (MADB), available via the Internet;
b   Follow up complaints received from businesses about barriers to third countries, whether in the WTO (see page 11) or in bilateral consultations with the countries concerned;
c   Ensure EU trading partners effectively comply with their international commitments;
d   Contribute to the creation of a suitable framework for international trade.

The EU MADB has the following three functions:

a   To list all trade barriers affecting European exports by sector and by country and to ensure systematic follow-up and action for every single barrier identified;
b   To provide basic information of interest to European exporters: the rate of duty for individual products, validity of patents in specified countries, import licence obligation and any special customs clearance formalities;

c   Interactive means of communication between business and the European Authorities allowing an exchange of information online.

The MADB contains the following main sections: sectoral and trade barriers, and applied tariffs exporters' guide to import formalities services; WTO role and WTO bound tariffs. The service embraces over 100 countries and is available free on www.mkaccdb.eu.int.

The EU has facilitated creating a pan-European distribution strategy as the geographic borders between European countries have become almost nonexistent. Cross borders are easier with few frontier constraints. Moreover, import duties are few and the Eurozone featuring 13 countries has eliminated currency risk within the zone. Overall this has reduced trading cost and encouraged trade development (see page 152).

Nationalism is being replaced by a pan-European philosophy as companies find their country-specific logistics networks are neither cost-efficient nor effective as European countries band together for the common good.

As awareness of the benefits of a pan-European approach to logistics increases, organisations are reviewing their strategies. No decision to examine the logistics network should be made without considering three factors: the company and its resources, the customer and the supply chain. Emphasis must be placed on the value-added benefit and extolling good practice.

Planning is an essential ingredient in any pan-European approach to logistics. Many stakeholders will be affected by any change and their needs must remain paramount. The following considerations arise:

a   Ensure the needs of the supply chain – existing customers, vendors, suppliers, and alliances – will be met and improved upon;
b   Ensure that future business growth is part of the logistics strategy;
c   Ensure that the needs of the organisation will be met through streamlined cost, concentration on core competencies and focused technology and communication. Basically develop and improve on the elimination of inefficient elements in the logistic network (see page 27).

The design of a logistics network, no matter where it is located, is dependent on a range of factors such as type of product, range and volume of products, geographic spread of service area, level of service required and number and type of customers. The infrastructure in the 27 Member States varies from the developed networks in the UK, France, the Netherlands, Germany and Belgium to the less developed found in the 12 new members, as from 1 May 2004–1 January 2007.

The way to achieve pan-European logistics excellence is to apply strategic planning methodology of the network design within the company business plan. The objective of network planning is to establish the economic way to ship and receive products while maintaining or increasing customer satisfaction. Overall, the objective is to maximise profits and optimise service, adding value to the service. Strategic logistics network planning must respond/comply to the following:

i How many distribution centres (DC) should exist and their location;
ii How much inventory should be stocked at each DC and this should reflect the trade cycle;
iii What customers should be serviced by each DC;

   iv How should the customers order from the DC;
   v How should DCs order from vendors;
   vi The frequency of shipment to each customer and the level of service;
  vii The method of transportation.

The methodology of redesigning a European logistics network begins with a strategic plan that moves seamlessly from a concept to an efficient and effective reality. The first step of any configuration redesign is identifying the mission of the organisation. This involves outlining achievable baseline results of the plan and developing a strategic business plan. Once the strategic mission is clearly defined, the organisation must evaluate its current position and market resources in the context of pan-European logistics, and in particular, focus on the infrastructure and their adequacy. Overall, it entails collecting information from sites about the following:

a   Equipment and layout including high-tech;
b   Standard operating procedures (SOPs) including transportation, and any deviations/ inconsistencies in actual facilities operations;
c   Staffing levels and employment law;
d   Labour resources rates and degree of flexibility to handle volume variations in receiving and shipping cargo;
e   Building characteristics – for example, clear height, lighting levels, column spacing;
f   Annual operating cost (e.g. rent, taxes, insurance, maintenance and energy);
g   Inventory (e.g. turns, fill rates, safety stock, skill velocity);
h   Performance metrics and reporting procedures;
i   Freight classes and discounts;
j   Replenishment weight/cube;
k   Degree of twenty-first century technology.

Collecting information on customers means understanding where the market is, who it is and what features will ensure a competitive advantage inherent in such a location – overall, its market position.

    Each EU nation differs slightly in what drives customers to purchase reflecting differing cultures (see page 143) and what constraints are made to their ability to buy. It extends to culture, lifestyle, technology, climate, economic/social factors, education, language and religion. Italy and France are design fashion-conscious. Germany focuses more on engineering and quality/durability. Some countries do not favour a Western profile, but favour the customer focus and are very nationalistic. Key elements of the customer profile include the following:

a   Target market area – concentration of customers by country, clusters of high volumes. Conservation areas, high population density countries like the Netherlands, and multicultural countries all have different expectations. Cluster markets strategy involves servicing a collection of countries contiguous to each other with similar cultures and market needs. One country can be the distribution centre, thereby encouraging volume shipments and reducing distribution cost. Overall, it encourages development of the market through lower cost and extols the economies of scale and a more effective logistically driven organisation within the markets served;
b   Current order profile and factors contributing to variations and any scope of mitigation such as price, discount and the benefits of a more effective logistics network. An

analysis of type of products ordered, any associated ordering patterns, seasonality issues, and terms of order;

c   Market direction – which products are growing in popularity and which have declining product lifecycle, changes in packages, changes in legislation, changes in product specification/technology, competition and prevailing supply chain issues;
d   Sales growth by year, country and product;
e   Emerging demographics and geographic shifts.

Formulating a European strategy begins with a strategic European network plan that meets requirements over a specified planning horizon. The best strategy is the one specifically tailored to the organisation. Categories can be subdivided and more categories created (see page 83) to manage the process more effectively. Alternative strategies should also be designed and analysed and tested to ensure that the most effective solution is implemented. A risk assessment should also be made.

One of the last steps of network design is adding the management and IT infrastructure. Traditionally, freight and warehousing have been supervised by logistics organisation, but today the supply chain management should take the lead.

Many firms are finding these traditional structures too expensive and not as knowledgeable in how individual EU states work. This particularly applies to the 10 states that featured in the enlargement (see page 126). As a result, countries are employing regional specialists and maintaining centralised control, particularly in former Eastern countries where cultures are very similar.

The design of a pan-European logistics network or redesign of a European logistic network is neither an easy task nor one that should be pursued without research, analysis and justification.

A time-phased implementation effort – complete with training and piloting – is critical to the success of the EU logistics challenge. However, the ultimate result is to become more competitive, with higher profits and value added to the consumer. The former Eastern bloc countries need a higher learning curve in the logistics operation/culture compared with the 15 Member States prior to May 2004.

Asia

Global trade continues to expand in the Asia–Pacific region with more than 84 per cent of companies operating in the region relying on 3PL services. China and India in particular have increasingly attracted global 3PLs to operate in these developing countries, but challenges such as poor infrastructure, complex regulations and industry readiness, still remain.

China is the third largest market in the world, with its outsourced logistics services growing by 22 per cent per year. Opportunities to drive logistics services abound as China continues to be a global powerhouse, exporting USD760 billion worth of goods in 2005. The growth in transportation witnessed in the country has been in tandem with the increase in trade volumes. In 2004, rail freight traffic increased 6 per cent and inland waterways tonnage was up 8 per cent year-on-year while port traffic rose by 18 per cent.

Moreover, the huge availability of cheap labour for manufacturing has driven the country's growth of exported goods, while the Chinese logistics market itself is estimated to be worth more than USD120 billion by 2010. However, foreign 3PLs operating in China need to face challenges such as infrastructure limitations, regulatory restrictions and domestic competition. Road handling capacity accounts for only 10 per cent of the container traffic received at ports. Rail systems are old and poorly coordinated and can cope with only 30 per cent of the demand placed upon them.

Regulatory restrictions in China prove another complication. Licences are required for many activities that foreign 3PLs often take for granted. Also, there is no one central authority that issues those permits and licences and 3PLs need to negotiate with local government for service permits.

It is also difficult for 3PLs to create a pan-China network without engaging the assistance of Chinese 3PLs as they have to face many domestic 3PLs, which not only have a rich customer base, but also a good relationship with municipal, regional and national governments.

Many companies from developed markets, particularly the EU and North America, have chosen to outsource (see page 133) their production/assembly base to Asia and in particular, China. This embraces the investor selecting an economic development logistics supply chain zone, usually under a joint venture (JV) basis.

An example of future investment in China involves US-based ProLogis – a global provider of distribution facilities and services, which has signed an agreement launching two projects in Chengdu – the capital city of western China's Sichuan province. The two projects are a standard storage facility, located in the city's Jinnui District, and the ProLogis Chongqing Logistics Park, which covers 53.3ha. This involves an investment of USD40–60 million and embraces storage facilities that will be completed by 2009. It is a JV with the Chongqing Economic and Technological Development Zone authorities.

ProLogis will construct the facilities and lease them to clients, embracing the many car parts manufacturers and electrical engineering companies emerging in Sichuan and the neighbouring Chongqing municipality. By May 2006, ProLogis built 12 logistics parks in China, involving an investment of over USD200 million. It is envisaged that ProLogis will embark on two further projects in Chongqing's export processing zone, together with a bonded logistics centre in Chongqing.

ProLogis also has logistics parks in Shanghai, Guangzhou, Lingang – south-eastern Shanghai, Yantian Port Logistic Zone in Shenzher, a bonded park in the Guangzhou free trade zone, Tianjin ProLogis Technological and Development Zone and the ProLogis Park at Beijing's Capital Airport.

In 1980, China had five special economic zones designed to encourage inwards investment. Between 1984 and 1986 a further 14 economic and technology development zones emerged. A further 54 economic and technology zones emerged featuring one in Tibet and another in Qinghai. Later came zones for 40 coastal cities and those for hi-tech companies. Cities from Shenzhen to Urumqi operate 16 bonded zones and 38 export processing zones, which waive import-related fees for companies that ship out whatever they bring into China. Logistics zones with warehousing or transportation links operate alongside other zones. There are zones for science and zones for industry. Today, hundreds of economic development zones operate in China.

An example of a major economic zone with a mature infrastructure and access to power in the peak demand seasons of winter and summer is Tianjin economic development area, which includes 4,100 companies and two hi-tech zones. It is located close to China's fourth largest seaport and in 2008 the city opened a freight airport.

Zones under the central government permit foreign investors to pay income tax of 15–24 per cent compared with the normal 30 per cent. Local government can charge 3 per cent local income tax, but often cut it to attract investors. Land prices may also be discounted. Better breaks go to companies that strategically help a local economy.

Investors should study which zones are near suppliers, markets and international transportation routes. Furniture factory investors are located in the Pearl River Delta Zone, because plywood suppliers are close by while laptop manufacturers prefer zones between Shanghai and Hangzhou because they have access to continuous local delivery from ports air-freighting in chips and finished computers out. Zones in western China are less attractive because of their distance from supply chains or transit hubs, but may attract investors seeking minerals not found elsewhere.

Manufacturing regions in China embrace Beijing – Tianjin Corridor (Beijing, Tianjin, Hubei); Yangtze River Delta (Shanghai, Zhejiang, Anhui, Jian, Hubei), Pearl River Delta (Hong King, Macau, Guagdon, Guangxi) and Pan-Pearl River Delta.

Doing business in China is much like doing business throughout the whole of the EU (see page 126); crossing from one province into another is much like crossing the border from one EU country to another. China might be one country, but with around 17 independently governed regions and many different languages or dialects being spoken – not to mention each region having its own customs or other local regulations – the business entrepreneur has to manage each region independently.

To conclude, there are four types of logistics in China:

a   Companies that have evolved from state-run storage and transport businesses: Sinotrans Group; Cosco, China Overseas Shipping and China Merchants Group;
b   Companies that began as units of major domestic shippers: Haier Logistics, Shanghai Hualian – Supermarket Logistics;
c   Private or joint stock logistics companies: Guangdon P.G., Beijing Huashand, Beijing Xiashongmao and Beijing ZIS;
d   Foreign-invested joint ventures.

Another huge, but unexploited logistics market in Asia, is India. However, unlike China, the development in India's logistics market is relatively slow and still in the infancy stage. Global 3PLs could harness the opportunities in driving IT-enabled logistics in the Indian IT powerhouse through the development of systems such as logistics planning. Agricultural logistics could be another focus for 3PLs, while the large infrastructure projects available provide yet more room for proper logistics management.

But as in other developing nations, poor infrastructure and transport vehicles in India hinder the proliferation of logistics services. Complex tax laws on the implementation of VAT that vary across states are another major concern for 3PLs in India, holding back investment. Another tax issue discouraging the 3PLs in India is the service tax on warehousing. Hence it may be cost-effective for a company to keep warehousing as an in-house activity, as outsourcing this activity means factoring in the service tax.

The governments of both India and Pakistan are conscious of their poor infrastructure. India is building a container terminal at Vallarpadam, capable of handling 8,000–9,000 TEUs. Surrounding the port will be a special economic zone with an area of 115.25 hectares and another at Puthuvypeen with 285.84 hectares. Overall, the Indian government has earmarked USD320 billion investment for infrastructure development of which USD11 billion has been allocated to ports, which will double the port capacity by 2012.

Pakistan's largest port, Karachi, completed its first phase of expansion plans in 2009. Gwader deep-sea terminal – Pakistan's second largest port with 500,000 TEU capacity, plans to have a free trade zone connected via a 700km coastal highway between the two cities.

Another factor contributing to inefficiency is the complexity of the international trade documentation process. While places such as Singapore and Hong Kong have implemented automated trade systems, there is a lack of such IT infrastructure in India. The Port of Singapore Authority (PSA) remains a leading world port and primarily a transhipment hub port in the region. It has a continuous investment programme and has state-of-the-art technology in all areas of its business. A further factor is the challenge of the Indian industrialist to meet the opportunities. There is currently a lack of sophistication of the equipment and technologies used in the Indian logistics market, compared with those commonly used in developing countries.

In Taiwan, APL Logistics has recently obtained a licence to operate at Taiwan's Kaohsiung FTZ as an international logistics provider. Some of the benefits at the FTZ include simplified customs procedures, exemption from customs checks and inspections in some situations, as well as duty, commodity and sales tax exemptions. Not all FTZs are equal. FTZs are widely used in Hong Kong, Singapore, mainland China, Korea and Taiwan. Customer procedure in Hong Kong permits 24-hour customs clearance, with all cargo from foreign countries exempt from customs duty and VAT. Singapore FTZs offers similar incentives and permit cargo to be stored within the zones without any customs documentation until released. In mainland China, customs auditing is implemented in bonded areas; cargo access between bonded areas and the areas outside the customs territory is serviced as a record; and cargo assessed between bonded area and tax area has to be declared. Korea offers transhipment cargo, exempt from declaration; consumption cargo and office equipment for self-use of enterprises in FTZs, and other items that are not used for the purpose of operation, need not be declared; and bonded transportation is allowed for foreign cargo between different FTZs. Finally, in Taiwan, foreign cargo stored within an FTZ and cargo transhipped from a FTZ to foreign countries or to other FTZs, the FTZ enterprise shall declare to customs. These cargoes cannot enter or leave the FTZs until they have received computer clearance/authority.

Finally, the Port of Dubai is an example of outstanding growth in less than 30 years. In the mid-1970s, Jebel Ali in Dubai in the United Arab Emirates (UAE) consisted of little except desert and the seashore. The completion of phase I of the Port of Jebel Ali's expansion raised port capacity from 4 million TEU to 5.7 million. Today, it has been transformed by the building of roads, distribution centres and industrial plant gathered round one of the world's busiest ports. It is the eighth largest container port in the world, handling 8.9 million TEUs. The TEUs in 2006 compared with Rotterdam's 9.7 million TEUs. Singapore was top with 24.7 million TEUs, followed by Hong Kong's (China) 23.9 million TEUs, Shanghai's 21.7 million TEUs, Shenzhen's 18.4 million TEUs and Bussan's 12 million TEUs.

Today there are 11 seaports and 6 airports with satellite links to 230 countries in the UAE. This is supported by a number of free zones embracing the Hamriyoh Free Zone and the most recent, Sharjah. The flagship ports are Jebel Ali and Port Rashid. Jebel Ali has become the transhipment point for goods serving many other ports in the Gulf and for some ports in the Indian subcontinent. Overall, the ports of Dubai have become major global hub ports and trading ports of the Gulf region with the ongoing development of free zones, which attracts global investors and entrepreneurs.

North America

The United States has a large and diversified economy with a broad base of natural and human resources and a well-developed physical and technical infrastructure, logistically driven. Buoyed by a steady flow of immigrant labour, and a large domestic market, it remains a global leader in technological innovation and product dissemination.

Canada is an industrial country of mining and industry, and the culture is similar in many areas to the US. Canada, the US and Mexico are members of the North American Free Trade Agreement (NAFTA), formed in August 1992 and which by 2007 saw the abolishment of all tariffs and trade barriers. The US is a leading trading nation and is the leading importer of Chinese goods.

Global sourcing and the growth in international trade are resulting in a record volume of goods crossing US borders. According to US foreign statistics, in 2004, the US freight transport network carried USD2.2 trillion of imported and exported goods, an increase of 168 per cent from 1990.

Understandably, the infrastructure is struggling to absorb this amount of trade. With more than 400 freight gateways across the US, the bulk of the traffic is concentrated on a few ports, airports and highways, which are becoming bottlenecks. Because infrastructure developments are usually long-term projects, current improvements will not be visible for a while.

Ports currently deal with 10 super post-panamax container ships and airports are getting ready for the additional 30 per cent capacity of the Airbus 380–800F. Road transport remains a major distributor, but facing higher fuel costs. Consequently, rail is becoming a growth market. Also, inland waterways are being developed. Overall, despite the extensive infrastructure throughout the US, the freight network was under pressure in 2006.

In consequence of extended lead times due to outsourcing and congestion, levels of stock have increased, resulting in higher inventory carrying costs. In January 1992, US retail inventory was valued at USD242 million, but by January 2006 the figure had risen to USD475 million. Inventory being nothing more than capital in motion, it was also affected by US interest rates. Hence it can become more costly to carry inventory in the US when interest rates are rising.

Besides infrastructure and the traditional compliance requirements, supply chain managers have now to comply with new regulatory requirements resulting from the Sarbanes-Oxley Act. This law, covering corporate governance, was passed following accounting scandals, and introduced transparency and control of processes across the company. Several aspects of logistics are concerned such as the accuracy of the inventory.

A further area is customers' compliance requirements. To standardise receiving and tracking, large organisations impose on their suppliers a set of rules covering various areas from delivery to labelling. Failing to comply with these rules can result in a chargeback by the customer, or a non-compliance note, ultimately affecting the supplier performance results.

The US logistics environment is fast moving, and logistics managers – on completion of the finally designed cost-efficient network mitigating congestion, limiting inventory and compliant with all requirements – must keep it under continuous review. This will add value to the network and ensure full compliance. Overall, many believe the US supply chains have a shelf life of around one year.

Consequent on all these constraints, the US supply chain management team has generated even greater efficiency – the most successful adaptation through change and innovation. Automation is one answer. By using software, linking customers directly to the back-office operation, they reduce the manipulation of data, increase the speed of collecting information and are able to react immediately to any event.

Radio frequency identification (RFID) is the most recent development. Hitherto, the large upfront cost required by RFID and the doubt over its efficiency had stopped many organisations adopting the technology, but an independent study by the University of Arkansas commissioned by Wal-Mart had demonstrated the benefit of the tool. The study shows that Wal-Mart had been able to reduce out-of-stock by 16 per cent and items tracked with an electronic code were replenished more quickly than those tracked with a bar code. They also noticed a reduction in manual orders and excess inventory.

Wal-Mart is China's eighth largest trading partner and an estimated 70 per cent of the US retailing giant's goods are made by mainland manufacturers and these shipments represent 10 per cent of the US total annual imports from China.

Behind automation and technology business, practices are changing in US and other developed economies, especially the EU, Dubai (see page 133) and Asian/Japanese markets. Consequently, different models are being developed. Demand-driven supply networks (see page 101) are supply chains managed from the sale side. Instead of having products pushed through the supply chain from the suppliers to the customers, goods are pulled through the value chain from the customer when needed, which in turn creates a series of reactions from replenishment to reordering. In this format the supply chain is driven by actual demand and not a forecast. This model demands a new strategy, an extremely agile supply chain and skilled and knowledgeable managers.

A further area of development in the US is the concept of total cost, which emerges from 'lean' school of thinking. Logistics costs are often limited to transportation, handling, inventory and a few other elements. Managers, operating in a lean supply chain management (see page 27) environment are starting to include all factors that affect the cost of supplying the goods, taking the logistics function to the heart of corporation finance including trade finance (see page 51).

An efficient supply chain in the US is not only complex and expensive; it also has an enormous competitive advantage. Logistics has become a strategic and corporate function under the responsibility of chief logistics officers.

To conclude our analysis of the global trade scene, it is appropriate to tabulate the growth of the logistics market in 2004. Much of the growth can be attributed to not only trade expansion, but also mergers and acquisition (M&A) of logistics companies. The rationale of M&A is that larger companies generate higher volumes with a more flexible costing system. Current market conditions are set for an extended period of radical change, which would put pressure on medium-sized companies which, to survive, would need to focus on using technology to integrate much better with partners and customers. Customer focus and partnering remain the most important features to develop the global logistics company.

Logistics companies must devise a strategy by choice and not by default and make the investment to ensure it is a success with a clear focus.

The percentage growth of global logistics markets in 2005 produced a world average of 6.2 per cent. This was made up of Domestic China 11 per cent, Intra-Asia 9 per cent, Asia–North America 7 per cent, Asia–Europe 6.5 per cent, Europe–South-West Asia 6.25 per cent, Europe–South America 6.16 per cent, South–North America 6 per cent, Europe–North America 5.7 per cent, Intra-Europe 5.4 per cent, Europe–Africa 5 per cent, Europe–Middle East 4.7 per cent and Intra-North America 4.1 per cent. Estimated logistics supply chain cost as a percentage of GDP reflects the following data: direct cost European 9–10 per cent, Asian 13–14 per cent; indirect cost European 4–5 per cent and Asian 9–10 per cent. This produces a total figure of European 13–15 per cent and Asian

22–24 per cent. The foregoing demonstrates the growth and competitiveness to develop an efficient logistics supply chain strategy in export-led markets.

An Analysis of a Houston (TX) Headquartered Freight Forwarder and 3PL Association International Freight and Logistics Network (IFLN)

To provide an insight into a Houston-based freight forwarder and 3PL association, the IFLN identified the manner in which business is conducted. Moreover, it reflected the logistic culture in the US, which may be regarded as a market leader in the logistics field and its interface with a major 3PL global associated IFLN.

For many small- and medium-sized freight forwarders and 3PLs participating in global tender with large multinational shippers, it is not a feasible option. Unlike the major global 3PLs – such as DHL, Keuhne + Nagel (K + N) and Penalpina – the smaller players tend to specialise in a particular region, transport mode or cargo niche. If, however, they operate globally, they are often co-loading on the services of their larger competitors. Clearly, without a global network of offices, or range of IT capabilities, they are at a disadvantage in gaining high-volume shippers' business.

However, this is not always the case. An example is found in a Houston (Texas) head-quartered freight forwarder and 3PL alliance, International Freight and Logistics Network (IFLN). A feature of IFLN among air and ocean freight alliances is its global coverage and the wide range of industrial sectors in which it serves. It has over 170 members in 90 countries, embracing multi-modal freight forwarders, NVOCs, airfreight and project cargo specialists, which all work together to provide shippers with comprehensive solutions.

Some 3PLs cover more than one country, such as: Crowley Logistics being represented in El Salvador, Guatemala, Honduras and Cost Rica; Dart Express in several countries (including India, Kenya and Vietnam); and SIF in Argentina, Brazil and Chile. However, major markets are represented by several logistics and transport providers, each with its own specialisation in terms of service offerings or geographical coverage.

In the US there are 15 IFLN members embracing Associated Container Line, Customs Clearance International, and K2 Logistics China and Hong Kong. Overall, they are represented by 10 service providers, and India by 5, while there are 4 IFLN members located in Singapore.

To facilitate its members' growth, IFLN provides them with value-added services that support their container and other business, through cooperation with other companies. These include an online cargo insurance programme and a cooperative venture between IFLN and Syncho Net for the repositioning of empty equipment on a large number of trade lanes.

IFLN's extensive network continues to grow to the point where the alliance can now provide comprehensive door-to-door solutions by all transport modes and for all goods worldwide. The group vision statement is:

> We intend to be a leading worldwide alliance, well positioned to compete with multinationals, 3PLs and 4PLs and project forwarders on a global basis in specific trade-lanes and in niche markets.

Examples of IFLN success are associated with the establishment of a key account structure. Under the key account structure, the IFLN supports its members involved in the tender or go into the tender under the IFLN brand. This support includes IFLN providing a forum for members to contact each other on a one-to-one basis to enable them to bid for tenders jointly. This is realised via a detailed exchange of information using the IFLN website as the contact point, and also through meetings between members, many of which are arranged at the IFLN's biannual conference. IFLN employ people dedicated to global accounts and a sophisticated supply chain visibility IT system – an important marketing tool for the alliance when it bids for global tenders. The system is also used for the generation of reports and KPIs, which can be used both by IFLN members and its customers.

The success of IFLN is attributed to its flexibility and enthusiasm in its approach to global tenders. Unlike many global 3PLs, IFLN members do not have departments dedicated to tenders, and the owners themselves manage many of these companies on a day-to-day basis. Examples include gaining the GE business. This involves the supply of a wide variety of construction and other material from multiple origins (50 per cent from Italy) to Algeria, where Africa's largest destination plant is being built. The IFLN handle GE's shipments from the purchase order stage and deal with all of its suppliers. It has daily contact with the company's purchasing and project teams, with respect to establishing shipment dates from suppliers and manages all the logistics activities into Algeria. GE relies on the IFLN IT system to track its shipments.

Another example is the UK-based industrial automotive and building products manufacturer Tomkins. Four service providers, including IFLN, were selected to handle the contract globally. The Tomkins Group has a total of 88 facilities in 22 countries and embraces all of its air and ocean freight business. The latter embraces 7,000 TEUs and a large number of Overseas Container Ltd (OCL) shipments over a two-year period, covering multiple trade lanes. The IFLN's participation involves managing shipments to and from the US, Belgium, Germany, France and the UK, and it is being extended to Spain and Eastern Europe.

In 2004, a total of 250,000 TEUs were handled by IFLN members with 45 separate service contracts and a large number of carriers. The IFLN's major advantage is to negotiate as a group – under one entity – with global carriers.

India's Automobile Industry Supply Chain Development

The benefits of global supply chain manifests itself in the ongoing growth of one of the major markets in the world – India – which we will now examine together with two case studies.

It is being driven by a domestic market growth embracing a rise of 8 per cent in the last five years per capita disposable income, resulting in increased purchasing power. Other factors include the lowered age of first-time car users, shorter replacement cycles, rising dual-income families, new technology lowering the basic cost of car ownership, a generally low car penetration in the country and India's growing steel production. Domestic sales grew 14 per cent from 2001–02 to 2005–06 while the commercial vehicle segment rose by 24 per cent.

The most extraordinary development is found in the export growth, which rose by 45 per cent during the period 2001–02 to 2005–06. Motorcycle exports rose by 45 per cent and three-wheelers by 50 per cent. India's auto components industry grew by 20 per cent during the same period to reach a value of USD10 billion from USD8.7 billion. The forecast is USD18.7 billion by 2009 and USD40 billion in 2014.

India's production of auto components includes: engine parts 31 per cent of total production; drive transmission and steering 19 per cent; body chassis 12 per cent; suspension and braking parts 12 per cent; equipment 10 per cent; electric parts 9 per cent; and other 78 per cent. The growth of IT in the design, development and simulation processes has contributed to the growth rates.

Auto components exports registered outstanding growth rates of 24 per cent during the period 2000–02 to 2005–06. Europe attracted 31 per cent; US 26 per cent; Asia 16 per cent; Africa 10 per cent; Middle East 10 per cent; Oceania 1.5 per cent; and other 0.5 per cent.

India is emerging as a major destination for investments from non-Indian automobile and auto component multinational companies (MNCs). Global automobile manufacturers are streamlining their business processes by outsourcing non-core activities to lower cost countries like India. Cost is not the only consideration, but also the availability of skills in process, product and capital engineering. The basic cost of a car is likely to remain constant over the next decade as major manufacturers outsource their components and plant from high-cost economies to low-cost economies, particularly China and India.

The rationale of development in India and China is the availability of a good education system extolling the skill required. India's process-engineering potential is used in the redesign manufacturing processes and make them more labour-intensive and less capital-intensive, thereby enabling MNCs to substantially reduce their overall costs. For example, 'de-automating' production processes, as found in Western factories, can reduce overall manufacturing costs for some components by up to 20 per cent.

India has emerged as a leading destination globally in product engineering design, resulting in reduced development cost and lead times as found in the Maruti Alfo's steering system, realising a weight reduction of 15 per cent. In India there are 456 auto component companies possessing ISO 9000 certification, 248 companies possessing TS 16949 certification, 136 companies possessing QS-9000 and 129 possessing ISO 14001 certification (see pages 74–8).

Indian logistics costs are very high, especially when compared with developed countries. However, while India is emerging as a major global automobile source, it is inhibited in its growth by its inadequate logistics network, which is fast improving. However, the Indian Government and Port Authorities are developing their road and rail/port network, the latter with a focus on containerisation (see page 83). Currently it costs about 14 per cent of the GDP, transportation 35 per cent, inventory 25 per cent, losses 14 per cent, packaging 11 per cent, handling and warehousing 9 per cent and other categories 6 per cent. To redress the situation, many Indian automobile manufacturers are taking proactive measures to control their logistics costs and improve customer services, such as to improve their supply chain adopting e-sourcing. This helps companies reorganise purchasing processes and support aggregated buying across business units with the help of Internet-based tools or B2C Internet portals. The process reduces time spent on negotiation, accelerates information gathering and speeds up communication channels among buyers and sellers. Some companies have implemented this e-sourcing for procurement of high-value commodities yielding considerable savings as a result.

Supply chain management succeeds when it coordinates information and goods flow between customers and networks linking supplier, manufacturers and distributors. Over 70 per cent of India's software houses have expertise in SCM.

The automotive sector is one of the market leaders in implementing SCM. The IT market is growing at 40 per cent annually and this is due to the following reasons:

a   Tier 1/2 suppliers to original equipment manufacturers (OEMs) (whether based in India or abroad) reduce time to market the goods and product lifecycles. This puts pressure on manufacturers to integrate with OEMs, Tier 1 suppliers, sub-contractors and distributors during the product development and manufacturing process.

b   The manufacturing base wishes to improve operational efficiency variable costs.

c   Dwindling product lifecycles, the rapid customisation of products and growing globalisation have all led to encouraging IT investment by India manufactures.

In 2005–06 the Indian IT services rose by 30 per cent in each year: software experts totalled 75 per cent and the domestic market the remaining 25 per cent.

Given below are examples of two companies, Ashok Leyland and Mahindra and Mahindra, extolling the benefits of SCM:

Case Study: Ashok Leyland

Ashok Leyland, one of India's largest private companies, is a part of Hinduja Group. It is one of the country's largest automobile and auto component companies. The company offers a range of trucks, buses, special application vehicles and engines across more than 40 countries.

During 2005–06, the company produced a total of 65,000 vehicles out of which it has exported 4,879. In the domestic market, it sold 56,776.

Rising raw material cost has been a serious concern for the company. A steep rise in steel and copper prices meant the company decided to streamline its supply chain process and start an SCM project to optimise its supply chain process and rationalise its sources. The project, Oscars Inbound, includes supplier partnership vendor base rationalisation, tiering of suppliers and cluster information, inventory optimisation through JIT and LCL, total cost management, logistics initiatives, e-sourcing and global sourcing.

Gains:

a   supplier partnership covers engineering and technical support, global market leader, global availability of spares, testing capabilities, improved field performance, system supplier, JIT supplies and world-class technology;

b   partnership gains include vendor consolidation under tier-1, continuous technological upgrading of products without in-house investment, shorter development lead-time, value engineering and cost reduction, improved field performance, inventory efficiency through JIT supplies and human power rationalisation;

c   vendor base rationalisation. Gains from source reduction include pricing on volumes, improvement in quality and reliability, vendor improvement programme for continuous improvement, tiering for ease of fitment, system buying and reduction in paperwork;

d   vendor tierisation includes economies of scale, system buying and rationalisation of supplier base. Cluster formation includes 55 adherence-mistake proofing, process improvements leading to self-certification;

e   inventory level has reduced from 23 days to 18 days;

f   total cost management includes various initiatives such as daily management, process control, design, technology and capacity. Total savings were 3 per cent of total operating cost;

g   logistics initiatives include transporter-based rationalisation, Kanban pull from satellite warehouses, enhancement of truck, turnaround, load, space and route optimisation;

h   stores outsourcing covers activities outsourced to 4PL service providers. The services are receipt accounting/documentation, binning and debinning, issue accounting, perpetual inventory and reverse logistics for pallets. All these services have saved 42 man-days;

i   e-sourcing includes global benchmarking, gain through bidding, identification of cost-competitive sources, introducing best sourcing practice, increasing efficiency and minimising costs, improving the value chain's bottom line.

All these activities saved 11.5 per cent of total material cost.

Case Study: Mahindra and Mahindra

Mahindra and Mahindra (M&M) is another of the largest private companies in India. Its farm equipment unit, the third largest producer of tractors in the world and one of two major operating divisions, produces more than 100,000 tractors a year. In 2005–06, the company sold 85,000, achieving a growth rate of 30 per cent on the previous year. India's 6 million farmers depend upon them.

The company's tractor exports to the US, Africa, and several countries in South East Asia face stiff competition. M&M set up its assembly/manufacturing facilities at multiple locations, which increased the complexity of the supply operations. Hence, the company needed an integrated solution that could link all plants to optimise costs and operational efficiency and respond quickly to customer requirements.

For M&M, cost reduction was very important. It has to spend more money on raw materials, but cannot increase prices due to high competition.

Thus, SCM was the only solution to keep its margin healthy – minimising costs by reducing the cost of production, logistics, working capital (inventory) and the cost of lost sales. Pull-based replenishment helped in optimising the logistics and manufacturing operations to improve margin and minimised costs by enabling quick customer requirements.

Successful implementation of SCM has helped M&M reduce its inventory by more than 50 per cent.

Replenishment lead-times, which cover planning and execution, were around 52 days before the SCM project began. Now this has been reduced to 19 days. The company has established a strong web component for its 400 dealers to collect sales information and its 800 suppliers to submit SCM planning information and material requirement planning (MRP) schedules.

The company started with dealer stock of 12,000 tractors and company stock of 7,000. But the change in business model and implementation of pull-based replenishment enabled the company to reduce its dealer stock to 6,000 and company stock to 3,500.

With ongoing implementation of SCM, the company expects to further reduce its dealer inventory to 4,000 tractors and company stock to 2,000.

The continuous growth of the Indian automobile and auto components industry provides immense scope for management to enhance the supply chain sector. It has become a favourable destination for foreign companies to establish facilities and form alliances with domestic companies. The low cost of manufacturing and government support have been the major drivers for foreign companies investing in India. The Indian economy is gaining momentum in the world of free trade and liberal movement of goods and services between countries. Hence efficiency in supply will be critical for India's automobile success.

Logistics Focus on 'Ceylon Tea' – Sri Lanka

Sri Lanka is the largest exporter of tea in the world with 94 per cent of its total production shipped to overseas markets. Exports total 300,000 tonnes and containers are the principal mode through which the tea is shipped.

Exporters/growers face many logistics, challenges to ensure that a good quality product arrives at consumers' premises on time. Most tea is transported by truck from the tea estates, which are located in the high regions of the country, to the various warehouses of the plantation companies. In common with many agricultural products, the quality of the tea at the final destination is determined by how well it is handled throughout the supply chain and, in particular, at key transfer points in the system – for example, truck to warehouse. A critical part of the process starts with the actual picking of the leaf, as any damage at this stage will have a long time to take effect.

Tea was originally packed in lead-lined wooden boxes, eventually giving way to plywood-panelled tea chests with aluminium linings. However, following environmental concerns, and problems over the disposal of these units, tea is now packed for export in multi-walled paper sacks, which are stowed in containers. The advent of the container has both streamlined the logistics process and much reduced claims attributable to rain-water damage. As a result, 75 per cent of all exports are containerised.

Sri Lanka faces competition from Indonesia, Vietnam, Kenya, Malawi, Uganda, India and Bangladesh. 'Ceylon teas' are classified mainly into three categories: low-grown, medium-grown and high-grown – and the markets for each type are different. The strongly flavoured and coloured low-grown teas are in great demand by consumers in the Middle East; buyers in the UK, Australia, New Zealand and Pakistan seek the redder full-bodied medium-grown teas. Meanwhile, high-grown teas are lighter, and contain an aroma and flavour that is in demand by buyers throughout Europe, North America and Japan. Russia has emerged as the largest importer of Ceylon tea, embracing 31 per cent of total imports. Elsewhere, the UAE and Syria buy most of their tea from Sri Lanka. Hong Kong remains a significant market, both in terms of local consumptions and as a distribution hub for China and other areas in the Far East. Hence, bulk tea is often imported into Hong Kong, and is then blended with teas originating from other areas of the world.

Sri Lanka does undertake some value-added processing, blending and packaging activities of specialist teas, but its role in this sector is limited because of government restrictions on importing other 'orthodox' teas. Heavy duties are imposed on imported teas similar to those produced in Sri Lanka. Specialised teas are a growth market with the demand for green tea rising more than 55 per cent in the past year. Prices for instant tea rose by 28 per cent in 2006.

Sri Lanka faces keen competition with Dubai emerging as a large centre for this activity. The port city is trading, blending and packing huge volumes of tea every year for customers across the world.

Most of Sri Lanka's tea is shipped on CIF, CFR or FOB terms with few buyers preferring DDP, ex-factory, or FCA contracts. It appears that most buyers do not want to get involved at the export end. Sri Lanka is well placed as a regional port hub in Colombo as the original gateway for South Asia, resulting in a large number of logistics/ freight forwarders and shipping lines being based in the city. Hence a competitive freight market exists from the extensive network of liner services and multitude of destinations these links serve. Colombo is often the last port of call for westbound vessels in the east–west route before European/Far Eastern destinations. Very often, ships call at Colombo with excess capacity and the shippers have the opportunity to negotiate very attractive rates.

A key area in the SCM is controlling and managing the transport and packaging cost. A further focus is the need to have a comprehensive EDI system and improve port productivity. Undoubtedly the completion of the south port project will provide an impetus to the development of the Port of Colombo as a high-tech facility with good productivity.

Thailand Food Supply Chain

The development of the global food supply chain in the past decade can be attributed to many factors, embracing changing culture in taste in many developed countries, rising living standards in the developed world, the development of a global infrastructure – in particular e-commerce – and the development of food plantations in many overseas countries. A key factor is inward investment by many brand names such as Del Monte, Nestlé and Cadbury Halls. Moreover, food hygiene is the paramount factor, plus quality control and the good chain standards as demonstrated by ISO (see page 74). The fundamental aspect is the development of logistics and SCM, which has transformed the channels of distribution in the global supply chain, whether it be by road, sea/container, or air. We will now examine the Thailand food industry.

Thailand has a fertile soil and abundant water supply, which favours strongly its food manufacturing. It is the world's top exporter of rice and pineapples, including canned pineapple juice and concentrates. It is among the top 10 exporters of sugar, frozen chicken, and shrimp and seafood, especially tuna. Currently it earns USD10 billion per year from food manufacturing.

Thailand brand food exporters include Mead Johnson, the dairy product subsidiary of Bristol-Myers Squibb, Dutch dairy Campina, Del Monte, Nestlé and Cadbury Halls.

For Japanese seafood supplier Kyokuyo, it serves restaurant chains, takeaway sushi kiosks and convenience stores. Kyokuyo can tap into ready supplies of raw materials and a skilled workforce available at low wages. For Del Monte, it is the year-round supply of vegetables and fruits such as rambutan and longan.

Both companies have opted for joint ventures to realise a shorter time frame. Japan's Kikkoman Corp-Del Monte's is sole licensee in Asia except India and the Philippines. It teamed up with Thailand's sweetcorn producer Agripure Holdings and major pine-apple grower and exporter Samroiyod Corpo to establish Sian Del Monte. Samroiyod brings pineapples and other fruits, Agripure sweetcorn and Del Monte the distribution capability.

Kyokuyo formed K&U Enterprise Co (KUE) in a joint venture with leading Thai frozen food exporter Union Frozen Products. It has an annual production of 4,000 tonnes: 70 per cent to Japan, 20 per cent to the US, Canada and Europe, and the residue to the domestic market.

For the US Jelly Belly Company, the push factor is the key element in its maiden venture overseas. A further factor to choose Thailand is the high cost of sugar in the US, which is significantly higher than on the world market. The new plant has an annual capacity of 6 million kilograms of jelly beans. It is located on Thailand's Eastern Seaboard Industrial Estate and was selected because of its strategic location, logistics and direct access to 25 markets. The jelly beans are shipped in climate-controlled containers to Europe, Asia and other markets.

Swiss food and beverage giant Nestlé has one of the biggest production facilities in Thailand, producing coffee, chocolate, beverage, infant formula and children's products, pasteurised and canned liquid through four Thai subsidiaries.

Thailand continues to develop its export food production base.

To conclude, we focus on future trends in the global food supply chain. Containerisation will continue to increase its market share while the specialised reefer tonnage will decline. The data on perishable food container shipments was 1990 – 25 per cent; 2000 – 43 per cent; 2006 – 50 per cent; and forecast for 2015 – 60 per cent. The shorter haul/ distant markets embracing intra-European, Morocco/Europe, Turkey/Europe and Mexico/US trade sectors, favour economically the road haulage/trucking services. New Technology will see advances in controlled atmosphere solutions while the machinery will be more fuel-efficient and emit fewer ozone-destroying gases. The new technology will mean that even more time-sensitive cargoes will be moved, while it is increasingly likely that the container or ship will become the storage facility where ripening actually occurs. This will reduce the need for expensive land-based cold stores and distribution centres, as more cargo is likely to move direct to the stores and/or retailer-controlled regional distribution centres. Such developments favour the container and the seamless through transport mode with ocean carriers more aggressively adopting marketing concept such as 'farm to fork'. The receivers, such as retailers/supermarkets, are becoming more influential. Today they are dictating the freight contracting process, with the result that cargoes are being shipped in lower-sized lots and on a more regular basis.

Culture

The global logistics operator and international supply chain manager must develop an empathy with their clients and fully understand their culture. Culture has been defined as the configuration of learned behaviour and result of behaviour, whose component elements are shared and transmitted by members of a particular society. Overall, it features in all areas of the global logistics operation, embracing protocol, law and politics, social/ economic factors, technology, material, culture and social organisation.

Culture is driving a fast-changing market in many countries and regions of the world. Entrepreneurs must monitor such changes to identify opportunities. This is evidenced through education, youth culture, tourism and immigration. It extends particularly to lifestyle and social/economic structure of economies. Areas of culture that generate change are given below:

a   Material culture includes all artefacts, that is, all physical objects that are made, such as pottery, paintings, housing, roads, dams and airports. Material culture is a useful guide to a society's standard of living.

b   Education. A highly educated population is easier to communicate with and usually quite sophisticated and more demanding in terms of product quality/durability/technology/performance. Educated populations have a higher standard of consumption and are more discerning on product choice development and knowledge of the product.

c   Culture differences. The 'in one in all' principle can be applied to cultural as well as economic groups. Culture is usually taken to imply such adornments of a civilisation as music, art and language. Society's culture is about everything that human beings conform to, resulting in a distinctive way of life for its people.

d   Religion. Characteristics, attitudes and taboos often result from religion that extends to food and people's attitudes to a whole range of products from deodorant to alcoholic drinks. It embraces philosophical systems, beliefs and norms. Muslims regard Fridays as the Sabbath while other religions regard Saturday or Sunday as the Sabbath. Additionally, colour has different meanings in different countries: white is for mourning in China and orange has political significance in Northern Ireland.

e   Special organisations, customs and roles. The social fabric and structure are changing in many countries through the influence of education, investment, travel, communication, migration, immigration, the Internet, inwards investment and technology. It develops a new era of networking and a changing business environment is emerging.

f   Language. While English is regarded as the international business language of the world, it is very advantageous to communicate in the client's language, which is often a vehicle to understanding their culture.

g   Aesthetics. This embraces beauty and good taste in art, music and architecture. Local aesthetics have a strong appeal to the local populace.

h   Ethics and more. It is all perception – the customer's expectation and experiences of the product/service identified in the brand image of the company.

i   Political systems. These are unique to particular societies, trading/economic blocs and are widespread in their implications. It extends to human rights, recognition of international conventions, protectionism and negotiations. It has widespread social and economic implications. A change in government can result in a different political allegiance.

j   Protocol. Basically how one presents oneself in dress code, mannerisms and codes of behaviour when negotiating change body language and non-verbal messages. Contrasting protocols exist in European and Asian countries, particularly China and Japan.

k   Economic systems. The structure of the economy.

l   Legal systems. These embrace a range of measures such as trade barriers, market access, commercial environment, and so forth.

m   Management culture. The manner and protocol in which a company conducts its business.

n   Immigration and migration. This embraces movements within the population strata, which can change the culture, taste, protocol and a whole range of areas within society

Finally, the cultures globally differ widely as, for example, the US and China, Japan and India, the EU and Africa.

International Agencies

International agencies are very much in the lead, forming the framework under which trade is conducted globally. The global logistics operator and supply chain manager must be very conscious of the role in terms of compliance and developing best practice.

We have already examined in this book the salient ones influencing logistics. The ISO (see page 74), the transport conventions (see page 9), security (see page 107), trade finance (see page 51), cargo delivery terms (see page 46), IMO (see page 107), WTO (see page 14), IATA (see page 9) and UNCITRAL (see page 9). It is important to bear such regulations in mind when designing the global supply chain and initiation ideas/proposals to add value to it.

Useful Sources of Information

The Economist (2007) *Pocket World in Figures*, Profile Books: London

Chapter 12

A Strategic Focus

Introduction

This wide-ranging book within global supply chain management and international logistics has now reached the final chapter. The continuous growth of the subject content adds to its complexity and this is in line with the growth of trade, redistribution of markets, extension of the supply chain, development of technology and the changing profile of the consumer. The consumer demands more choice, earlier response rate to the product order process, and more value added. Moreover, as countries across the globe enjoy higher incomes and more disposable income, their product choice becomes more discerning. This places increasing pressure on the supply chain manager to develop a greater level of efficiency in his/her supply chain sourcing.

Supply Chain Operations: A Focus on Adding Value to Brand Management

Brand management is the process of effectively managing, developing and sustaining a brand in the marketplace. This is primarily achieved through advertising and the buyer evaluation of the product/service and continuously adding value to the brand. It is essential that strong empathy be developed with the buyer. Brand marketing is the process of marketing the brand image of a product/service and in so doing extolling the perceived benefits of the brand to the user/customer.

Supply chain management crosses the organisation in both strategic and tactical terms. It embraces both cost and service mandates; it can be global in scope and reach. Success requires process, technology and people. The question arises: How do you distinguish the supply chain to satisfy both internal and external requirements? How do you focus to create branding to position and build competitive advantage? The value-added concept.

Branding is a way to position the company in the marketplace. It is the organisation identity. Branding must be dynamic and innovative, to maximise value to its customers, both nationally and internationally. It should be more than just an image: it should have substance to create value. Above all, it should reflect reality, not perception, and have depth and longevity to be viable.

The branding must reflect and embody a value proposition. It is not a financial figure such as sales, profits or assets, but the value placed on the SCM by the customer. It must be tangible and should define the benefit and solution that customers gain. It identifies the reason why a particular logistics operator is preferred in relation to another. Sometimes the value proposition is based on fundamentals such as low price. This strategy ignores the service, cycle time and inventory impact of supply chain management, and reduces SCM and 3PLs to a commodity service where price is the determining factor. Branding and a value proposition, based on low cost, may be tactically viable, but is weak strategically. Costs can only be lowered to some limit. Competitors can do lower prices too. It can make customers wait for even lower prices rather than acting now. A low-cost proposition can create a somewhat negative image about the supply chain service and its value. Basically, pursuing lowest cost can divert the supply chain organisation from its primary purpose with both short-term and long-term impact.

Value-added benefit emerging from the supply chain represents an 'in-depth' evaluation. With consumer goods being a dominant part of the world economy and especially for the SCM executives and for 3PLs, the value proposition must be focused as a critical supply chain need. This may be difficult to identify and address. Research is the route to this objective.

Yield management is primarily associated with the airline and hotel industries where reservation-based companies attempt to maximise revenue from a fixed capacity: seats on a flight or rooms in a hotel. The analysis can involve research tools, such as linear programming and simulations to determine a pricing model at the micro-level. It recognises that the price or revenue-creating ability of the item in supply decreases with time.

Yield management is applicable in SCM when inventory is viewed as the supply whose yield is to be maximised. Inventory is key to success for manufacturers, wholesalers, distributors and retailers. Formulating the right inventory is difficult and challenging. Insufficient inventory means lost sales opportunities. Too much inventory means markdowns – and reduced profits – to sell it. Companies working on their margins especially feel such pain.

Ocean carriers practise a form of yield management, balancing the timing and value from the service contract period through peak season, when space may be at a premium, regardless of pricing, and into slack season, where price reductions are given to freight forwarders to fill ships.

Retailers experience a short shelf life for their products, relative to demand and the price customers are willing to pay. This reflects changing taste, fashion, new technology and culture garments, and computerised products fall into this category. Sales promotions, discounts and markdowns are common practice to draw customers. Firms that are in dynamic, volatile businesses, such as fashion, know the impact of short product lifecycles and pricing decisions on the bottom line.

The operations research approach determines the 'optimal' markdown(s). However, it does not address the underlying problem of demand planning and uncertainty and how to manage it.

The length of the inbound supply chains has increased significantly with global sourcing. Longer supply chains have resulted in longer times to produce and deliver products from suppliers.

The yield management value strategy realises inventory velocity with its focus on product supply and not on placing it at customers or in stores. It puts the focus where it belongs at the beginning of the supply chain where the product originates.

Firms can turn inventory from purchase orders into cash. Inventory in a long transit, inventory that sits in warehouses and sits on store shelves and floors does not increase in value with age. Inventory follows a route of depreciation. The only solution is price reduction and lower profit margin or even a loss. This applies to fast-moving markets such as computers or the fashion-conscious market of garments.

Traditional procurement approaches focus on product price, as do traditional logistics approaches that focus on freight price. Overall, there is a need to have a composite pricing strategy embracing all the elements reflected in the supply chain. The result of these pricing efficiency approaches is to place prices before inventory requirements by treating the product supply as two separate events. They create discord in the development of an effective supply chain that can minimise time, inventory and cost while maximising service and profits.

The dual-price approach hinders the development of inventory management at suppliers to create yield management as a benefit of supply chain management by focusing on having the right inventory at the right quantity at the right place and at the right time – the core of the logistics definition. Basically, the place to implement this strategy is at the supply origins with suppliers.

Developing a value proposition by embracing yield maximisation of inventory beginning at the supplier level converts an operations research tool into a supply chain operations paradigm to manage the product and its flow. It expands the supply chain focus, supplier management and creates substantial benefit together with competitive advantage. Yield management success requires supplier management in order to bridge supply chain planning and supply chain execution.

Basically, supplier management controls supplier performance. It examines the timing of the product, the quantities, how and where delivered, product mix and so on. Overall, the objective is to maximise yield.

Effective supplier management is based on technology, process and people. Technology is the method used to place orders with the supplier such as via the Internet, EDI, or others. A key point is the relationship with the supplier and credit rating. It is supply chain execution. More importantly, it is how purchase orders and suppliers are managed with event management and exception management.

The technology enables revising orders, their priorities, style and other mixes, their timing, quantities, and more. Technology gives visibility/transparency to directing and controlling supplier performance and what is in the supply chain, including what is happening with transport and other logistics service providers.

Process takes purchase orders from being transactions to being part of a process that flows through the organisation. Overall, this links all elements of the supply chain, integrating it within the company and between trading partners. It provides the dynamics for controlling product flow and inventory positioning. That control is key to placing the right inventory, right as to quantity and timing and location, so as to achieve higher price yield.

People are logistics personnel, located in China, India, Malaysia, Thailand or wherever the suppliers are located. They speak the same language and are in the same time zone as suppliers. They are the day-to-day operational spears that make process and technology work; global supply chains cannot be managed with emails. Managing suppliers embraces people.

Value proposition is needed for C-level supply chain executives and for 3PLs and 4PLs. It must bring significant bottom-line benefit within the company and to its customers. A value proposition budget on yield management is unique, creates competitive advantage and drives increased profits. The challenge is to move beyond traditional functions and tasks.

An interesting global brand case study is found in the phenomenal expansion of the Seattle-based coffee giant Starbucks. It focuses attention particularly on running an effective supply chain. It has revenue of USD4 billion from 7,700 outlets in 36 countries. Underpinning this growth in large measure is a successful brand, to which the company executives refer as the 'Starbucks Experience'. It can be described as a kind of modern holistic branding exercise that essentially means all senses of consumers walking into any Starbucks outlet in the world are met with identical sensations.

In Asia–Pacific there are 1,100 outlets, which involves very complex supply chain processes. The complexity of the task is found inasmuch that business models exist in different markets or market business units and each varies considerably. In Thailand and Australia the corporation wholly owns them; those in Taiwan and Hong Kong are joint ventures with local business partners, and those in Malaysia, Indonesia and the Philippines are licensed operations.

In 2001, to cope with the growth of Starbucks, all supply chain outlets for Asia were moved from Seattle to the company's Asia HQ in Hong Kong. The supply chain is critical, embracing not only coffee, but also furniture to merchandise, blenders, express machines and paper cups. Starbucks moves over 5,500 TEUs annually in Asia of which 30 per cent are shipped from Singapore to 13 Asian markets, while the remainder consist of direct shipments from a variety of locations worldwide. Most of the stock goes either directly to Japan, or one of two regional distribution centres in Hong Kong or Singapore. Dairy products are sourced from New Zealand, store merchandise from Yantian and Shanghai, and furniture and espresso products from Italy, and which go directly to the Asian markets.

Retention of full control over all major inventory planning and forecasting is essential to the efficiency and uniformity of the company's supply chains. Starbucks would not outsource. This involves inventory planning, increasing velocity, maintaining KPIs, monitoring the financial performance and the interface plant capacity for supplies, and predicting where supplies are required. Strategic items such as coffee are all joint venture companies and licences are required to purchase direct from Starbucks.

Starbucks sources all its green coffee through a wholly owned trading company in Lausanne, Switzerland. Shipments go direct to the company's roasting plant in Kent, Seattle, from where the Asian markets are supplied through the Singapore distribution centre. Japan, where 518 outlets make it the company's largest Asian market, is an exception and gets its coffee shipments direct from the US.

Items the company classes as leveraged, decentralised or generic can be sourced locally. These basically consist of items that cannot be imported, due to regulatory restrictions in various markets, or have such a minimum impact on brand that sourcing them locally will not have any significant effect on the character of the stores. When local sourcing occurs, data in outlets is maintained by performance specification from Hong Kong.

The Hong Kong central supply chain team is divided into three groups embracing procurement, distribution and planning. The three groups support two major supply chain streams, retail supplies and store development. Store development embraces the capital goods necessary to build a store from scratch, including espresso machines and blenders, as well as furniture. These goods are handled through Starbucks' second Asian distribution centre in the Tradeport facility at Hong Kong International Airport.

Retail supplies includes all operating supply chain activities such as paper cups, napkins, tea and coffee, which are moved through the Singapore distribution centre. It is the distribution team that takes responsibility for outsourced supply chain activities, which contrary to the general industry trend, tend to be kept to a minimum.

DHL Danzas is the strategic logistics partner in Asia, responsible for: handling customer service and distribution to the joint ventures and licensees; processing orders; and managing and operating the distribution centres in Hong Kong and Singapore.

Training is an essential key to maintain efficiency in the company's supply chain, which also embraces an annual forum to provide best-practice training and distribution guidelines for supply chain executives in the various markets. Furthermore, the opening of any new Starbucks store involves bringing supply chain executives to Hong Kong for workshops on ordering forecasting, planning and distribution.

Basically, the essential ingredients of Starbucks' strategy is full control of planning, forecasting, sourcing of strategic brand items, servicing the customers assiduously, and providing regular training to keep employees fully conversant with the technologies and processes involved.

To conclude, logistics operators must strive to add value to the supply chain continuously and so improve their competitive situation in the marketplace.

Product Outsourcing

Product outsourcing is a core element in the logistics strategy of both the manufacturing and the service sectors. Product outsourcing may involve a single product in the product process, or multiple sourcing, embracing a range of suppliers/component parts often in different countries to complete the production cycle. Usually, multiple sourcing is the cycle, such as an automobile plant in China. It basically embraces 3PLs (see page 130).

The rationale of outsourcing may embrace a variety of reasons as follows:

a   Lower cost in all elements of the business. This embraces labour; access to materials – such as transport cost, including shorter supply chain; lower taxation such as corporate tax; lower rental, warehouse, building cost; political incentives to encourage inwards investment; lower overheads; arbitration; and access to highly trained workforce at low cost.

b   Closer access to markets, both industrial and consumer, with lower distribution cost. This is a key factor and the rationale of why many companies have relocated their manufacturing/assembly plant to the Far East and subcontinent. An important aspect is the essential element to have a high-tech supply chain network and with a modern infrastructure, particularly containerisation and unitised multi-modal transportation. Closer access to Chinese and Japanese markets such as Dyson products (see page 151).

c   Employment law – conditions of employment is another incentive to outsourcing. The employment law features areas of redundancy, work councils, industrial disputes, minimum wage, pensions, national insurance, employee rights, disciplinary and grievance procedures, health and safety at work, training, discrimination in recruitment, trade unions and their relations with employers and members; human rights; minimum possible amount of intellectual property that might be stolen and employment tribunal. The EU may be regarded as a highly regulated employment market, but regulations do differ marginally in Member States.

Employment law differs widely. A contrasting situation exists in France, which is based on social welfare, while in the US the commercial climate prevails, but varies by individual state. Employment law also differs widely globally, with the developed countries having a more regulated employment system. There is a sharp difference between employment law/conditions in the US/EU compared with the situation in many countries in the Far East/subcontinent.

d   The range of support services. This includes the range of telemetry systems, which allows exporters to measure different levels of inventory in warehouses and thereby reduce the supply chain cost in a logistics-driven environment: global breadth and depth with the ability to comply with the changing rules and cross-border regulations connected with international trade between buyers and sellers around the globe; trade-specific applications that replace the manual process of documentation within the trading process; and a system that must be able to function around the world supporting different measurement systems, providing for currency conversions, and multiple languages for export form filling.

e   Access to 3PL operators, which provides a strong export infrastructure such as warehouse tracking systems to back up the exporters' online presence; also to ensure there is a delivery network in place to deliver goods globally.

f   The geographical strategic location to maximise the benefits of outsourcing, especially items a, b, d and global logistic hubs (see page 79).

g   Outsourcing is now featuring extensively a strategy of joint ventures, licensing, and trading companies. Joint ventures are particularly common, enabling the two trading companies from different countries – at least one being local – forming an agreement and a new company to manufacture/produce/market the goods on a joint basis. It applies to the automotive industry, a wide range of consumer goods, industrial plant and pharmaceuticals.

It is important that under the joint venture both companies have the same management and culture and the credit rating is established in the host country. The following areas require evaluation: capital construction; land availability; labour-free deployment training and redundancy; timescale; product and plant specification constraints; technology; expatriate employment terms; procurement – raw materials and components sourcing and any constraints; marketing – domestic/globally; quality control; legal environment; attitude to competition, domestically and internationally; and arbitration.

h   An increasing number of manufacturers now focus in their geographical location strategy on logistic hubs at Rotterdam, Dubai, Hong Kong, Singapore (see page 130) and economic zones such as Shenzhen. The Shenzhen economic zone represents the South China hinterland and is served by the Shekour container terminal and is contiguous to Hong Kong. It has a range of value-added services and state-of-the-art facilities.

Outsourcing represents a major step in a company's logistics strategy. It must be well researched and a visit to the market is essential. Companies like Dyson identified the benefits by sourcing their component parts in the Far East – particularly Malaysia, and shipping them to Malmsbury, England for assembly and distribution globally. Ultimately, Dyson transferred their production to Malaysia with substantial cost benefit and market access involving lower transportation cost. Design and research remains in England. A key factor is quality control, and encouraging component suppliers to develop new technology in production and product specification.

An essential part of outsourcing strategy is to check out the government policy. A friendly government, which is stable and offers favourable terms, is essential (see Dubai). Planning and a financial evolution is essential. It is a major step in the company strategy.

Product outsourcing usually involves outsourcing the logistics and freight business instead of keeping it 'in house'. To reduce overheads, shippers are replaced by 3PLs and 4PLs and supply chain management providers. In so doing it is important to acknowledge that the business must fulfil its legal responsibilities. This embraces the trade terms that a company applies to its customers or suppliers and the financial arrangements (see page 46).

Key factors are the need to establish, negotiate, monitor and review KPIs and service contracts that take account of the evolving needs of the company, the supply chain and its business strategies. This can be undertaken in house (within the company), or by engaging a smaller third-party provider to represent them. This has the benefit to give more attention to detail and satisfy the specific, individual requirements of the client. A further area on which to focus is security.

Future Growth and Related Constraints of Global Supply Chain Management and International Logistics

Over the past few decades the transport industry has changed dramatically through the demands of an increasingly integrated global economy. Maritime and air transport services are no longer associated with the port-to-port and airport-to-airport movements, but rather an integral component of comprehensive door-to-door transport services. Several elements have contributed to this evolution including advances in technology (e.g. containerisation, and information and communication technologies), infrastructure modernisation, and globalisation of production and manufacturing processes.

Additionally, there have emerged other services to international trade such as warehousing, freight forwarding, consolidation, electronic tracking of consignments, FTZ, ICDs and hub port/airports. Logistics companies or third-party logistic providers – 3PLs – provide some or all of these services. Each of the following companies – Nippon Express, Keuhne & Nagel, Schewker, DPL, and Panalpina – moved over 0.5 million TEUs during 2004 on behalf of shippers. In the same year companies among the top 10 providers of logistics services worldwide realised revenues above USD4 billion per company with the top two companies achieving revenues of USD14.8 billion and USD11.1 billion, respectively. Most major liner shipping companies have subsidiaries focusing on the same business and often serving primarily the parent sea carrier.

We will now examine the rationale and comparison of the developed economies with those of the developing economies in logistics terms and how the developing economies can become more logistically focused.

The expansion of the 3PLs has been under way over the last few years, mainly through the acquisition of lesser competitors. During 2005, in Europe, Keuhne & Nagel took over ACR Logistics for USD525 million and DPL took over Exel for USD6 billion. Freight forwarding features prominently among the activities undertaken by these companies and is usually the one undertaken in developing countries, often in competition with local companies.

Over the past few decades the transport industry has been transferred by the demands of an increasingly integrated global economy. Maritime transport services are no longer associated with strictly port-to-port movements, following the demise of the liner conference system, but rather are integral components of comprehensive door-to-door transport services.

It is important in our analysis that we recall the definition of the essence of logistics services as defined by the Council of Logistics Management: 'the process of planning, implementing, and controlling the efficient effective flow and storage of goods, services and related information from point of origin to point of consumption for the purpose of conforming to customer requirements.' Overall, it is often referred to as a single set of services – in reality, logistics services involve a myriad of activities. Logistics may be asset-based and non-asset-based and, as such, heavy capital investments are not always required to supply logistics services. Not all suppliers of logistics services are multi-national. Operators in developing countries can differentiate themselves by establishing a niche market and providing individualised services. Addressing drivers of cost levels, focusing on logistics services areas with low capital investment requirements, specialising in areas with a clear competitive advantage and tailoring commitments to reflect real commercial interest and national regulatory frameworks are many elements that could contribute to developing countries' active participation in the logistics services market. Hence, under the right conditions, logistics services suppliers from the developing countries could tap into global markets where they could learn from their interaction with other business partners and exposure to the ways of modern logistics networks.

World trade has seen a constant increase in containerised freight since the intro-duction of containers in the mid-1960s. In 1965, world container throughput at ports was practically non-existent. It reached 387.7 million TEUs in 2005, an annual growth of 8.7 per cent. This figure is expected to reach 500 million TEUs by 2010.

Containers are the major vehicle driving global logistics and countries that do not have a modern container port and supporting dedicated infrastructure also serving land-locked countries are seriously disadvantaged in terms of trade development. It substan-tially increases the freight cost of overland distribution (see page 8) and very much extends the transit time. It is a major challenge to the management of the supply chain.

Containers are easy to handle and store, offer protection against damage and theft, and allow interchange among various transport modes. These features have encouraged the widespread use of containers and facilitated multi-modal transport operations. Add-itionally, containerisation has brought about greater efficiency in cargo handling in ports and inland freight stations through the use of specialised equipment, which has contributed to the changing patterns and practices.

In addition to containerisation, the transport industry is being increasingly shaped by developments in the field of information and communication technologies (ICT). Transport and logistics services have been heavily influenced by the widespread use of electronic commerce, which in turn has enabled the growth of this particular ICT area. E-commerce allows consumers to place orders on the Internet and enables trade trans-actions to be rapidly concluded. This results in frequent deliveries of small packages to many different destinations, thus compelling transport and distribution services providers to modify their operations, business strategies and practices.

Another element to consider is the modernisation and the liberalisation of ports and international transport services that have taken place in many countries since the early 1990s. These developments have resulted in improved port and logistics operations, including speedy turnaround of vessels and containers in ports. To ensure that these efficiency gains are not undermined by inefficiencies that may occur in other segments of the transport chain, a comprehensive door-to-door approach to delivering goods is increasingly adopted by traders and transport providers.

Global manufacturing and distribution processes bring together raw materials, ports and other semi-finished inputs from different parts of the world. Trade in components, whose delivery is time-sensitive and which are essential to production operations, accounts for around 30 per cent of global trade in manufactured goods. This trend is reinforced by the growing importance of intra-company trade, which accounts for approximately one-third of this trade.

The new production processes require the implementation of supply chain management techniques to ensure timely receipts of inputs and delivery of finished products to the marketplace. The just-in-time (JIT) production processes require that supply and demand be matched in real time to reduce inventory and warehouse storage costs and free up working capital and equipment. The demands of the consumer and industrial market-place have resulted in manufacturers increasingly entrusting the logistics functions of their supply chain operations to third-party providers. Outsourcing logistics has allowed the manufacturers to focus on their core business activities to benefit from the economies of scale of their 3PL partners and the broad range of services offered by specialised logistics services providers. Table 12.1 (below) is a list of the top 10 logistics services providers, ranked on the basis of their revenues in 2004.

Logistics costs, including transport, packaging, storage, inventories, administration and management, are key considerations for all players in the international logistics chain. Controlling logistics costs allows companies to maintain a competitive edge and countries to experience trade growth, since lower logistics costs translate into competitive export and import prices. Within global logistics expenditures, the share of transport is growing while that of inventory holding is decreasing. For example, in 1980, expenditures on inventory holding were estimated to be higher than expenditures on transportation in the United States. In 2002, this trend was reversed since transport-related expenditures were 90 per cent higher than expenditures relating to inventory holding.

Although of relevance to all economies, logistics costs are more important for develop-ing countries – in competitive times – where they have been estimated to be the highest in the world. Several factors contribute to differences in cost levels and structure, includ-ing the efficiency of distribution systems, the quality of transportation infrastructure, the weaker currencies in developing countries, and the regulatory and institutional frameworks.

An examination of Table 12.2 indicates that in 2005, the international freight costs of African countries as a proportion of the value of their imports represented 10 per cent – nearly twice the world total (5.9 per cent) and almost one and half times the costs for developed market economies (4.8 per cent). These costs are even higher for land-locked developing countries, given the additional constraints caused by their geographical

Table 12.1 Top 10 logistics providers

TOP 10 LOGISTICS PROVIDERS
REVENUES IN 2004 (million US dollars)

Logistics services provider	Revenue
Nippon Express	14,840.8
Excel Group	11,122.9
Schenker	9,658.4
Deutsche Post Logistics	8,168.2
Kuehne & Nagel	7,036.6
UPS SCS	5,015.0
TNT Logistics	4,912.3
Panalpina	4,721.7
CH Robinson	4,341.5
Geodis	4,057.2

Source: Containerization International, September 2005.

Table 12.2 Estimates of total freight costs on imports of African countries, 2005 (in billions of dollars)

Year	Country group	Estimate of freight cost of imports	Value of imports (c.i.f)	Freight costs us a percentage of import value
2005	World total	632.4	10,712.2	5.9
	Developed economies	341.1	7,035.7	4.8
	Developing economies	259.9	3,359.0	7.7
	Economies in transition of which	24.1	317.5	7.6
	Africa	24.6	246.9	10.0
	America	19.4	441.1	4.4
	Asia	153.0	2,588.1	5.9
	Oceania	0.8	8.8	9.6

Source: Calculations based on UNCTAD Handbook of Statistics 2006/2007, IMF Balance of Payments Statistics and IMF Direction of Trade Statistics.

situation, which led to higher transport costs and longer delivery times. For example, in Namibia, the cost of all trade-related transactions for a 20-foot full container load (FCL), including inland transport from the port to the factory gate, is slightly over USD3,000, while in Germany and Sweden, these costs amount to only USD813 and USD500, respectively. The foregoing analysis demonstrates the disadvantage developing nations experience in logistics terms, to develop their global markets on a competitive basis – a serious impediment to the global expansion of the logistic network.

Proponents of logistics services liberalisation, whether through individual or collective requests, seek the removal of measures indentified by the logistics services industry as impediments to the efficient provision of logistics services. Overall, logistics providers seek the removal of market access and national treatment restrictions on local presence and investment as well as non-tariff barriers arising from burdensome and non-transparent regulatory regimes. Measures and practices identified include: restrictions in the form of establishment and foreign equity capital (e.g. only in the form of joint venture with a 49 per cent capital cap on foreign participation); cumbersome, discriminatory and non-transparent customs regulations; lengthy inspection procedures; non-transparent costly and time-consuming licensing practices; absence of bilateral trade agreements on land-locked countries; failure to develop FTZs, ICDs, economic zones; and abuse of monopoly power.

Additionally, the negative effect of common market barriers are numerous. These include restrictions on the use of shipping agents, discriminatory taxation measures and port dues, discrimination against foreign carriers in the use of port services, anti-competitive business practice, and finally the burdensome ship and cargo examination procedures.

According to industry stakeholders, border clearance procedures, including customs and inspection, constitute the greatest impediment to the supply of global logistics services. They indicate that on balance, logistics services forms are more concerned with limited transparency and discriminatory practices than establishment restrictions. It is argued that limited transparency and inequitable access to information result in a slight to significant adverse impact on operations, while little or no adverse impact or costs result from establishment restrictions such as joint-venture requirements, ownership/equity restrictions or investment limitations.

The WTO are endeavouring to address a range of these issues where consensus can be sought. It is an ongoing process. Evidence exists that important trade transactions costs faced by developing countries indicate that transport and logistics services in developing countries are not at a stage where they could compete on a level playing field with global logistics suppliers that offer state-of-the-art services. Unlike in the case of global players, developing countries' logistics services face a wide range of challenges, including uncertain legal status of transport intermediaries, cost and availability of banking and other financial services, and limited and insufficient access to know-how, modern commercial practices and ICT. As a result, the logistics services sector is still at an initial stage of development in most developing countries.

The large gap between the requirements for modern logistics services and the capacity of developing countries' suppliers to meet market demand requires an intervention at all levels, as well as internationally through WTO trade agreements such as the general agreement on trade in services (GATS).

The way forward to develop and contribute to the growth of the global market by the developing countries is complex. For developing countries to positively contribute and to capitalise on related business opportunities that may emerge, a number of objectives need to be sought. These include: an effective market access request-and-offer-process; tailored technical assistance and capacity buildings; and building on synergies resulting from progress achieved in other negotiation areas, such as trade facilitation.

It is important to bear in mind the linkage between liberalisation of trade in services via commercial presence and foreign direct investment. Trade liberalisation should be a careful balancing act between gains that could be secured from relaxing certain access rules, changing ways of doing business and seeking opportunities that could be realised by penetrating markets opened by trading partners.

Future Strategic Focus – Global Supply Chain Management and International Logistics

Logistics is the driving seat for the continuous expansion of world trade. This will continue, as mentioned earlier in the book, so that while in 2000 some 10 per cent of goods purchased were imported, in 2020 the figure will rise to 80 per cent. A dramatic increase is needed in the reconfiguration of trade and extending to all sectors of the global supply chain business. Hence the need for entrepreneurs to have a strategic logistic focus. The following points are relevant:

a   The board of directors must be focused on a logistics strategy and one board member must be designated Logistics Director, as found in the Starbucks organisation (see page 148). Moreover, it must feature in the company mission statement and business plan composition. Additionally, the company organisation must be logistics-integrated and a company without a logistics presence will need to reposition itself with emphasis on differentiation.

b   Planning, forecasting, customer focus, sourcing, training, technology and processes are key factors – in particular to keep focused on the customer needs and the market environment.

c   There is a need to have a high-tech focus on the business to keep pace with latest developments and extol efficiency at all levels.

d   Reduce cycle time on processing/information data/decision-making. Information is vital to the supply chain.

e   Added value is a key factor, both in the supply chain and the overall logistic operation. It can be aligned to cost benefit and in particular, efficiency and productivity/return on investment, related to time-based inventory reduction.

f   The sourcing and buying terms need constant review. The cash to cash cycle needs continuous review.

g   Adequate professional resources are essential to have professionally qualified and experience personnel.

h   Flexibility is a key factor.

The above is a formidable list and individual companies will vary their emphasis in various circumstances.

Accordingly, it is hoped that this book will facilitate the development of global supply chain management and international logistics. It is a very complex area with increasing complexity as the global business expands. This book is compelling reading and an aide-memoire to comprehend the ingredients of the subject and should be on the bookshelf of every global supply chain manager and international logistics operator and student of the subject.

Glossary

abnormal load A consignment necessitating special arrangements.

absolute advantage An individual has absolute advantage in the production of two goods if, by using the same quantities of inputs, that person can produce more of both goods than another individual.

acceptance credit The process of specific banks arranging acceptance credit involving the acceptance of a 'bill of exchange' drawn on any of its members.

accepting bank/paying bank A bank that accepts a 'usance bill of exchange' payable upon a stated or determinable future date.

active inventory The provision of raw material, finished products, which will be sold or used within a specified period without extra cost or loss.

air bridge Part of an overall transit in which an air transit features and is integrated with at least one other transport mode such as maritime transport, thereby forming an intermodal transit.

air consolidators An agent who usually offers a regular service on scheduled flights and in so doing despatches as one overall consignment under one document, the master air waybill, a number of individual compatible consignments from various consignees to various consignors.

air waybill An air freight consignment note made out by or on behalf of the shipper that evidences the contract between the shipper and carrier(s) for the carriage of goods over routes of the carriers.

ANDEAN A trading bloc embracing Bolivia, Colombia, Ecuador, Peru and Venezuela.

APO Advanced planning and optimisation.

arbitration Method of settling disputes, which is usually binding on the parties concerned.

ASEAN Association of Southeast Asian nations embracing Brunei, Indonesia, Malaysia, Myanmar, Philippines, Singapore, Laos and Thailand.

asset productivity The productive use of an asset.

ATA (Carnet) A simplified import and export documentary procedure, backed by an international guarantee chain for temporary importations.

aval An unconditional guarantee for each bill of exchange or promissory note from an internationally recognised major bank.

average inventory The average inventory over a specified period.

average total cost Total cost divided by the quantity or service produced in a given period.

backhaul A transport unit return movement from original destination to original point of origin.

bankers' guarantee A written instrument usually issued on behalf of a customer in favour of a third party.

bar coding A method of encoding data for fast accurate electronic readability (see RFID entry).

best practice The classification description of an acceptable code of practice adopted to execute/undertake/perform a specific activity.

bill of lading A receipt of goods shipped on board a ship signed by the person (or his/her agent) who contracts to carry them, and stating the terms of which the goods are carried.

bill of materials A list showing all raw materials or components required to make a final product.

bill of sight A custom import form used when the importer is unable to make a complete customs entry owing to insufficient information from the shipper.

BIMCO Baltic and International Maritime Council.

bonded warehouse Accommodation under Customs surveillance housing highly dutiable cargo, which may be stored in importation and withdrawn at importer's convenience on payment of relevant duty.

break bulk General cargo conventionally stowed as opposed to bulk, unitised or containerised cargo, which has been stripped from containers (or other forms of bulk carriage) for forwarding to final destination or the process of commencing discharge.

broker One who puts buyer and seller in touch with one another for a fee or commission.

BSI British Standards Institution

budget The process of formulating forecast and objectives of either expenditure and/or revenue including traffic volume during a specific future period for a particular service/trade or company.

business logistics The process of planning, implementing and controlling the efficient, effective flow and storage of goods/services and associated information from point of origin to the point of consumption for the purpose of responding to customer needs.

business acumen The ability of a person to identify, create and cultivate maximum advantage of business opportunities, which may be self-created or simply arise through a particular circumstance.

business cycle The process of the business environment going through various phases of its development embracing the peak, decline, trough and growth.

buyer credit The process of providing finance direct to the buyer (or to a borrower, e.g. a bank in his/her country) in the form of buyer credit.

buying cycle The sequence of events/the process of the client buying a product/service.

C&F Cost and freight (named port of destination) – Incoterm.

CAD Cash against documents.

CAE Customs and Excise.

CAP Common Agricultural Policy.

capital The equity or shares (authorised and/or issued in a company/equity) equity plus reserve plus profit retained plus loan and debenture stock in a company/entity.

capital employed The aggregation of capital employed in a particular situation/business usually related to the income and level of profitability.

cargo insurance The insurance of cargo in transit.

carriers' liability The shipowner as a common carrier is liable for all events except act of God, war, kings/queens enemies, general average, inherent vice, etc.

certified invoice A commercial invoice bearing a detailed statement of the value and origin of the merchandise described thereon and signed by the exporter.

CFS Container Freight station.

channel of distribution The route followed to enable the goods to reach the buyer/end user from the point of origin in the supply chain.

CIF Cost insurance freight – Incoterm.

CIM Convention Internationale Concernant le Transport des Merchandises par Chemin de Fer.

CIP Carriage or freight and insurance paid to (named point) – cargo delivery term Incoterms.

CKD Completely knocked down – consignments that are assembled at destination as distinct from being transported as a complete unit or for example cars knocked down.

Clean Report Of Findings (CRF) The document issued by the Inspection Agency under the pre-shipment inspection arrangements.

CMR Convention relative and contract de transport international des Merchandises par route.

commercial invoice An accounting document prepared by the exporter (seller) in the name of the importer (buyer) or agent.

contract logistics Third-party logistics relationship where a contract exists between provider of 3PL service and client.

CPFR Collaborative planning forecasting and replenishment.

CPT Carriage paid to named place of destination – Incoterm.

correspondent bank A bank that acts as the agent of another bank to provide specified services cost benefit analysis. The measurement of resources used in an activity and their comparison with the value of the benefit to be derived from the activity.

cost-effective The process of determining the general efficiency of a particular service/facility/process, etc. in cost or value for money terms.

cross-docking The process of scheduling of road haulage vehicles/trucks into a cross-docking facility whereby the cargo is unloaded from several trucks and then immediately reloaded into one container for delivery to final destination.

cross-dock operation Sometimes referred to as stockless warehousing. In this type of operation, goods are moved to a warehouse where they may be pre-palletised, pre-configured or pre-packed and then assembled, usually across the loading docks into consolidation outbound loads.

C-TPAT The US Customs Trade Partnership Against Terrorism – December 2004.

Customs invoice A document prepared by the exporter in accordance with the requirements of customs authorities in the country of the importer, serving the customs authorities of the importing country as a basis for establishing the customs value of the goods and for the calculation of the customs duty.

Dangerous goods Refers to certain commodities such as corrosive substances, explosives, flammable liquid, flammable solids, infectious substances, liquid and compressed gases, magnetised material, oxidising substances, poison and radioactive materials.

DDP Delivered duty paid (named point) – Incoterm.

DDSN Demand-driven supply network.

DDW Demand-driven workforce.

demand chain Basically another name for the supply chain with focus on the customer or end user demand pulling materials and product through the chain.

DGN   Dangerous good note.

distribution centre   A depot which is issued as a break bulk point for a region, area, or continent and from which individual shipments will be reforwarded to final destination. Part of the supply chain.

documentary credits   Documentary credits are used as a means of guaranteeing the transaction of both importers and exporters in the conduct of international trade.

documentary letter of credit   Document whereby the buyers require the importer's bank to authorise the exporter to draw in financial amounts by a specified date for a particular shipment, subject to the detailed documents being forthcoming.

dutiable cargo   Cargo that attracts some form of duty, that is, Customs, Excise, Value Added Tax, Sales Tax, etc.

duty free zone (DFZ)   A designated area where goods or cargo can be stored without paying import customs duties awaiting further transport or manufacturing.

EAN   UCC (leading global numbering system for supply chain stakeholders).

Economic zone   An area designated for economic development to improve wealth and employment in the zone with focus on industrial and services sectors – often sponsored by governments.

EDI   Electronic data interchange.

EN 2000   European Standard for qualtiy management.

end user   The person/company who uses/consumes the product/service provided by the vendor – in effect the final buyer in the supply chain.

exchange control   The exchange control regulations imposed by a government regulating/controlling the acceptance of foreign exchange as payment for goods sold overseas.

export declaration   The process of an exporter declaring to Customs the fullest details of the consignment being exported.

export sales contract   The initial document in any international transaction: it outlines the specifics of the sales agreement between buyer (importer) and seller (exporter).

Ex Works (EXW)   An Incoterms 2000 applicable to all modes of transport.

FAK   Freight all kinds.

FCA   Free carrier (Named place).

FCL   Full container load.

FEU   Forty-foot equivalent unit – container term.

fixed costs   Those costs that remain at a constant level, irrespective of whether the service is operational or immobile, such as depreciation.

FOB   Free on board – Incoterm.

fourth-party logistics (4PLs)   A company that assembles and manages the resources, capabilities and technology of its own organisation with those of complementary service providers to deliver an extensive supply chain.

freight forwarders   An entity/company responsible for undertaking export/import cargo arrangements on clients'/shippers' behalf at a seaport, airport and so on,

GDP   Gross domestic product.

GE   (major indutrial company).

general merchandise warehouse   A warehouse used to store goods that are readily handled/available, are packaged and do not require a controlled environment.

Hague Rules   The complete code of rules for the carriage of goods by sea.

hard currency   A currency that is consistently appreciating or stable in terms of other currencies.

Harmonised Commodity Description and Coding System (HCDCS) An international classification system that assigns identification numbers to specific products. The coding system ensures that all parties in international trade use a consistent classification for the purpose of documentation, statistical control and duty assessment.

hedging The establishment of an opposite position on a futures market from that held and priced in the physical commodity.

hub The control transhipment point in a transport structure serving a number of consignees and/or consignors by means of spokes.

hub airport An airport that acts as a hub of a transport network and relies on feeder services which may be rail, road, sometimes sea transport and air.

hub and spoke system An example arises in international distribution whereby packages are collected by road and delivered unsorted to a central point called the 'hub'. Handling and sorting takes place at the hub, taking advantage of automated handling and sorting procedures involving bar coding to scan in and scan out the individual packages. At this stage the hub movement involving a dedicated truck or aircraft convey the packages to an overseas hub centre where the goods are sorted and distributed, usually by express road services to the consignee.

hub port A seaport that acts as a hub of a transport network and relies on feeder services, which may be road, rail, inland waterways or feeder shipping services. In so doing, it is often termed hub and spoke with the spoke being the feeder service.

IACS International Association of Classification Societies.

IATA International Air Transport Association.

ICC International Chamber of Commerce.

ICD Inland Clearance Depot.

ICS International Chamber of Shipping.

in-bond goods Goods liable to Customs duty placed in bonded warehouse under Customs surveillance or in transit under Customs seal.

inbound logistics The process of adopting a logistic strategy for importing products. This involves receiving goods.

Incoterms 2000 International terms drawn up by the International Chamber of Commerce relative to the delivery trade terms of international consignments and as specified in the export sales contract, usually evidenced in the export invoice. There are 13 terms, for example, FCA, CPT, etc.

INMARSAT International Maritime Satellite Organisation.

integrated logistics A comprehensive system embracing the entire supply chain as a single process, from raw materials supply through finished good distribution. Overall, all functions that make up the supply chain are managed as a single entity rather than managing individual functions separately.

intermodal transportation The provision of through connecting transport service(s) involving different modes of transport, that is, road, rail, sea and air.

international buying The process of purchasing goods/services which cross international boundaries.

inventory A record of goods received, stored and delivered.

inventory cost The cost of holding goods, usually expressed as a percentage of the value includes the cost of capital, warehousing, taxes, insurance, depreciation and obsolescence.

ISO International Standards Organization.

land bridge   The provision of through international, dedicated multi-modal transport service operation on a regular basis. It may be the Far East/European service involving sea/rail with the containers being rail conveyed between the West and East coast ports.

LCL   Less than container load.

LDI   Logistics data interchange.

lead time   The period required, for example, to prepare for the introduction of a new facility/scheme/plan/product, etc. It includes time for order preparation, queuing, receiving, inspection and transport.

logistics   The process/mechanism of moving/distributing goods in a cost-effective and efficient manner and the related organization and technology required to achieve this objective, which can be conveniently summarized as the ability to get the right product at the right price and right time.

logistics chain   The process of moving/distributing goods through all the elements of the logistic chain originating from the supply source and moving to the manufacture/assembling/processing stage and terminating at the distribution point.

long-term planning   The process within a company or particular set of circumstances to devise a plan for future action, which may be five, seven, or in exceptional cases rather longer, up to ten years.

manifest   Inventory of cargo and stores on board a ship/aircraft for a particular sailing.

marginal cost   The additional cost of producing one more unit of output.

marine insurance   The process of providing insurance cover for a vessel (hull and machinery) and cargo shipped.

non-vessel owning common carrier (NVOCC)   A carrier issuing bills of lading for carriage of goods which s/he neither owns nor operates.

NPDI   New product development initiatives.

order cycle time   The time that elapses from placement of the order until receipt of the order. This embraces time for order transmission, processing preparation and shipping.

order picking   Assembling a customer's order from items in storage.

order processing   The process of executing customer orders.

outbound consolidation (break-bulk)   Consolidation of a small number of customer consignments in larger load. Subsequently the goods are shipped to a location near the customers and ultimately the small shipments distributed to the customers.

outbound logistics   The process of adopting a logistics strategy for exporting products. This involves distribution of goods.

outsourcing   The process of a company contracting out the process of sourcing products/components/materials etc. for a company.

packing list   A list of the contents of a package/consignment.

pallet   A steel or wooden platform of 800×1200 mm and 1000×1200 mm designed to accommodate and facilitate cargo transhipment and through cargo movement.

physical distribution   The movement and handling of goods from the point of production to the point of consumption or use.

piggyback   The carriage of unaccompanied road vehicles and trailers on wheels on rail flat cars; in international marketing terms the process of an exporter fresh to the business in a particular overseas country joining forces with an established exporter and thereby promoting/selling both companies' products/services on a joint basis.

point of sale   Place where goods are retailed/sold.

productivity   The relationship between the quantity of an item produced and the resources used to produce it.

push/pull strategy   Basically it is the two options available to an entity to move its products through a distribution channel. The push strategy involves trade and sales-force incentives such as cash discounts, direct mailshots, credit facilities, competition – trade and sales force, exhibitions and demonstrations. Alternatively, the pull strategy is based on consumer incentives. This includes consumer competitions, free samples available offered in store demonstrations, packaging, sponsorships, price reductions by the manufacturers and so on. Overall, the promotion strategy involves extensive advertising and consumer protection.

radio frequency identification (RFID)   Basically it enables potentially hundreds of tagged items to be read within a second. Further, depending on the materials, tags can be embedded within the product packaging and read without ever having to open the transport unit. Modern RFID systems enable reading of all tags, product tags, transport unit tags or any combination of packaging levels.

RDT   Radio data terminal.

reefer cargo   Cargo requiring temperature control.

reverse logistics   The process of collecting, moving and storing used, damaged or outdated products and/or packaging from end users.

RO-RO   Roll on/roll off ship designed for the conveyance of cars, road haulage units, and unitised cargo.

SAD   Single Administrative Document.

safety stock   A quantity of stock planned to be in inventory to protect against fluctuations in demand and/or supply; or in the context of production scheduling, safety stock can refer to additional inventory and/or capacity planned as protection against forecast errors and/or short term changes in the backlog.

Sales and Operations Planning (S&OP)   The translation of upstream demand data into an actionable operational plan that reflects rapid product commoditisation; short product lifecycles, higher product mix and higher product volatility are all putting pressure on margins and accelerating the importance of sales and operations planning. An AMR research definition.

SBS   Leaver uncharged.

SCP   Supply chain planning.

ship agent   The ship's agent represents the shipowner/master at a particular seaport.

shipbroker   A person having one or several occupations: chartering agent, owner's brokers, negotiating the terms of the charter of a ship on behalf of a charterer or shipowner respectively, or sales/and purchase broker.

shipper's agent   The agent representing the shipper whose name appears on the consignment note as the party contracting with the carrier for the carriage of the goods.

shrink wrapping   A form of packaging, which is provided by placing the goods on a covered base – such as pallet – and covering it with a film of plastic, which is shrunk to enclose the items by the use of hot air blowers (thermo-guns).

soft currency   A currency which is consistently depreciating in terms of other currencies over the long term.

software   The programmes that enable computers to operate; instructions to a computer.

strategic alliance   A joint venture or marketing cooperation are two examples whereby a company joins forces with another operator with identical objectives.

strategic planning   The process of planning within a company the available resources on an optimum basis, including investment project(s), with a view to taking maximum advantage of business opportunities based on profit motivation.

strategy   A course of action including the specification of resources required to achieve a specific objective.

supply chain management   The management mechanism/structure and strategy/objective to supply goods on an international trade basis involving not only the exporter/seller/supplier and buyer/consumer/end user, but also all the intermediaries and their management in the supply chain.

supply warehouse   A warehouse that stores raw materials; a company mixes goods from different suppliers at the warehouse and assembles plant orders.

tariff   A list of duties payable on imported or exported cargo imposed by the government; published freight rates/charges and/or related conditions of the carrier.

Terms of Delivery   The terms under which the goods delivered to the buyer/importer and this is found in the export sales contract that embraces Incoterms 2000.

Terms of Sale   The terms of the sales contract agreed between buyer (importer) and seller (exporter).

TEU   Twenty-foot equivalent – a standard size for an intermodal container.

third-party logistics provider (3PL)   The process among manufacturers to outsource logistics thereby taking cost advantage of consolidation and other benefits.

Total Quality Management (TQM)   The total involvement of an organization's workforce into quality achievement and excellence, both relating to the final product or service and guarantee.

tramp vessel   A vessel engaged in bulk cargo shipments or time chartering business.

UCP 600   The Uniform Customs and Practice for Documentary Credits 2007 revision are rules drawn up by the ICC, which apply to any documentary credit (including to the extent to which they may be applicable to any standby letter of credit) when the text of the credit expressly indicates that it is subject to these rules. They are binding on all parties thereto, unless expressly modified or excluded by the credit.

UNCITRAL   United Nations Commission For International Trade Law.

UNCTAD MMO   United Nations Conference Multi Modal Transport Convention.

value-added chain   The process of adding value – improve the benefits to the shipper from the supply chain management system.

value chain activities   These can be categorized into two primarily types: primarily activities (inbound logistics, operations, outbound logistics, marketing and sales service) and support services/infrastructure, human resources management, technology and procurement.

vendor management   The management responsible for selling activities.

workforce performance management   A category of labour management technology that mirrors and supports the integrated workforce performance management process.

XML   Extensive Markup Language.

Readers are urged to study: Dictionary of Shipping International Business Trade Terms and Abbreviations by Alan Branch and David Branch, 6th Edition 2009 – 20,000 terms published by Seamanship International Ltd, 4 Dunlop Square, Dean Industrial Estate, Livingston, West Lothian, Scotland, EH54 8SB Email: info@seamanship.com

Index